Herbert Goldstein
New York, April 1985

T3-BVR-459

The Book of Mordechai

A Study of the Jews of Libya

The Book of Mordechai

A Study of the Jews of Libya

Selections from the *Highid Mordekhai* of Mordechai Hakohen
Based on the complete Hebrew text as published by the
Ben-Zvi Institute, Jerusalem

Edited and translated, with introduction and commentaries, by

Harvey E. Goldberg

A Publication of the
Institute for the Study of Human Issues
Philadelphia

Copyright © 1980 by ISHI,
Institute for the Study of Human Issues, Inc.
All Rights Reserved
No part of this book may be reproduced in any form or by any electronic or
mechanical means including information storage and retrieval systems without
permission in writing from the publisher, except by a reviewer who may quote
brief passages in a review.

Manufactured in the United States of America

Library of Congress Cataloging in Publication Data:

Ha-Cohen, Mordecaï, 1856–1929.
    The book of Mordechai.

    Bibliography: p.
    Includes index.
    1. Jews in Libya.   2. Libya—Ethnic relations.   I. Goldberg, Harvey E.
II. Title.   III. Title: Highid Mordekhai.
DS135.L44H32213   961'.2004924   80–11470
ISBN 0–89727–005–3
                              B543 60
This publication was made possible in part by Grant BNS–7825107 from the
Anthropology Program of the National Science Foundation.

For information, write:

Director of Publications
ISHI
3401 Science Center
Philadelphia, Pennsylvania 19104
U.S.A.

TO MY PARENTS

Preface

Highid Mordekhai was first published in Hebrew in 1978, almost half
a century after the death of the author, Mordechai Hakohen. Thanks are
due to the Hebrew Manuscript Division of the Jewish National and
University Library in Jerusalem for permission to publish the manuscript, and to the members of its staff for their continual assistance. The
publisher of the Hebrew edition, the Ben-Zvi Institute for the Study of
Jewish Communities in the East, was a supportive and helpful partner in
that endeavor.

The present publication differs from the Hebrew edition in several
ways. As I mention in the Editor's Introduction, this is a translation of
only Parts III and IV of the work. That Introduction itself has been
considerably expanded from the Hebrew, for the benefit of an audience
with an interest in anthropological questions but without a special
knowledge of Jewish history and culture. Similarly, the division into
chapters is new, and the editorial forewords to the chapters do not
appear in the Hebrew. The notes, too, have been rewritten with an
English-reading audience in mind.

Hakohen's book consists of 114 Sections (Hebrew: *simanim*) and
ninety footnotes of various lengths. References to the original work are
given mostly by Section number, but sometimes by footnote number and
manuscript (ms.) page number as well. A reference to a "Note," with an
uppercase "N," indicates one of the author's footnotes. In the few
instances where only the manuscript page number is given as a reference, the appropriate Section may be found in Appendix I of this book
and easily located in the Hebrew. In this edition, Hakohen's Notes are
not numbered. Some are indicated by an asterisk and located at the foot
of the page; two very long ones have been treated as text. My own notes
(referred to with a lowercase "n") appear at the end of each Section.

Parentheses in the translation correspond to Hakohen's usage in the
Hebrew, while brackets indicate editorial additions. Where brackets en-
close a question mark, the translation is uncertain.

Hakohen's writing has a style of its own; his detailed, often lively, narrative is replete with phrases and images from classic Hebrew texts. I have tried to preserve the flavor of his text, while providing the reader with comfortable English. The punctuation and paragraphing have been changed to follow English usage. Here and there the notes give technical references to the original language, but these, and the citations of biblical verses, have been kept to a minimum.

Hebrew and Arabic words appear in a fairly careful transcription, except when there is a conventional English spelling, in which case the precise transcription is provided only when it may be of linguistic interest. Thus "Mordechai" (the conventional English spelling) is rendered *Mordekhai* when it appears as part of the Hebrew title of the work in question. That the French title page in the Hebrew edition uses *Mordecaï* only proves that there is no perfect solution to these problems. Other orthographic conventions are explained in the Note on Orthography.

Good maps of Libya are hard to find, and those contained herein are my own constructions. They are based on a variety of other maps, not on the information supplied by Hakohen, and in some cases do not agree exactly with Hakohen's descriptions.

A number of people offered valuable criticism on earlier drafts of this work. For this assistance I wish to thank Haim Blanc, Ken Brown, Brad Martin, Jonathan Oppenheimer, Ismar Schorsch, and Walter Zenner, and gratefully remember the late H. Z. Hirschberg. A partial subvention from the National Science Foundation aided in the publication, and the final product reflects the skill of the editorial staff of ISHI.

HARVEY E. GOLDBERG

Contents

List of Illustrations

Note on Orthography of Words in Hebrew and Arabic

I have tried to achieve some degree of precision in transcribing Hebrew and Arabic words, including place names, but there is no perfect solution to the problems in this area. Besides the various spellings suggested by literary as opposed to spoken Arabic, place names in Libya have the added complication of different "Latin" spellings according to whether an author is French, Italian, German, or English. The spelling adopted here corresponds closely to the Hebrew in Hakohen's text, except if there is a well-known English variant. This also holds true for words other than place names. The following list shows the correspondences between Arabic and Hebrew script and the symbols used in this book:

Transcription	Arabic	Hebrew
ṭ	ط	ט
ṣ	ص	צ ס
q	ق	ק
kh	خ	כ
gh	غ	ג
ḥ	ح	ח ה
ʿ	ع	ע א
ʾ	ا	א

Sh is to be pronounced as it normally is in English. Vowel length is usually ignored in Hebrew, but is given for Arabic. In the word list in Section 94, stress is sometimes indicated (based on Hakohen's text), and the vowel *schwa* (ə) is used where it is appropriate. Where phonological precision is not demanded, as in the title of a book, *schwa* may be indicated by a ' or an *e*, but these conventional representations should be clear from the context.

Editor's Introduction

Libya is over twice the size of Texas, but its population numbers only about three million people. Most of the country's inhabitants are found in Tripolitania, the northwestern province that belongs both geographically and historically to the Arab West, the Maghreb. However, Tripolitania differs from other regions of the Maghreb in that it has only thin lines of settled and cultivated areas separating the desert from the sea. In recent times, Libya was one of the last of the North African countries to be colonized by a European power; Italy appropriated the area long after France had established itself in the richer lands to the west. In other words, Libya has traditionally been a marginal land within the Maghreb.

Unfortunately, this situation is reflected in the extent of scholarly interest in the country. With some notable exceptions, the researcher looking for an able portrayal of Libyan society and history is faced with a dearth of material. Although the discovery of oil aroused interest in the area, most writers have been concerned with economic and political matters, leaving a vacuum in the study of the country's institutions and folkways. It is not an overstatement to claim that Libya has suffered from scholarly neglect.[1]

This scarcity of material stems from more than simple lack of interest. In at least several instances it may be traced to the time lag separating the completion of a manuscript from its publication. This is particularly true of Tripolitania. At his death in 1928, Ettore Rossi was nearing the completion of his work *Storia di Tripoli e della Tripolitania,* which was not to be published until forty years later (1968). Rossi was able to consult the work of L. C. Féraud, the French consul in Tripoli from 1879 to 1884, whose *Annales tripolitaines* appeared posthumously in 1927. An important source for both these authors is the Arabic chronicle of Ibn Ghalbun, a Tripolitan[2] writer of the eighteenth century. Ibn Ghalbun's history was summarized in a Turkish book published in 1867–68, and it appeared in Arabic only in 1929–30.

1

LIBYA

Zuara   TRIPOLI

Khoms

Mesallata   Misurata

Ghuryan

Jado   Yefren

Nalut

JEBEL NEFUSA

TRIPOLITANIA

Sirte

Benghazi

Derna

CYRENAICA

N

FEZZAN

● Zawilah

Marzuk

~mountain escarpment~

An American visitor to Tripoli in 1904 mentions hearing that an "attaché of the French consulate had once found certain valuable historical data" in the archives of the local Jewish synagogue (Furlong 1909:102). I suspect that this refers to Féraud, who may have consulted the manuscript of Rabbi Avraham Khalfon (1735–1820), which dealt with the history of Tripoli from ancient times through his own. This work, like Ibn Ghalbun's, had never been published, and in 1945 fifty-three pages of it remained in the library of the Rabbinic court in Tripoli (Raccah 1945). However, a considerable part of Khalfon's work was included in the historical narrative of Mordechai Hakohen (1856–1929), a portion of whose book, *Highid Mordekhai,* is presented here for the first time in English.

II

Mordechai Hakohen was born in Tripoli in 1856 to a family of Italian descent. Since there was no separate Italian community in the town (Benjamin 1859:241), his early years were spent like those of the other Jewish children in Tripoli. He recalls that he had a deep interest in learning from a very early age. He had no opportunity for an extended formal education, but his inquisitiveness and intelligence led him to pursue many subjects on his own, including the study of languages. Although he began his career as a humble teacher and peddler, he later worked as a clerk in the Rabbinic court and was able to spend many hours in its archives. There he began work on his manuscript, *Highid Mordekhai,* or "Mordechai Narrated,"[3] a record of the history, customs, and institutions of the Jews of Tripoli and Tripolitania. In the historical section, he draws extensively on the unpublished manuscript of Avraham Khalfon,[4] but also includes a great deal of information from the nineteenth century based on his own research and observation.

In 1906, Hakohen met Nahum Slouschz, a Russian-born Jewish scholar, then working at the Sorbonne, who visited Tripoli to conduct research into the history of the Jews of North Africa (Slouschz 1927:vi). Slouschz, like other visitors to the region, was directed to Hakohen, who agreed to be Slouschz' guide. Hakohen and Slouschz took two trips together, one to the east of Tripoli as far as Benghazi, and the other to the interior, returning to Tripoli via the coastal oases to the west.

When Hakohen showed Slouschz the manuscript of *Highid Mordekhai,* Slouschz reacted enthusiastically (Hakohen 1969:49). Slouschz suggested that a French translation might be published by the Alliance Israélite Universelle in Paris and corresponded with Hakohen about this matter for several years. In the course of their correspondence, Hakohen supplied Slouschz with further information on Tripolitania, material that Slouschz incorporated in his own publications over the next thirty years.[5]

In 1920 Hakohen was appointed as a magistrate in the Rabbinic court of Benghazi, where he lived with his wife and younger children until his death on August 22, 1929. In his later years, while he worked on other matters, he seems to have continued to enlarge and revise the *Highid Mordekhai*.

III

The manuscript of *Highid Mordekhai* is housed in the Jewish National and University Library in Jerusalem (no. 8° 1292). It was written by the author in ink on plain paper (14 by 21 cm.) and bound so that it takes the form of a 262-page book, each page having a recto and a verso. The author wrote in a formalized cursive script known as *mashait*,[6] which differs very little from standard Hebrew. For the most part, the work is quite legible, except for an occasional blurring of the ink or passages in which the writing is somewhat crowded.

There must have been several copies of the manuscript. One of them was sold to the Italian Ministry of Colonies and was published in part, in Italian translation, by M. Mario Moreno (1924, n.d.). The manuscript in the Jerusalem library was given to Professor E. Urbach by a member of Hakohen's family while Urbach was serving as a military chaplain in Tripoli in 1943. Later, Hakohen's children donated a collection of their father's personal papers (4° 1256) to the library. The manuscript itself, according to the Author's Introduction, is divided into four parts, as follows:

Part I (Sections 1–65):   The History of the Jews of Libya
Part II (Sections 66–89):   The Jewish Community of Tripoli
Part III (Sections 90–110): The Jews in the Libyan Countryside
Part IV (Sections 111–114): The Italian Conquest of Libya

This translation presents only Parts III and IV.

Part I (Sections 1–65) deals with the history of Libya from ancient times until Hakohen's day, with special reference to the Jews. It combines traditional North African historiography with the author's own modern research. In the first half, Hakohen relies extensively on the unpublished chronicle of Avraham Khalfon.[7] At several points, it seems that Hakohen copied directly from Khalfon,[8] while at others he says that he "drew upon" Khalfon's work.

Hakohen's narrative of Libyan history contains no novel information. However, the final sections of Part I depend extensively on his personal knowledge of and involvement in events in Tripoli during the last quarter of the nineteenth century and the beginning of the twentieth. This material, which we hope to present in a later publication, provides an important view of Ottoman attempts at reform.

Part II (Sections 66–89) deals with the customs and institutions of Tripoli's Jews in Hakohen's own days. A portion of this part, based on a somewhat different version of the manuscript, was published in Italian by M. Mario Moreno, an orientalist in the colonial service assigned to Libya. Many of the sections in Part II of the Jerusalem manuscript are simply lists of information on a variety of matters. These include a list of synagogues in the town, books published by Tripolitan authors, words which differ in the Jewish and Moslem dialects of Arabic,[9] and excerpts from Rabbinic works dealing with the local customs. In Appendix I, I have set down a table of contents for Parts I and II, giving them my own section headings, to provide a sense of the breadth of Hakohen's interests and research activities. An especially valuable section in Part II discusses the workings of the Rabbinic court.

Part III (Sections 90–110) makes up the first portion of the present book. It discusses the Jews of the villages, or, to be more precise, the small market centers scattered throughout the Tripolitanian countryside.[10] Hakohen first came into contact with these communities through his itinerant peddling and later was to focus his scholarly attention on them. The end of this part (Section 110) discusses the Jewish community in Benghazi, where Hakohen took up residence in 1920 and spent the last years of his life. Part IV, also translated here, describes the Italian conquest of Tripoli in the fall of 1911. In both parts, while adding my own section headings, I have retained Hakohen's section numbers for convenience of reference.

IV

A sample of Hakohen's manuscript is reproduced on the following page. Like Jewish authors throughout the Arabic-speaking world, Hakohen wrote not only in the Hebrew of the *Highid Mordekhai* but also in Judaeo-Arabic, the local Arabic written in Hebrew characters. Some of his personal letters are in that language, as is a short monograph, composed for the Jews of Benghazi, dealing with Rabbeinu Gershom Me'or ha-Golah.[11] Hakohen's use of Hebrew in *Highid Mordekhai* is evidence that he was writing for a wider Jewish audience. In fact, Jewish education and language were of particular concern to Hakohen, as seen in the following lines:

> One wishes that the honorable leaders of those groups who are attempting to revive the Hebrew language would agree on both an

ר'עו   עי 96

בשנת התרע סיפן באו ברברים בלילה גנבו דים
גם הליתו רש בהיכל הפת ושאר הפגרים הנשלחים שם,
היהודים נכבדי טריפולי הודיעו בחכתבים לרש
רבני תוגרמה וגם לחכית אשר בעיר הבירה, ואריד
חדי נתקבלה פקודה מקושטא שי נכבדי החמשלה
אשר בטריפולי ובכפר יפין לחקור בעין חודרת לתת
עונש חמור על האנשים אשר שלחו ידם בקרש גם על
תושבי החצון לשלם כסף ענושים לקומס הרסות הבהכנ
הנז

שרי החמשלה שם חתרו להשקיע את הדבר וילחמו
את רש היהודים ואחוזת קרעיהו אשר ערכו לטריפולי
כתב הקבלתא ויחתמו כגד רלונם לאחר לא חלו בה ידי
חדם רק נר אחד הדליק בבהכב נתד חמנו נכון להיכל
הקדש ותהי השרפה . אך קודם גמר הדבר נהפכה החמשלה
כי נכבשה טריפולי לפני האיטלקים ורגזה הארץ
הבהכנ אשר בעיר ריטיר הנזל אין לה עלי זית
הקדיש ולא שום תמיכה רק מתקיימת ממחיר העליות
לסת כ שאר כל בתי כנסיות של החצון של היהודים
(חולם בתי התפלות של החשולמים בכל החצון כלים
מתקיימים חפירו' הווק ף (ההקד ש) לחזיק הבדקים
ושמן להוחנר ושכירות החזן וכיולא, והות החמן קרקעה
ועלים יקדישו אותה הקתמדכים על הרוב החשוכי
בנים להיות וק ף נ(היקדיש) לבית תפלה אייוחדת להיות
הקרן קים לעולם והפירות לתחיכה לבית תפלה פלונית
וזה

A sample (p. 215a) of Hakohen's manuscript, reproduced by courtesy of the Jewish National and University Library, Jerusalem (call number Heb 8° 1292).

adequate system of pronunciation, *i.e.* one that differentiates each sound, and on one script—whether Rashi script[12] or cursive—for all of Israel scattered in many lands. Then the language would be more vital because it would be understood, in its spoken and written forms, in every Jewish community. In addition, all Jews would be united by a single script and a single tongue, in contrast to the present situation in which the European Jew and the African Jew, each familiar with the traditional Hebrew of his own country, are estranged from one another in speech and in writing. In particular, the language could be enriched with words from the Bible, Talmud, and Midrashim, or from Arabic, which is related to Hebrew [Note 62, ms. p. 160a].

This passage shows the significance of Hakohen's remark, in the "Biography of the Author," that he was influenced by the literature of the Haskalah, or Hebrew "enlightenment." The Haskalah originated in Germany and spread to the Jewish communities of Eastern Europe. Its purpose was to bring the Jews into the modern world and to bring the "world" to the Jews by creating a Hebrew literature as cosmopolitan as the literature of any other contemporary language.[13] The Haskalah itself was no longer an important movement in Eastern Europe in the last decade of the nineteenth century, the period in which Hakohen probably started his work. It had, however, established a legacy of modern Hebrew writing, as well as a Hebrew press. Hakohen read Haskalah and post-Haskalah literature, even though these movements had minimal impact on the Jews of Tripoli. He also contributed news items on his community to Hebrew papers in Warsaw, London, and Palestine (see Appendix II). In this way, Mordechai Hakohen was open to intellectual innovations from the European world, innovations that reinforced his belief that his search for knowledge need not be constrained by religious tradition.

As shown in the passage quoted above, Hakohen sensed that a special effort was necessary if the Hebrew language was to be adapted to the needs of modern life. Unlike the Haskalah writers, who consciously eschewed Rabbinic Hebrew in favor of the biblical language, Hakohen drew freely from both sources. His extensive familiarity with traditional Hebrew is apparent from his writing, which despite its richness betrays a certain repetition of phraseology. Here and there, the influence of the local pronunciation of Hebrew creeps in, as when an *'alef* is substituted for a *he'*. A glimpse at the Hebrew of Khalfon, which appears here and there in the manuscript, suggests that the continuity in this genre of writing, independent of the influence of the Haskalah, might be profitably studied. Indeed, a linguistic analysis of the text would be a study in itself.

V

We do not know enough about the history of Tripoli at the turn of the century to describe Mordechai Hakohen's social world in detail. A full study of his life and writings would surely enrich our understanding of that period. But a few words can be said here about the Tripoli of his day and its Jewish community.

The Ottoman empire had retaken Tripoli in 1835, but did not gain complete control of the interior till 1858. From mid-century, the administration of the Turkish pashas advanced certain policies of reform, but these were not well received by the local population.[14] The imposition of new taxes was resisted, the extension of equality to Jews and Christians was resented, and there was relatively little response to the Ottoman authority's educational programs. Thirty-three pashas governed Tripoli from 1835 through 1908. Under their reign, some features of modern technology—the telegraph, regular steamship mail service, and modern water and sewage facilities—were introduced. However, the administrative and technological changes instituted from above[15] had little effect on the attitudes and social structure of the native population.

The latter half of the nineteenth century saw the decline of the slave trade with its terminal at Tripoli (Martin 1978). However, Tripoli continued to be an important node of commerce linking Europe with Central Africa. Recent studies have shown the continued vitality of the caravan trade up until the first decade of the twentieth century (Johnson 1976; Baier 1977). In the middle of the nineteenth century, Turkey had enlisted the aid of European countries in exploring the interior for natural resources, but later she forbade this activity for fear of aiding foreign intelligence operations. This suspicion was heightened, of course, by the establishment of the French protectorate in Tunisia in 1881. Throughout the latter half of the nineteenth century, European political influence was on the rise, given voice by the foreign consuls in Tripoli.

The Jewish community had always made up a significant portion of the capital's population, and Jews were prominent in the commercial life of the country. Jewish merchants were active in financing trans-Saharan caravans from Tripoli. From the middle of the nineteenth century, there was a steady and rapid population growth among the Jews, along with an influx from the hinterland to the town.[16] This probably was due to the greater physical security to be found in the city. Toward the end of the century, the growing Italian presence may also have been a factor in luring immigrants to Tripoli.

Under Ottoman rule, the office of Ḥakham Bashi (Chief Rabbi) was established, giving religious tradition greater leverage in local community affairs. Most of the Chief Rabbis were men from abroad who had been appointed to the post. This reflected both a dearth of Rabbinic competence within the Tripolitan community and the fact that most local scholars had devoted their energies to the mystic tradition of the Kabbalah. The first Rabbi to officially bear the title of Ḥakham Bashi was Eliahu Bekhor Ḥazzan, who led the community for fourteen years (1874–1888) and was a prominent Sephardic Rabbi.[17]

Rabbi Ḥazzan's term in Tripoli appears to have been, in the words of a talmudic adage, the provision of a remedy before the onset of an illness. Having previously served as a Rabbinic emissary[18] in Tunis, he was well acquainted with the intellectual currents of the European enlightenment. One of his books, *Zikhron Yerushalayim,* depicts a confrontation between traditional religious conceptions and the spreading Western ideas. Ḥazzan reacted to this challenge not with vociferous arguments or extremist withdrawal, but rather with reasoned debate and sympathetic persuasion.

From his second year in Tripoli, Ḥazzan began to work toward educational reform within the Jewish community by modernizing the methods of instruction, teaching European languages and mathematics, and encouraging the development of vocational training. His efforts met with some opposition from conservative elements in Tripoli, who were somewhat derisively referred to by Hakohen as the "assembly of judges." However, the controversy seems to have been confined to the elite of the community, with few echoes among the Jewish population at large, who were yet to be affected by the winds of the enlightenment. Nevertheless, the timing and social disposition of this confrontation were crucial. By the first decade of the twentieth century, many Jewish youngsters had been drawn into modern educational systems, either those run by the local community or the Alliance Israélite Universelle, or those sponsored by Italian institutions.[19] The battle for European-style schooling had been won, fought by men who were at the same time defenders of religious tradition. Among the local leadership of this movement we find, not surprisingly, the figure of Mordechai Hakohen.

VI

Mordechai Hakohen, the scholar, was also very much involved in community affairs. Having worked in his youth as a teacher, he placed education among his central interests. In the local reform movement, he provided continuity while innovating Chief Rabbis like Ḥazzan, Qimḥi, and Shabbetai[20] came and went. In 1888, he proposed a way to simplify the teaching of basic reading by having students match written consonants and vowels with natural syllabic sounds, eliminating the need to memorize the names of the letters. Although this suggestion was rejected, he was eventually able to bring about some changes in the method of instruction.

Hakohen came into contact with people from all walks of life—villagers, petitioners to the Rabbinic court, Turkish governors, and even foreign consuls. In 1903, he helped organize a merchants' protest, in the form of a day of prayer and fasting, against an attempt to impose the military exemption tax on the Jewish population. His intellectual encounters with representatives of other religions are noted in his manuscript. His research interests and activities were so well known that historically minded travelers, both Jewish and non-Jewish, were directed to him.[21] Eventually his Rabbinic learning, gained through his own efforts, was given local recognition and he was appointed to serve on the Rabbinic Tribunal in Benghazi.

Hakohen thus had firsthand knowledge of a wide range of people and social experiences. At the same time, there is a distinct sense in his writings that he was a man who found life's fullest meaning in the world of ideas and words. The following description, even allowing for the patronizing tone of the author, conveys the same impression (Furlong 1909:102):

> I found the rabbi [Hakohen] buried in a pile of old books in the library of the synagogue. Touching his hand to his forehead,[22] he welcomed us; then brought from a dark corner a musty old book on magic and science and a glass sphere on which he had pasted paper continents. These proved to be his two greatest treasures, which he exhibited with all the unconcealed glee and pride of a child.

Perhaps the same glee was felt in his encounters with members of other religions, described in several footnotes,[23] in which he successfully upheld a Jewish point of view.

> In 5648—1888—a respected Moslem named Ḥmida al-Mrabeṭ asked me, "Why are the Jews so strict with themselves in refusing to eat meat slaughtered by Moslems, although it is excellent slaughtering and does not inflict suffering on the animal?" I answered that the Torah had compassion for animals and was also concerned with human physical and spiritual well-being. Therefore, the animal has to be checked for infectious diseases and has to be slaughtered with a very sharp knife; in addition, the blood has to be totally drained, as it is defiling and may also contain microbes. He told me that the Moslems eat without inspecting the lung, and also use defective knives,[24] but do not seem to suffer from this. "What felicity there is in the Moslem religion, with no restrictions of diet—not like the Jewish religion!" I answered him, saying, "If this is so, why do you reject the religion of Christianity, which can provide even greater happiness, for it permits the eating of strangled animals and of

pork?[25] You should adopt Christianity, which permits everything."
He then cried out, saying, "I have been trapped by error because I
debated with you. But wait, the matter is not finished yet."

One night Ḥmida arranged a feast for a learned guest, Sheikh
al-Khaḍir, together with other Moslem notables. I went to his house
for some business matter and Ḥmida whispered to the sheikh, "See
if you can introduce the matter of religion to the Jew and entice him
to accept the pure religion of Islam." Then the sheikh began
smoothly and slyly, saying, "My son, you are not to blame for not
having followed Islam, for you did so innocently, because there is
nothing written in the *Sura*[26] of Moses concerning Mohammed. But I
should tell you that at one time the Jews falsified the Torah,[27] leaving only a few things intact, such as the Ten Commandments, which
were not tampered with."

I replied to him thus: "You know that formerly the Ottoman Government, may its Glory be upheld, decreed the establishment of a
trade school for the Moslems, and after spending a great deal of the
treasury's money, issued another decree ordering the closing of the
school. How is it that the Government builds and then dismantles?"
The sheikh answered that the Government thought at first that the
youth of Tripoli were cultured and would learn easily, but when it
found out that the results did not justify the investment, the project
was abolished. I then answered, saying, "But the Holy One, Blessed
be He, is not a man who is capricious or a mortal who changes his
mind [Numbers XXIII:19]; he knows hidden things and sees the end
of matters from the beginning. How could he first decree, in the Ten
Commandments, 'Remember the Sabbath Day . . . You shall refrain
from doing all manner of work'[28] and then change his mind and say,
'Let us accept the Moslem religion, work on the Sabbath, and cease
work on Friday'? God forbid that we take such a view." The sheikh
then became incensed and forbade those gathered at the table to
speak to the despicable Jew or to have anything to do with him.

The same sheikh later traveled to the Ghuryan. The Governor,
Ḥasuna Qaramanli, also prepared a feast for him. The Moslem notables began to argue with the head of the Jewish community.[29] At
this, the sheikh forbade them to debate with the Jews, saying,
"When I was in Tripoli, at the home of Ḥmida al-Mrabeṭ, I began to
debate with a Jew whose tongue was sharp as a sword and whose
voice was the voice of evil temptation. Even though I am learned, he
almost succeeded in making me doubt. Had it been in my power, I
would have sentenced him to death. But praised be God that I was
saved and did not abandon my Holy Religion as the result of his
poisonous words" [Section 5, Note 8, ms. p. 10a–b].

When it came to matters of intellectual and religious principle, Hakohen
did not mince words in order to smooth social relationships.

This incident may strike the reader as highly stylized, following a set

pattern that raises some doubt as to its actual occurrence. While Hakohen's narrative definitely fits into a classic cultural format, this does not
mean that we are simply being told a tale. I have heard similar accounts,
though less elaborate, from other Tripolitanian Jews, and I doubt that in
all these instances the informants were trying to take advantage of my
naiveté. Instead, their stories reflected a cultural milieu in which these
religious questions were live and immediate and individuals acted out a
drama which seemed to them peculiar to their own experience but which
the outside observer recognizes as a variation of a well-known script.

We do not know enough of the Moslems of Tripoli to document this
assumption, but it is supported by the fact that Hakohen's arguments
reflect the impact of classic Moslem concerns. Even when he is debating
with non-Moslems, as in the following quotation (Section 9, Note 12),
the argument revolves around an issue more relevant to Jewish-Islamic
polemics than to Jewish differences with Christians.

> Present-day researchers, who have discerned that Hebrew and
> Arabic are related, as two sisters, have sought to discover which of
> them is older, which has primacy over the daughter language. In
> 5665—1905—my friend, the scholar George Na'ama, who is Cath-
> olic, told me that he had irrefutable proof that the Hebrew language
> emanated from Arabic. The word *misraim* [Hebrew for Egypt]
> means two *misr*s [*misr* is the Arabic word for Egypt, and the Heb-
> rew would therefore be derivative], *i.e.* upper *misr* and lower *misr*.
> The *mem* at the end of a word signifies a plural [or dual], just as in
> Arabic a *nun* at the end of a word signifies a plural [or dual]. There-
> fore the *mem* at the end of *misraim* is the same as a *nun* in Arabic,
> and since Hebrew adds a plural form as in Arabic, this shows that
> the Arabic form [the "singular" *misr*] is older.
>
> I answered him as follows: "It is known that personal names and
> place names do not take an affix; neither the definite article *he'* nor
> the plural *mem* is used. One can say neither *ha-avraham* [the
> Abraham] nor *avraham-im* [Abrahams]. Therefore the original name
> of the country is not *misr,* but *misraim,* taken from the personal
> name of the sons of Ham, as it is written, 'The descendants of Ham:
> Cush, Misraim . . . ' [Genesis X:6]. Also, I could bring definite
> proofs to the contrary. For example, the following, from the begin-
> ning of humankind, the story of Eve: 'She named him Seth, meaning
> God has placed [placed, the Hebrew *shath,* sounds like Seth] for me
> another offspring . . . ' [Genesis IV:25]. If she had spoken Arabic
> she would have called him Ja'al [from Arabic *ja'ala,* meaning put or
> placed], to sound like the spoken word" [ms. p. 19a].

It would be a mistake, however, to assume that Hakohen's intellectual battles simply reflected the obvious religious cleavages in his society, even though the position of the Jews as a minority under Islam was

of great concern to him. His independent judgment allowed him to consider people and situations on their own merits. He had high hopes that the Italian conquerors would ensure freedom of religion, but he encouraged any progress toward this goal, wherever he found it. In several letters to the Hebrew press[30] he praises Turkish officials, "to whom religious prejudice is foreign," for acts of fair administration. In his discussion of Ahmed Razem Pasha, he attributes the governor's pressure on Tripolitanian Jewish families who sought Italian citizenship to his "love for the Ottoman empire, not his hate for the Jews" (Section 58, ms. pp. 107b–108a). In the passage quoted above, he describes the Catholic scholar, whose name is obviously an Arab one, as a friend. He was thus fully capable of combining personal regard with firm intellectual opposition.

I had the opportunity to talk with two of Mordechai Hakohen's daughters, who also described him as a man for whom intellectual integrity and commitment to the written word were the highest of values. In Tripoli, he confronted the religious and lay leaders of the community in Rabbinic court, besting them through his legal acumen and his familiarity with the written codes. His move to Benghazi was due, in part, to these conflicts, in which, in the words of his daughters, he refused to "bow" before those in power, insisting instead on the correct judgment based on legal texts. He appears to have been a man who was deeply involved in, but at the same time capable of detachment from, the social fabric of his times. While a panorama of classes and personalities unfolds in the pages of his manuscript, there is almost no indication of comradeship within the Jewish community or of a relationship that might be called collegial.

Hakohen was obviously aware of this situation. In his introduction, he clearly states that those who scorn (*mevazim*) his efforts outnumber those who respect him. Ya'aqov Guweta', a former resident of Benghazi, recalls that the Jews of that city scoffingly referred to *Highid Mordekhai* as *siddur rebbi mridikh,* little Rabbi Mordechai's book. Hakohen did not see the Jews of Libya as the audience for his book. Instead, he wrote for a wider international community of scholars whose books he read and to whose work as a whole he felt he was contributing. When I asked his daughters if their father had any close friends, they did not mention anyone in the local community, but told of three non-Jewish scholars—M. Mario Moreno, a man named Rossi, and Allessandro Allessandri[31]—who came to their home in Benghazi to study Hebrew with Hakohen.

In his last years, his daughters said, Hakohen became more and more removed from daily affairs, and was primarily concerned with making an important contribution to science. He would sit and work with single-minded concentration, even ignoring the cat if it jumped on his shoulder as he sat at his desk. He had become preoccupied with a classic challenge of the physical world, the invention of a perpetual motion machine. In the midst of his work, on August 22, 1929, he died of a stroke, having succumbed, in his daughters' view, to the pressures of solving the problem. The medical facts are lost to us, but the story befits the image of a man who was committed to the unity of the natural and moral universe.

VII

The special quality of Hakohen's book is apparent when it is compared with works in two separate genres, the accounts of Jewish travelers and the Rabbinical treatises on local customs.

There is a long tradition of travel literature which describes the conditions of Jewish communities in various countries. Best known is the twelfth-century work of Benjamin of Tudela, who traveled through the Mediterranean countries and the Middle East, and whose narrative has become a major historical document of the period (Adler 1911). More recently, the work of David d'Beth Hillel of Vilna has given us a valuable picture of Jewish life in the Middle East and India in the first part of the nineteenth century (1832). In that same period, many Rabbinical emissaries from Palestine traveled throughout the Diaspora collecting funds and published descriptions of the Jewish communities they visited (Yaari 1951). It is particularly interesting to compare Hakohen's work with that of two other Middle Eastern Jews who accompanied European explorers in North Africa and the Middle East in the latter half of the nineteenth century. One of these is Mordechai Aby-Serour (1830–1886) of Morocco, who served as guide to the explorer Charles de Foucauld, known for his study of the Berbers. The second is Ḥayyim Ḥabshush (Goitein 1941), the Yemenite Jew who assisted Joseph Halevi, the noted orientalist, in his search for Sabaean inscriptions in the Najran in 1870.

Mordechai Aby-Serour (see Semach 1928 and de Foucauld 1939) was familiar with wide areas of southern Morocco as a result of his commercial activities. He established regular trade links between Timbuctoo and Morocco. At the age of thirty-five, calamity befell him when his brother and brother-in-law, both partners in his commercial ventures, died. The governor of Timbuctoo used this opportunity to confiscate his wealth, leaving him little to show for his former successes.

Around this time, Aby-Serour came into contact with the French consul at Mogador, Beaumier. At the latter's suggestion, he wrote a paper on the Jewish community that he had founded at Timbuctoo (Aby-Serour 1870). The Société de Géographie then brought him to Paris on two occasions, hoping to train him to carry out scientific explorations in

Morocco. However, these missions proved disappointing, and the original enthusiasm of the scientific community waned.

In 1880, Aby-Serour contributed a paper to the Alliance Israélite Universelle on the topic of the Daggatouns (Aby-Serour 1880), whom he described as a people scattered through the western Sahara, under the patronage of the ruling Touareg nomads. The Daggatouns are nominally Moslems, but they stand out from the rest of the population by virtue of their fair complexion. In his paper, Aby-Serour develops the thesis that these people were originally Jews from Tafilalet and other towns of southern Morocco who were converted to Islam. He bases this belief on local legends, claiming that the Daggatouns received him "as a brother."

Of course, legends such as these must be understood in terms of their social setting; myths claiming Jewish origin can be found all the way from West Africa to Afghanistan. They are often attached to marginal groups whose social position is parallel to that of the Jews—politically weak and requiring protection, practicing specialized trades, and preserving customs distinct from those of the Islamic majority. In his introduction to Aby-Serour's paper, I. Loeb apologizes for the author's lack of ethnological sophistication. It is difficult to take a man who survived the Sahara through ruse and imagination and reshape him into a detached and disciplined researcher.

Mordechai Hakohen was also fascinated by his coreligionists in remote and exotic areas. Their origins intrigued him, and he searched their past for hints of a dramatic and glorious history. He observed present-day customs, suggesting ways in which they might illuminate biblical passages, and collected myths about past centuries in which the Jews and the Berbers ruled the land. At the same time, in spite of this romantic theme, Hakohen had a scholar's sense of the limits of evidence. He emphasized the fact that written documents were in short supply, and he recorded oral history without automatically accepting its validity.

Hakohen entertained a variety of alternative hypotheses, and when data were not available, he admitted that positive conclusions were not within his reach. He fully appreciated the canons of legitimate inference, even more so, at times, than his European traveling companion. While Aby-Serour was a man who was prematurely cast in the role of scientist, we would seriously miscast Hakohen by viewing him as a native raconteur.

The other travel writer mentioned above, Ḥayyim Habshush, a Jewish coppersmith from San'a, did not pretend to contribute to European geographical research. Had it not been for his contact with Halevi, the French orientalist, and later with other explorer-scholars, we may assume that his work would never have been written.[32] Halevi's journey provides the framework for the organization of Ḥabshush's manuscript, which takes the form of a narrative. This, of course, does not detract from the value of the report, which reflects Ḥabshush's intelligence, inquisitiveness, and broad interests (Goitein 1941:7). It does, however, mean that the work does not attempt to synthesize existing knowledge of the Yemen with the author's special contribution.

In contrast, Hakohen's manuscript may be viewed in precisely that way. He acquainted himself with earlier works on the history of Tripoli, notably the chronicle of Avraham Khalfon and the history of Ibn Ghalbun.[33] He read geographical works written in Hebrew and published abroad,[34] and consulted Italian works as well. His historical accounts include many specific events but also describe their ethnographic and sociological background. While much of Ḥabshush's journal is built around personal episodes, Hakohen attempts to remove himself from the narrative, confining personal incidents to footnotes. When writing of historical events in which he was an active participant, he normally identifies his source as "Mordechai Hakohen," and places the phrase "the author" in parentheses. In brief, his work is an independently conceived intellectual effort rooted in the author's own scholarly interests and cultural background.

VIII

Hakohen may also be compared with writers who described the details of local custom from the perspective of Rabbinic law. Two who shared a background similar to Hakohen's are Rabbi Avraham Ḥai Adadi (d. 1874) and Rabbi Eliahu Bekhor Ḥazzan (1846–1908). The former served as chief magistrate of the Rabbinic court in Tripoli and wrote two treatises discussing the customs of the local Jewish community.[35] The latter, only ten years older than Hakohen, was Chief Rabbi in Tripoli from 1874 to 1888. He then moved to Alexandria to head the Jewish community there.[36] As we have seen, Hakohen knew Ḥazzan and worked with him toward educational reform in Tripoli. Ḥazzan's book, *N'veh Shalom,* discusses the customs of the Jews of Alexandria.

Works such as *N'veh Shalom* and Adadi's *Maqom she-nahagu* are organized according to well-established Rabbinic codes. Their aim is to evaluate, justify, or criticize local practices in terms of the legal tradition. They are written in a conventional Hebrew-Aramaic style, filled with terminology and phraseology from the Talmud and the commentaries, and are replete with references to other Rabbinic authorities. They can often be important sources of historical information concerning local customs and social institutions. This is not, however, their main purpose.

Hakohen was completely familiar with this genre of writing, so much so that in Sections 71–72 of *Highid Mordekhai* he includes two long excerpts from Adadi's work. As a religious man, he accepted the importance of these Rabbinic judgments, and in his later years, when serving as magistrate in the Benghazi court, much of his energy seems to have been devoted to the correct administration of Rabbinic law. But his religious background merely highlights the special character of *Highid Mordekhai,* which aims to *describe* contemporary practices, not to prescribe or to proscribe.[37]

To illustrate this difference, compare Adadi's account of mourning practices among the Jews of Tripoli with a parallel account by Hakohen describing mourning among the Jews of Yefren about thirty years later. Adadi states (1865:126b):

> It is customary in most Jewish communities for the relatives and friends of a mourner to visit him, dine with him, and offer consolation, each man bringing food, meat, and wine. This is not the case in this city . . . where they run from the mourner and avoid him as if he were excommunicated.

Hakohen's account (Section 101) treats the same custom with empathy, even while seeing it as foolish. He does not compare it unfavorably with standard types of behavior, but confines his criticism to a footnote. He takes the trouble to detail specific practices, and by using legal terminology (such as "derive benefit from his possessions")[38] he accords these customs the status of a comprehensible system with its own internal coherence. Thus we find that Hakohen, though never explicitly making the point, distinguishes the role of the historian-observer from that of the representative of traditional law, and accords importance to both of these activities.

Although Hakohen was an intellectual innovator, we should not exaggerate the extent of his emancipation from his surroundings. For example, he accepts the traditional view of North African historiography that the origins of the Berbers may be traced to ancient Palestine (Section 14). More generally, he accepts a genealogical-migratory framework of history as a means of discovering the genetic relationships and geographical positions of nations. In a footnote to the section that describes the fauna of Libya he mentions Darwin and his colleagues, taking issue with their theory on the descent of man. Hakohen opts for the traditional explanation that monkeys were once men, but were punished by the Creator for having sinned.[39] This view is not merely stated; it is defended with logic and with reference to observable facts. These "quaint" views should not detract from our appreciation of Hakohen's scholarly contribution.

IX

In discussions of various approaches to the study of society, a contrast is often made between "text" and "context." Anthropologists are usually said to emphasize the latter and ignore the former. While my own work among the Jews of Tripoli has been that of an anthropological field researcher, I need not apologize for turning to the task of editing another man's ethnography, particularly if that ethnography can "enlarge a specific experience to the dimensions of a more general one, which thereby becomes accessible *as experience* to men of another country or another epoch" (Lévi-Strauss 1963:17). Moreover, I believe it is possible, without great misrepresentation, to view Hakohen's work from the perspective of twentieth-century anthropology.

To begin with, we find in the *Highid Mordekhai* a combination of detachment and empathy that would do credit to many an anthropologist. We have already cited Hakohen's attempt to present unusual mourning practices in Yefren in understandable terms. This attitude may be contrasted with the standard townsman's view of the village Jews as uneducated, simple, and unkempt.[40] Hakohen recognizes the native intelligence of the Jews of the Nefusa region, even though they are not learned men (Sections 94–95). Since he came from an Italian family, we may assume that he was exposed to all the common stereotypes concerning the native village Jews, but these are hardly felt in his writings. His positive view of the Jews of the Jebel Nefusa can be seen in his attempt to emphasize their closeness to tradition (see his Note in Section 97 below), in his belief that their spiritual welfare was strengthened by their correct observance of the commandments (Section 98), and in his efforts to aid the indigent among them (the second Note in Section 92).

There is no aspect of life which is foreign to Hakohen, and he organizes his material in a manner quickly recognized by ethnographers. He deals with climate, crops, and other ecological matters before describing social life. He is knowledgeable about the political organization of the Berbers, and understands how important this matter is in appreciating the situation of the Jews. Much of his material on the Berbers of the Nefusa appears in the context of his discussion of the Jewish community, but the Ibadis also receive separate attention, as in the paragraphs describing the Berber *waqf* (Section 96).

Hakohen uses a wide range of tools. He studies texts and collects oral history from Moslem and Jewish elders. Along with Slouschz, he carefully searches for inscriptions, particularly in Jewish cemeteries. He is concerned with grammatical precision when relying on linguistic evidence. When matters are uncertain, he presents the facts, inviting others to offer their own theories.[41]

It is also useful to compare Hakohen's treatment of the same data with that of his traveling companion, Slouschz, who viewed the Jews of the Tripolitanian interior primarily in an historical evolutionary perspective. Hakohen's point of view, by contrast, is mainly synchronic. While he has a keen eye for customs that hint of a biblical or talmudic past, he confines his historical interpretations to footnotes. His principal aim is a portrayal of the life of the village Jews as he observed it. His conceptualization of the material parallels the approaches of later anthropological research. Thus, the extensive account of the Nefusa community represents one pole of a continuum, the opposite being represented by the Jews of Tripoli (Moreno 1924, n.d.). Other villages are portrayed in considerably less detail but are summed up in terms of a continuum, either as being close to the Nefusa model or as consisting of a mixture of village traits on the one hand and Tripolitan practices on the other. Examining his work, one is inclined to agree with Darnell (1974:18) that anthropological inquiry has an internal logic of its own; various proto-anthropological investigators in different historical periods have all shown similar elements of a modern understanding of cultural diversity.

Any good account is dependent on good ethnography, and we may admire Hakohen here as well. Whether he is describing material culture, economic arrangements, or Jewish customs, the detail and richness of his descriptions are striking. This is not only an "outsider's" reaction; it was also the response of Rabbi Gabriel Megiddish (b. 1907), a former resident of Yefren in the Jebel Nefusa, who now resides in the village of Shalvah in the Lachish region of Israel. Rabbi Megiddish corroborated almost all of Hakohen's account of the region, disagreeing on only a few details. In brief, the quality of Hakohen's work can legitimately be compared with that of other ethnographers.

One aspect of Hakohen's concern with precision is found in his penchant for quantification. In describing the distances between various sites and villages he attempts to give exact information, usually in hours traveled. As a supplementary source of income, he taught himself how to fix watches, but his interest extended to the astronomical basis of timekeeping. He discusses this in two long footnotes (Section 9, Note 13, and Section 53, Note 42), in which he also describes the installation of a clock and chimes in a Catholic church in Tripoli.[42] In comparing the calendars of Moslems, Jews, Christians, and Hindus he reveals a fine appreciation of the relative nature of such reckoning.

Hakohen also strove for historical accuracy in dating. In several footnotes he takes issue with dates given by Moslem chroniclers, forcing himself to struggle with the problem of intercalating lunar and solar years. In one of these notes, he also offers a suggestion for reconciling contradictory dates that appear in the Bible.[43] Here, as in the problem of tracing the genealogical links between nations, he works under the assumption that one can arrive at the "correct" solution.

It has been noted (Gruber 1965) that modern anthropology, which concerns itself with both man's biological past and his cultural present, became possible only when geological time was accepted as relevant to man's experience. Anthropology, as a distinct discipline, is based upon a characteristic time scale which brings all human societies, regardless of area, period, or phenotypic peculiarity, within the purview of a single science of man. Although Hakohen's understanding of the Bible prevented him from accepting this extended historical perspective, he does sense the importance of a unified view in studying human history. His attempt to match Moslem and Jewish chronology is not simply a mechanical exercise revealing a compulsive attachment to numbers. Rather, it is an effort, like that of Bodin (1566; tr. 1945), to devise "a method for the easy comprehension of history" by establishing a single time scale for all histories.[44] In his two notes on time reckoning, he refers to the ancient Hindu calendar, as well as to those in the Western tradition.[45] When trying to reconcile the contradictory dates in the Bible, he notes that somewhere in central Africa a year is counted every six months, and that this might have been the system in ancient Egypt. His attempt to coordinate the time scales of different societies would not be sanctioned by modern anthropology, but it does imply *an* anthropology, a study of man in the broadest sense.

A second assumption taken for granted today is the continuity between animal and human life, or, in other terms, the link between biology and behavior. Hakohen had learned of Darwin's views and the controversy surrounding them. This was his reaction:

> According to our sages, apes were originally human beings who, because of their evil deeds, were cast down[46] by the Creator and turned into apes. The scholar Bondin[47] also demonstrated clearly to the academy in Paris that the ancestors of apes were human beings who, because of their sins and promiscuity, had been cast down and turned into apes. However, according to the scholar Darwin and the scholar La Mettrie,[48] our original ancestors were apes, and we have become civilized over the course of time, while the apes have retained their original form. Each scholar has his reasons and explanations.
>
> Now, we do not rely solely on the tradition of our sages, of blessed memory, if we cannot find conclusive proof. If we take the time to look carefully at the history of nature, whose laws have been constant since the time of creation, we can bring nature herself as evidence against Darwin and his colleagues.
>
> Nature, which does not change, clearly indicates that our ancestors were not apes. The ape is special in its nature: it does not reproduce in captivity; this is not true of human beings, who reproduce in every habitat. In addition, we witness species of plants and animals which can fertilize related species but which do not repro-

duce thereafter, except in the case of human intervention, as in the grafting of trees. For example, the horse and the donkey are related and can produce a mule that is similar to both of them, but the mule cannot reproduce. This is not the case, however, with regard to apes and men. Researchers in Australia have already tried to mate a man and an ape and produced nothing, not even a mule. Therefore, if we claim that our ancestors were apes, how did nature change so much that they [men and apes] cannot reproduce?

If it is claimed that the time involved is very long, and they have grown apart and therefore cannot cross-fertilize and reproduce, then we can bring an argument from the plants! Everyone[49] is in agreement that plants are older than animals, yet they still function as of old, fertilizing related species and bearing fruit. We thus see that their inner nature has not changed.

However, if we claim that apes were cast down by the Creator, we can also claim that the same act deprived them of the ability to fertilize other related species and reproduce. For there is also the case of the Whites and the Blacks, and, according to tradition, "have we not all one father?"[50] They have been separated from one another for hundreds of years, but not through a divine act. Even though Blacks differ from Whites in several respects, the power of reproduction is preserved; they can mate with Whites and yield offspring, and the offspring can yield offspring. They are thus different from the mule, which results from the horse and donkey; because they [Blacks and Whites] all have one father, the seed can yield more seed without outside intervention [Section 4, Note 7, ms. pp. 8a–b].

Several points deserve mention here. Hakohen does not build a barrier between himself and the Darwinian line of inquiry, nor does he suggest that his readers do so. He states his willingness to abandon traditional notions if they do not stand up to logical and empirical scrutiny. In yet another footnote, which has a Malthusian tone, he claims that the traditional Aramaic translation of a verse in Isaiah[51] cannot be correct. The *targum,* or translation, states that 2,600,000,000 Assyrian soldiers died outside of Jerusalem, but this must be an exaggeration because

> if we say that this number [of soldiers] was present in Sennacherib's army in addition to the population of other nations, and also imagine that the whole earth was covered with grain, it still would not suffice to feed everyone. For the circumference of the earth is forty million meters, and the land consists of only twenty-eight percent of the total area [Section 67, Note 49, ms. p. 127b].

As for Darwin, Hakohen attempts to meet him, so to speak, on his own grounds. Hakohen does not accept the premise of the antiquity of the earth, as he explicitly states. He does assume, however, that nature works according to regular principles, and by reference to these principles he attempts to show that Darwin's theories are untenable. What is interesting is that Hakohen does not oppose the premise that one can bring the natural world and the human world into the same universe of understanding. When he declares that "everyone is in agreement that plants are older than animals," he places Darwin's theory and the biblical narrative on the same plane. By implication, the biblical account of man's creation, like Darwin's version of evolution, is not to be divorced from the overall view of the natural world and its development. Hakohen's argument juxtaposes the reproductive powers of plants, animals, and men. Even the reported experiment in which a human being was mated with an ape receives no moral comment, despite the prohibition and abhorrence of this sort of union expressed in the Bible (Leviticus XVIII:22).

In view of all this, it is not "odd" (Harris 1969:83) that a belief in the creation stories of Genesis often goes together with a monogenetic view of human origins (see Hodgen 1964). Given a unified view of human history, as well as a belief in the continuity between the creation of nature and the creation of man, it is obvious that "we all have one father." In line with this position, cultural variation is seen as a matter of learning, as in the incidents in which the physical habits of people from different backgrounds come into direct contrast.[52] These assumptions, together with the relativism implied in his work, indicate a logical affinity of Hakohen's approach to contemporary anthropology.

If Hakohen had a view of man that was close to that of modern anthropology, it is also true that he did not formulate a specific concept, such as "culture" or "social structure," which expressed that view. Still, he shared a common attribute with many of the thinkers who promoted the comparative study of societies (see Lowie 1937:39–54). Hakohen, in addition to being a part-time scientist, historian, and interpreter of the Scriptures, was also, and perhaps foremost, a jurist. Traditional Judaism, while anchored in the biblical narrative, does not impose itself in daily affairs by demanding a literal acceptance of the cosmology of Genesis, but rather by its legal regulation of almost all aspects of everyday life. While Hakohen separated legal judgment from the detached observation and recording of various practices, his juridic orientation is felt constantly. Many of these practices are presented in legal terminology; a more casual observer might have let them pass simply as habits or customs. The legal bond relating Jews to Berber tribesmen in the Jebel Nefusa is noted, along with the balance of obligations which tied Jewish artisans to their clients (Sections 91 and 92). Domestic life is seen in terms of the duties specified in the Mishnaic code (Section 100), and the peculiar mourning practices mentioned above are understood as a prohibition against deriving "benefit from his possessions." The ban on gambling in Benghazi does not only take the form of moral exhortation, but implies that stakeholding documents are illegal (Section 110). In these and other passages it can be seen that Hakohen's legal background led him to stress the importance of institutions, rights, and obligations, and gave him a way of conceptualizing data which might be reported simply as exotic folkways by a more superficial observer.

Anyone who has read both the work of Nahum Slouschz and that of Hakohen is bound to ask about the relationship between the two men. Slouschz refers to Hakohen now and then, calling him "my friend," saying that he was "something of a Hebrew scholar," and acknowledging that his account of Tripoli under the Qaramanli reign (Slouschz 1908a) is indebted to Hakohen's work on Khalfon's manuscript.[53] The overall impression is that of a nineteenth-century explorer condescendingly appreciating his "native guide." In a similar fashion, Slouschz' teacher at the Sorbonne, Joseph Halevi, did not even mention his guide, Ḥabshush, in his reports on his travels in Yemen (Goitein 1941:9).

There are in existence fourteen different letters exchanged between Hakohen and Slouschz after their first meeting in the summer of 1906. Five were among Slouschz' papers and can be found in the archives of the Hebrew writers' association in Tel Aviv (Agudat HaSofrim Ha'ivriyim). Four of these have been published (Hakohen 1969). The remaining letters may be found in the archive of Mordechai Hakohen in the Hebrew manuscript division of the Jewish National and University Library in Jerusalem. Here the letters are recorded in a ledger kept by Hakohen which includes copies of incoming and outgoing correspondence. Several of the letters are available in more than one place. The letters sent to Slouschz are written in a *mashaiṭ* script, while the copies in the ledger are in a North African cursive. These various letters provide a glimpse of the relationship between the two men.

Hakohen accompanied Slouschz on two journeys in 1906, one to the east of Tripoli as far as Benghazi, the other to the Jebel Ghuryan and the Jebel Nefusa, with a return to Tripoli via the coastal oases to the west. Their visits to outlying towns are reflected in Part III of Hakohen's manuscript, which we present here, but Hakohen had been familiar with these places for twenty years before Slouschz' arrival. Slouschz requested that Hakohen keep a diary of the journey (Hakohen 1969) and send it to him after its completion. Hakohen also worked at copying tombstone inscriptions, and over the next several years he supplied Slouschz with other information concerning the area.

The correspondence between Slouschz and Hakohen ranges over the years 1906 to 1910, although the majority of the letters were written before March 1907. Most of them are from Hakohen to Slouschz, although one can reconstruct, from the former's replies, the latter's requests. In one letter, Slouschz asks Hakohen for information on place names and tribal names, estimates of the size of the Jewish communities, a word list of the peddlers' argot of the Nefusa region, details of local liturgical practice, lists of patronyms, and so forth. Slouschz at first shows impatience that Hakohen's replies did not reach him immediately. Later, however, in a letter written from Tangiers in 1906 (Slouschz visited the other North African countries after his trip to Libya), we find Slouschz apologizing for not having written sooner. He had taken sick in Morocco and had been hospitalized in Tangiers. He tells Hakohen that while he was lying in the hospital in Tangiers, a fire broke out in his hotel, destroying much of his material. He promises Hakohen a copy of his forthcoming book to help the Tripolitanian scholar with his own research.

Hakohen also made requests of Slouschz, usually of a highly specific and technical nature. In one letter, he asks Slouschz if there is some demographic law whereby a population equalizes its sex ratio if many men are killed in a war. In another letter, he discusses color terminology in Hebrew and Arabic and asks for reactions to his interpretation from Slouschz or his colleagues. He also asks Slouschz to send him detailed maps of Libya. He seems to have received no replies to these various requests.

Hakohen also discusses with Slouschz the possibility of publishing his book in France. Slouschz seems to have made the initial suggestion, and, in the letter from Tangiers, he says that he has already written to the Alliance Israélite Universelle in Paris about the matter. Hakohen worked at finishing the manuscript, which at that time included Parts I and II of the present version. In a later letter (January 27, 1907), Slouschz writes of a French translation of the work, and asks what kind of royalties Hakohen would expect. Hakohen does not reply to this question (at least not in the letters available) but merely writes, on May 17, 1907, that the manuscript is ready. He asks whether he should send it to Paris or wait for Slouschz' planned visit to Tripoli. Not having received a reply, he writes a month later (June 16, 1907) to say that although someone else is interested in publishing the work, he feels committed to Slouschz. In the few remaining letters, no further mention of the manuscript is made.

Slouschz made tentative plans to visit Tripoli again during a summer vacation, as reflected in Hakohen's letters from 1908 to 1910. Hakohen writes of coordinating his return from Jerusalem, where he planned to find a spot in which his mother could eventually be buried, with Slouschz' possible visit in 1909. Slouschz did not return to Tripoli. Instead he visited Cyrenaica in 1908, serving on a mission of the Anglo-Jewish Territorial Organization that sought alternatives to Palestine as a Jewish homeland (Slouschz 1907). Hakohen and Slouschz were never to meet again.

A great deal of the material found in Hakohen's manuscript also appears in Slouschz' work, but this is all the more reason to make the original manuscript available to the public. Slouschz is heavily influenced by nineteenth-century theories of history and culture, and he places the customs of the Jews of Tripolitania in the context of those theories. This is particularly true with regard to his descriptions of the small rural communities, in which Slouschz' theorizing is largely unfettered by historical documents.

Two themes of Slouschz' writing are worth noting. The first is a national romanticism, seen in his search for cultural traces of the biblical past and for evidence of groups boasting an autonomous Jewish existence.[54] Both Slouschz and Hakohen point to many place names, such as "castle of the Jews" or "wadi of the Jews," and state that these indicate a large, and perhaps dominant, Jewish population in the area. It is quite possible, if not probable, that the Jewish population in these regions was once larger than it is today, just as the general population was once larger. This does not, however, imply Jewish dominance. Elsewhere (Goldberg 1971), I have suggested that the multiplicity of Jewish archaeological remains might instead reflect the frequent movement of communities from place to place in a land which, both ecologically and politically, provided them only a precarious existence.

The second theme in Slouschz' work is one that is well known to anthropologists, a unilineal view of cultural development. Unilineal evolutionist thought had an impact in many scholarly fields, and Jewish studies was no exception. Slouschz, for example, believed that the Jews of North Africa had gone through the same stages of development, at a later date, as other Jewish communities. He refers to the shift in leadership at the end of the Second Temple period in Judea, in which the hereditary aristocracy of the Kohanim (priests) was replaced by the aristocracy of learning represented by the Rabbis. He sees the same development in North Africa at the end of the first millennium, and attempts to document this by referring to cultural "survivals" of the early power of the priests (1927:287–292).

Detailed consideration of this question is beyond the scope of this volume (see instead Hirschberg 1974:163–165). Suffice it to say that Slouschz, like other evolutionists, shows a penchant for building grand historical theories that overshadow the data on which they are based. In addition, the evolutionist assumption leads him to describe present-day customs as a means of interpreting earlier periods. Wherever necessary, we have offered alternatives to interpretations of customs cited by Slouschz, taking a more functional or synchronic view of these practices, but trying to keep history in mind as well.

While one must, of course, be wary of automatically applying interpretations based on Jewish history as a whole to the small communities in Tripolitania, it should be understood that these communities have been influenced by the major cultural forces which shaped North African Jewry (see Chapter Three). Their Judaism is based on the Rabbinic law which developed out of the Talmud, and, to cite a more recent period, their liturgy is infused with the innovations of Lurianic Kabbalism. Since they have always been in contact with the city of Tripoli, any attempt to categorize them as "vestiges" of a former period is clearly a misplaced exercise. There are, however—to give Slouschz his due—certain customs which may be best explained as the continuation of older patterns which have become extinct elsewhere. Each of these cases must be evaluated in its own right, and not be automatically attributed to an assumed stage of development.

XI

Hakohen's primary interest is the Jewish community in his own day, but some of the matters he mentions are worth considering in the broader context of North African ethnohistory. One that has intrigued students of North Africa has been the notion of the Judaized Berbers (Hirschberg 1963). This theory claims that before the advent of Islam, Judaism had been widely accepted by the indigenous Berber population. There are historical parallels in other regions of the world, such as the Jewish kingdom of Dhu Nuwas in the Yemen and the spread of Judaism in the Khazarite kingdom in southern Russia.[55] No less an authority than Ibn Khaldun indicates that some of the Berber tribes had accepted Judaism.

The assumed Judaization of the Berbers is sometimes used to explain the readiness of the North Africans to adopt Islam. It is a question that might be worth considering if there were any evidence about the nature of this Judaism, but there is none. Many people have also remarked upon the preponderance of Berber patronyms among North African Jews. This has been cited as evidence that a large proportion are descended from Berbers.

The historical evidence has been reviewed by Hirschberg (1963), who remains skeptical about the supposed predominance of a Berber element among these Jews: "It appears that the proportion of foreign ethnic elements in this North African group is no greater than in any other Jewish diaspora." Some of those who have been impressed by the Judaized Berber thesis have no doubt failed to appreciate the distinction between biological descent and cultural transmission. The question of a genetic similarity between North African Jews and their non-Jewish neighbors—and how such a similarity might be explained—should be kept separate from the discussion of how the Jews acquired their Berber surnames. With regard to the latter problem, Hakohen gives us an important clue (Goldberg 1972b).

In Tripolitania, as elsewhere in the Maghreb, many Jews lived in mountainous regions under the protection of Berber tribal chieftains. In the foreword to the next chapter, we will consider the nature of this protection at greater length. Here, we simply note that it was common for the client Jew to be called by the name of his patron, particularly when traveling outside the tribal area. In Hakohen's words (Section 91): "they are still called by the name of their lord, and treat it respectfully, as it stands at their side to protect them from the other Berbers."

The significance of the Berber name may be appreciated if we remember that the Jews were a mobile population, on both a short-term and a long-term basis (Goldberg 1971). As described in Chapter Two, many were itinerant peddlers and craftsmen. They frequently had to identify themselves outside their home communities, and invoking the name of their tribal protector was a common practice.

There appears to have been a continual movement of Jews from the interior to the city of Tripoli. This is a process that has been found all over North Africa, in both modern and precolonial times. In earlier periods, such movement has been ascribed to the increasing nomadization of the interior and the decline of settled agriculture; Despois (1935) has discussed these patterns in the Jebel Nefusa. If there has been a continuous movement of the peasant population from the interior to the city, and if Jewish traders were ultimately dependent on Moslem agriculturalists, then it stands to reason that the general urban-bound movement would extend to the Jews as well. If indeed, as stated by Hakohen (Section 73, Note 59), the Jewish population of the city is to a large extent composed of those who have come from the interior, it is also not surprising that many of them became known by the name of their tribe or their region of origin.

Another ethnohistorical problem to which Hakohen's work is relevant is the relationship of Arab and Berber. In recent years, there has been a reevaluation of the standard historiography of North Africa, which stressed the separation between the two groups. The earlier view emphasized the destructiveness of the westward movement in the eleventh century of the Beni Hilal and Beni Sulaym tribes, whose pastoral economy harmed both village cultivation and urban commerce. Another aspect of this historiography, emphasized in Moroccan studies, saw freedom-loving and marabout-worshipping Berber tribesmen continually resisting the imposition of a central government dominated by Arabism and official Islam. It is now clear that these distinctions have been overstated (Burke 1972, 1975). Camel nomadism existed among the Berbers in North Africa before the Arab invasions, and the raids of the Bedouin were not aimed at devastating rural or urban life. The elevation of the differences between

Arab and Berber to a basic cultural and national distinction must be understood in terms of French colonial policy in North Africa, which aimed to link the Berbers culturally and politically to France, at the same time separating them from the nationalism that would link them to Arab culture and Islam. Mordechai Hakohen does not directly address these issues. His use of the terms Berber and Arab is of interest, however, precisely because his accounts of the revolts against Ottoman authority by tribal leaders in Tripolitania are not colored by a particular political or ethnological stance.

Sections 42 through 46 of the *Highid Mordekhai* are an account of these revolts. The major figure is Ghoma, a chieftain from the Jebel Nefusa. Ghoma's wars with the Turkish pashas in the 1840s and 1850s are described by Féraud and Rossi.[56] Slouschz' version (1908a) relies on Hakohen's material, but he does not present all of it. Hakohen interviewed one of Ghoma's lieutenants, and his version of the rebellions contains details not found in the other histories.

Hakohen distinguishes between Arabs and Berbers in that the Arabs are the city dwellers and farmers living in the communities near the coast, while the Berbers are the tribesmen from the Jebel Nefusa. However, as in the case of French North Africa (Gellner 1972), the rebels do not fight in the name of Berberism. They are not trying to preserve their own linguistic identity, customary law, or special version of Islam, even though many of the Berbers of the Jebel Nefusa are followers of the Ibadi sect. Rather, the rebels are motivated by a warrior tradition which stresses honor, bravery, and manliness together with the quest of booty and the avoidance of Turkish rule and taxation. In this respect, the Berbers, whom Hakohen also calls mountaineers,[57] are no different from the Arabs of the coastal villages, except that the latter have little hope of resisting the Turkish military. Ghoma's rebels ally themselves with whomever they can, Arab or Berber, and no mention is made of any special tie between them and other Berber-speaking groups, such as the residents of Zuara west of Tripoli. In fact, the application of the terms Arab and Berber sometimes varies according to context, reflecting structures of segmentary opposition. While in many places the Berber mountaineers are contrasted with Arab peasants, Ghoma is called the "prince of the Ishmaelites" by the Bey of Tunis. His identity changes with the particular situation in which he appears.

Liberation from Tripoli is not an ideological matter either. At several points in the story Ghoma seems prepared to stop fighting if he is given recognition and authority by the Turkish governor. When this is refused, he continues to rebel. The distinction between Berber and Arab does not necessarily have any political content. When Hakohen refers to the Berbers in other parts of the book, he does so primarily with regard to language. In view of all this, Gellner's conclusion (1972) seems appropriate to Tripolitania: "The Berber tribesman is a menace *qua* tribesman, not *qua* speaker of a gibberish sounding language."

The question of Berbers versus Arabs was not a major issue in Tripolitania, and so we would not expect it to arouse strong ideological positions. There are only small concentrations of Berber speakers in the region, and even in the Jebel Nefusa Berber-speaking and Arabic-speaking communities stand side by side (Despois 1935). There are other matters, however, in which Italian colonial policy, with which Hakohen had some contact, might be expected to influence his ethnological inquiry. One is the archaeological perception of Roman antiquity and the interpretation of evidence concerning the region's agricultural potential (Segrè 1974:25–32). Another is the perception of local Arab society and its opposition to Turkish rule, which misled the Italians into thinking that their intervention would be welcomed (Evans-Pritchard 1949:108–109). In the case of the former, Hakohen frankly states that the natives do not work the land as diligently as they might, and that there is much untapped agricultural potential. This accords with the Italians' view that their rule will benefit the region. As for the latter, he looks forward to Italian rule, believing it will improve the condition of the country and the situation of the Jewish population. He does not, however, like later Italian writers, denigrate the rule of the Turkish governors. Neither does he suggest that the Libyan Moslems would welcome the Italians; instead, he stresses their religious opposition (Chapter Six). On these subjects, Hakohen seems to formulate his own view, which does not reflect an official ideological stance. Most of the manuscript was completed about five years before the Italian invasion, and his political opinions do not bias the ethnography.

XII

The manuscript appears to have undergone several revisions and to have existed in at least two, nonidentical forms. Hakohen's original plan was to make the *Highid Mordekhai* a two-part book, the first part dealing with history and drawing heavily on Khalfon, and the second dealing with contemporary Tripoli. This is the book he was finishing when Slouschz arrived; he describes it in one of his letters as divided into two parts. A similar division is mentioned by Moreno in the introduction to the edition that he translated (Moreno n.d.: 6–7).

However, the Jerusalem manuscript is not identical in either organization or content to that from which Moreno worked. The Jerusalem version is divided into four parts, as described earlier, while Moreno had in front of him a two-part text, with the second part subdivided into the following headings: (a) The Beliefs and Practices of the Jews of Tripoli,

(b) The Internal Organization of the Jewish Community, (c) The Jews of the Villages, and (d) The Jews of Cyrenaica. In the Jerusalem manuscript, headings (a) and (b) are included in Part II, while (c) and (d) are combined in Part III. Part IV, the account of the Italian conquest, is not mentioned by Moreno.

Moreno's actual publication, which includes only the beliefs and practices of the Jews of Tripoli, differs from the Jerusalem manuscript in several respects. First, it includes a more extensive explanation of general Jewish practices along with its description of local customs. It thus appears to be consciously directed toward a non-Jewish audience, suggesting that Hakohen had revised the work with the Italian translation in mind.[58] Second, Moreno's edition contains more ethnography, including detailed descriptions of amulets, local rituals, and proverbs and verses (in Arabic) to be cited on various occasions. Third, Moreno's volume does not have any of the lists of patronyms, personal names, and names of authors, some of which Hakohen had compiled at Slouschz' request.

Moreover, Toschi (1934:83) states that the Hebrew original is 489 pages long. The Jerusalem manuscript, in contrast, includes 517 pages of text and 6 pages of introductory material, and it does not appear to be a simple elongation of Moreno's text. The last section mentioned by Moreno, dealing with the Jews of Cyrenaica, ends on page 250a, or the 499th page, of the Jerusalem manuscript. It is therefore clear that there were at least two different manuscripts. Hakohen says that Slouschz was "a lamp unto my feet," and he probably inspired Hakohen to pay greater attention to the Jews of the villages. Some of these communities are mentioned in footnotes in the first part of the book,[59] but it appears that Hakohen decided to devote more attention to them after he saw the importance that Slouschz attached to the subject. The detailed account of Benghazi may have grown out of his residence there, from 1920 on. I cannot suggest any immediate reason for him to have written the last part, which describes the Italian capture of Tripoli, unless he felt that this was an appropriate "conclusion" to the long history documented in his book. He makes no attempt to conceal his pro-Italian leanings, but characteristically gives an unbiased picture of the period in which the conquering Italians begin to favor the subdued Moslem population at the expense of the Jews (Section 114).

According to the recollection of Hakohen's daughters, as well as the evidence in Hakohen's correspondence, Moreno had also hoped to publish the other parts of the manuscript. He was later appointed to diplomatic posts elsewhere in the Middle East,[60] and, with the growth of Fascism in Italy, his activities as a translator of Jewish manuscripts became impolitic. Two editions of Moreno's work appeared, one in Benghazi in 1924 and one in Rome. The Rome edition has no date, and I follow Attal (1973, item 1160) in assigning it to 1928. Aside from Moreno's translation, the manuscript of the *Highid Mordekhai* has been unknown (although "known about"), except to a handful of researchers and to individuals in the Jewish community. It is my privilege to make available a work which has too often *almost* been published.

NOTES

1. The point is well made by Roumani (1974). A general view of Libyan history is provided by Wright (1969). The history of Tripolitania is the subject of books by Féraud (1927) and Rossi (1968), while Cyrenaica, particularly the Sanusi order, is dealt with by Evans-Pritchard (1949) and Martin (1976). Martin also surveys the history of the Fezzan (1978). See Dearden (1976) on the Karamanli period and Cachia (1945) for details of the Ottoman regime in the last century. Khadduri (1963) and Roumani (1973) discuss more recent political developments. Various aspects of Bedouin social structure in eastern Libya have been described by Peters (*e.g.* 1965, 1968, and 1977). De Felice's study of Libyan Jewry (1978) appeared too late for me to consult it.

2. Throughout this book, "Tripolitan" refers to the city of Tripoli and "Tripolitanian" to the province of Tripolitania.

3. The title is taken from the Book of Esther, Chapter VI, verse 2, not the verse cited by Moreno (n.d.).

4. Khalfon (1735–1820) was one of the leaders of the Jewish community of Tripoli and served as its head for several years. He lived during the reign of 'Ali Burghul in Tripoli (Féraud 1927:289–304; Slouschz 1927:20–25; Rossi 1968:255–257; Dearden 1976:128–137). The tribulations facing the community at that time are commemorated in a poem he wrote which was incorporated into the liturgy of the Jews of Tripoli (Zuaretz *et al.* 1960:49–52; Hirschberg 1965a: 179–183). Although one of his Rabbinic works (Khalfon 1861) was published, his chronicle was not. His work is also mentioned by Càzes (1890) and came to the attention of other European scholars (Bergna 1925:243).

5. See Slouschz (1908a; 1909; 1927; 1938–43). More of Slouschz' publications on Tripolitania are listed in Attal (1973).

6. Used in many Rabbinic works, *mashaiṭ* scripts are discussed in the *Encyclopaedia Judaica* (vol. 2, pp. 729–743).

7. See Hakohen's introduction and, for example, ms. pages 31b, 37b, 46a, 48a, 56a, 66b, and 133b. Toschi (1934:83) states that Khalfon's manuscript was written in the Arabic language with Hebrew characters, but there is no evidence that this was the case. Toschi may have been misled by Hakohen's introduction, in which he mentions using remnants of Khalfon's manuscript and indicates that he drew information from various sources written in the Arabic language in Hebrew script.

8. For example, ms. pages 32a, 40a, 44b, 45a, 47b, 61b, 128a, 170b, and 188a. In some places, he says that Khalfon copied from sources available to him, including government records and earlier authors, including Moslem historians (see Authors's Introduction and ms. pages 34b, 35b, and 39b).

9. See Goldberg (1974b) and the Editor's Foreword to Chapter Two.

10. See Goldberg (1971) and the Editor's Foreword to Chapter Two.

11. Rabbeinu Gershom Me'or ha-Golah (Light of the Exile) lived in Mayence in the second half of the eleventh century. He is well known for his edicts—which were accepted by European Jewry—forbidding polygyny and requiring a husband to obtain his wife's consent to a divorce. The Jews of Benghazi had a burial society named after Rabbeinu Gershom, but were unaware of his historical importance. Hakohen's book was thus an effort to educate his community.

12. A type of *mashait* script.

13. See Mahler (1971: Chapter 13).

14. See the Editor's Foreword to Chapter Six.

15. Bono (1967) suggests that the material in the Turkish administrative archives in Tripoli has yet to be tapped. Rossi (1929) indicates that this material was preserved from about 1850.

16. See the Editor's Foreword to Chapter Five.

17. This account of religious and cultural development is based on Hirschberg (1965a) and especially Kahalon (1972).

18. An emissary of the Sephardic community in Jerusalem.

19. Very few Jewish children studied in Turkish schools.

20. Rabbi Yehuda Qimhi, a native of Turkey, was appointed to the post in 1896. Rabbi Ḥizqiyahu Shabbetai served as Ḥakham Bashi from 1904 to 1908. He wrote a *haskamah* (an approval of publication) to *Highid Mordekhai,* which appears in the manuscript on p. 3. In 1908 he accepted a position in Aleppo, and Hakohen corresponded with him for many years.

21. Carl Furlong (1909:102–104), an American interested in the incident of the warship *Philadelphia,* which was sunk in Tripoli's harbor, met him in 1904 and is mentioned by Hakohen in Section 37, Note 32 (ms. p. 62a). A letter from Hakohen to Slouschz tells of a visit by E. von Hesse-Wartegg, a Swiss geographer.

22. A common North African greeting.

23. The debate with a Moslem, quoted here, is followed in the text by a similar encounter with a Berber. A Catholic scholar appears in the next passage I have quoted. There is also an exchange with members of a Protestant sect (Section 66, Note 45, ms. pp. 122a–b).

24. Inspection of the lung and the use of a flawless knife are standard practices in Jewish slaughtering.

25. The dietary restriction concerning meat is one of the salient differences of daily practice separating Jews from Moslems. It is the same matter discussed in Hakohen's debate with the Protestants (Section 66, Note 45, ms. pp. 122a–b). Similarly, the issues of the falsification of the Torah and the Sabbath, in the continuation of the quote, are standard matters of Jewish-Moslem controversy (see Baron 1957: III, 80–86, and V, 86–94).

26. The text reads *surat mosheh,* but perhaps *torat mosheh* is intended.

27. See, for example, the Koran II:40–42 and III:70–71.

28. Koran II:63–65 and IV:154.

29. Presumably, Hakohen got this information from Sheikh Khalifa Ḥajjaj of the Ghuryan, whom he mentioned in Sections 102 and 103 (see Slouschz 1927:132–153 and Goldberg 1972a). Hakohen states (Section 95) that the sheikh

of the Yefren Jewish community participated in local council meetings with the heads of Moslem villages, and the same was probably true in the Ghuryan.

30. *Hayehoody* (London), vol. XII (1908), March 12, p. 4, and August 27, p. 3.

31. It is possible that Rossi was Ettore Rossi, but I have not been able to verify this; neither can I identify Allessandri. It also appears unlikely that Hakohen had colleagues in the Moslem community who were sympathetic to his work. El-Hachaichi, a Moslem scholar from Tunisia who passed through Tripoli in 1897, commented that "Moslem science has no representatives" among the inhabitants of the city (1903:275).

32. See Goitein (1939, 1941). We do not mean to imply that Ḥabshush had no awareness of, or interest in, European culture. The frontispiece to the Hebrew translation of his work (Goitein 1939) shows Ḥabshush with a copy of *Hamaghid,* a Hebrew periodical published in Lyck, in the pocket of his cloak. This, as Goitein has jokingly told me, was Ḥabshush's "entrance ticket into European civilization."

33. The relationship to Ibn Ghalbun's work is unclear. In numerous footnotes Hakohen mentioned the book *Ta'arīkh Ṭrablus al-Gharb* without giving the author's name (ms. pp. 27b, 28a, 39b, 40a, 50a, 95b, and 227b). There is a purported summary and continuation of Ibn Ghalbun's work published in Turkish presenting materials that date to Hakohen's own day (Rossi 1968:xx). Hakohen's references mention events that took place after the eighteenth century, when Ibn Ghalbun lived, but it is not likely that Hakohen could read Turkish. However, according to Rossi (1936:13–15; 1968:xx), there was an Arabic translation of the Turkish work, which was printed in Tripoli, without a date. Furlong, the American traveler who met Hakohen in 1904, gives the following account of the works consulted: "The book proved to be a modern Turkish publication in Arabic entitled 'A History of Tripoli in the West,' and briefly mentioned the circumstances of the burning of an American warship in the harbor. The manuscript was a local history compiled by himself from the papers and journals of an old rabbi, Abram Halfoom, who had lived in Tripoli . . . " (1909:103).

Ibn Ghalbun's original work was later published in Cairo (1930) and in an Italian translation by Rossi (1936). Hakohen often mentions in his footnotes that he found information in "Moslem books," but he never mentions the author. The one exception to this is his reference to Ibn Khaldun (Section 17, Note 22, ms. p. 31b). We can hardly believe that he was unaware of Ibn Ghalbun, and there are two other possible explanations for his lapse. The omission of exact sources of information was quite common among the European Haskalah authors. Another possibility lies in the religious stance of Ibn Ghalbun, who opposed the building of a synagogue in Misurata (Rossi 1936:170*ff.*). This might have led Hakohen to "eradicate his name," according to the words of a traditional curse of Jewry's enemies.

34. See Section 90 and the references to the geographical works of the Haskalah author Schulmann (ms. pp. 9a, 20a, 24a).

35. *Ha-shomer 'emet* (1849) and *Maqom she-nahagu* (1865), both published in Leghorn, Italy.

36. See Landau (1969:97–99 and *passim*).

37. Occasionally Hakohen mentions that a certain practice, such as gashing

the skin while mourning, is against the religious law. This remark is placed in parentheses.

38. The Hebrew reads *lo' yehenu menkhasaw*.

39. See the Midrash Tanhuma to the portion of Noah (Commentary on Genesis IX:20, midrash 13); Babylonian Talmud, *Sanhedrin* (109a); Koran II:65, V:60, and VII:166.

40. In a primer of modern Hebrew published in Tripoli in 1934 (Ben Yehudah 1934), the very first lesson includes a joke aimed at the village Jews. According to Hakohen's daughters, there was some objection to his publication of the material on village Jews because it did not fit the image that the urbanites wished to project of themselves among the Italians.

41. His conclusions were formed independently of those of Slouschz, and generally with more deliberation. Compare his consideration of the problem of the tombstone (the second Note in Section 90 below) with Slouschz' claim that this find is proof of his hypothesis concerning the Judaeo-Berbers (1908b:451; 1927:176–177, 200).

42. This innovation was opposed by Hafez Pasha because it competed with and disrupted the Moslem *adhan,* the call to prayer that was announced five times each day.

43. On the Moslem chronicles, see ms. pp. 20a, 40a, and 50a. The Note on the biblical dates is on ms. pp. 20a–21a.

44. One of the books written by Hakohen, not published but extant in manuscript form, is called ''*Y'mot 'Olam* (''Days of old''; see Deuteronomy XXXII:7). It coordinates the Christian, Moslem, and Jewish calendars (Section 87).

45. A partial inspiration for this effort is probably found in the commentaries of Ibn 'Ezra to Exodus XII:2 and XVI:1 (see Section 93, n. 3). In the latter passage, Ibn 'Ezra refers to the Hindu week.

46. The Hebrew *dehifah,* or push, indicates a one-time intervention, as contrasted with a regular happening in the normal course of events.

47. Hakohen's sources are unclear both in this instance and in other cases in which he cites ''factual'' information (such as the experiment in Australia, below). There was not a widespread awareness of Darwin's theory in the Islamic world (Bezirgan 1974), and it is likely that Hakohen is reacting to information that reached him through Europeans. The name *Bondin* closely resembles Bodin, the sixteenth-century French philosopher. Bodin (1566; tr. 1945) stressed the influence of environment and even said that there are certain nations who live almost like animals (pp. 145–146), but he predates the serious discussion of man's relation to the animal world. Another possible source is Buffon (1707–1788), a member of the French academy who presented the concept that ''degeneration'' had modified the form of species (1812). However, Buffon still believed that there were important differences separating apes from men, and did not posit a historical link between them.

48. See La Mettrie (1748; tr. 1912).

49. That is, both the biblical narrative and Darwin's theory.

50. Malachi II:10.

51. The *targum,* or Aramaic, translation of the Bible is sometimes incorpo-

rated in the synagogue service. Here the reference is to the *targum* of the *haftarah* (Reading from the Prophets) read on the last day of Passover, beginning with Isaiah X:32. The *targum* interprets these verses as a reference to the disaster that befell Sennacherib's army, as recorded in Second Kings XIX:35, and delights in embellishing the number of smitten soldiers. (See Goldberg 1978a on the atmosphere of the last day of Passover.)

52. See Note 17 ("Political Organization of the Berbers") on walking in the mountains; the footnote in Section 93 on positions while eating; Section 98 on squatting during the circumcision ceremony; and Section 100 on sleeping. His remarks on *potential* ability to learn (Section 94) are also relevant here.

53. Hakohen transcribed a section of his book and sent it to Slouschz. This pamphlet was donated to the National and University Library (28° 5775) in Jerusalem by Professor Dov Sadan, who received it from Slouschz. See Slouschz 1927:24, 44, 50–51, 66, 117–118, 124, 136, 156–157, 167–169, and 173–174 for mention of Hakohen. References to Hakohen in Slouschz' Hebrew works are less patronizing.

54. *Cf.* De Cenival's (1925) criticism of Slouschz' historical theories (1913) concerning the Jews of Debdou in Morocco.

55. See Baron (1957:III:66*ff.* and 196*ff.*).

56. See the references at the beginning of Chapter One. Two recent works deal with Ghoma's revolts (al-Misurati 1960; Streicker 1970).

57. Hebrew: *harariyim*.

58. In referring to the work, Toschi (1934:83) casts some doubt on Moreno's knowledge of Hebrew by inserting a parenthetical *sic* after citing him as the translator: "Tradotto (sic) dall ebraico da Martino Mario Moreno." Moreno was a scholar of Semitic languages, and he might easily have learned Hebrew under Hakohen's tutelage. It also appears that Hakohen collaborated actively in the preparation of Moreno's translation.

59. Yefren is discussed in a rather long Note (ms. p. 23a *et seq.*), part of which I have included in this translation as "Political Organization of the Berbers." Zawia is discussed on ms. p. 51a (Section 32, Note 30).

60. Beginning in 1926, Moreno served in Egypt, Yemen, Eritrea, and Addis Ababa (CHIÈ 1940:634). Hakohen's notebooks, containing a draft of an Italian translation of *Highid Mordekhai* alongside the Hebrew original, are still in the possession of his family.

Author's Introduction

Hakohen's manuscript includes several introductory sections, covering six unnumbered pages, which are translated below. Also included here is a footnote with supplementary autobiographical remarks.

This is the statement of the author, Mordechai Hakohen, son of My Lord, My Father Rabbi Yehudah, son of Marco (Mordechai), son of Abraham Israel Hakohen, born in Tripoli, Africa, on the twenty-fifth day of Elul,[1] 5616 years since the Creation, also called the year 1856: From the time that I was young I have sought to delve into the origins of my native country (even though my ancestors are from Genoa, Italy) and learn about the beginnings of Jewish settlement in it. In particular, my yearly trips in search of trade to the Atlas mountain communities where Jews have been living since the destruction of the Temple (may it be rebuilt speedily in our time), have moved me to study their origins and the ancient customs that they have received from their forefathers. I felt an irresistible urge[2] to investigate these things of the past, for whoever travels in the region feels that the world of antiquity is suddenly laid bare before his eyes.

Scholars have searched for the ancient past of the people of Israel and their history in the lands of captivity. But historians have not written the history of Tripoli and Cyrenaica, either in general or in detail. Neither have the Rabbis of the district, whose knowledge dwarfs my own,[3] laid the way for this effort to set down events and customs. Perhaps in the captivity and looting which they suffered their writings and precious objects were lost, leaving some room for my own contribution. I know very well that those who disdain me outnumber those who respect my efforts, and they say, "He has lost his sense of direction, he is pursuing worthless ends." But this book will please unprejudiced scholars and researchers. In addition, it will answer their complaint against Tripoli: "How shall we look upon her, for even though she is one of Africa's cities, no spirited man in her has risen up to gather and organize her history and customs?"

I searched diligently for documents and antique objects that would illuminate the past and its customs, until I found old records in the study[4] of Rabbi Shaul Adadi.[5] Among these manuscripts, I also found the writings of Avraham Khalfon, a local Chief Rabbi and the author of *Ḥayei Avraham*,[6] which explains and praises the commandments and customs; he died in Safed, well on in years, in 1820. It is clear from most of his writings that they were copied from chronicles in the government archives. A few old and torn pages of his work were also found in the Jewish archives. I have also drawn upon the works of the venerable Rabbi Avraham Adadi, who was head of the Rabbinical Tribunal here and who passed away in Safed in 1874. I have made use of the book *Ner Ha-Ma 'arav,* sent to me by _____ to complete my work,[7] as well as literature in Hebrew and other languages. That which I heard myself from trustworthy elders, or which I have seen with my own eyes, I have recorded at length.

I beseech the reader who may find a mistake in the spelling of a personal name[8] or a place name not to blame me, because I have copied from old and partially erased sources written in the Arabic language with Hebrew script. When words run together, I have tried to decipher the meaning, interpreting the unclear on the basis of the clear.[9] However, I may have erred in rendering several missing letters. This is particularly true of letters found in dates,[10] for some of the dates are given according to the Mohammedan[11] year, which begins in the month of Av, 4382 (July 622). The short Moslem year is based on twelve lunar months, or 345 days, 8 hours, and 876 seconds; but our solar year is just under 365 days and 6 hours. The Moslem year does not begin at the same time as the solar year; this means that when the source provides the year but not the month I may be mistaken by as much as one year.

In the notes, I have added some extraneous comments that may be of interest to scholars. I have called the book *Highid Mordekhai,* a title based on my name. From the beginning through Section 65 it describes general history; through Section 90, the organization and customs of the Jews; through Section 110, the villages as they concern the Jews; and from there till the end, the book tells of the Italian conquest of this land.

Signed by the Author,
Mordechai Hakohen of Tripoli, Africa

Biography of the Author

His father sailed to Candia [Crete] in about 1861, taking with him all his worldly goods. There he met his appointed end, and all his possessions were lost, since they were left as unclaimed property. However, the Italian consul in Candia looked after his orphaned countrymen in Tripoli, and was able to salvage about 800 francs. The Italian consul in Tripoli gave the money to the father's widow so that she could invest it and support her family. She did not want to accept charity from the consul's special fund for indigent Italian citizens; neither would she take anything from the Jewish community's charity fund. Instead, she worked as a seamstress and used the small amount of money she had to set herself up as a peddler so that she could support her children.

While at Hebrew School,[12] Mordechai Hakohen, orphaned from childhood, tried to earn a few pennies to help his mother and sisters[13] by assisting the teacher and giving instruction in the Bible and the Talmud. He longed to study languages, as well as subjects outside the religious curriculum, but this desire remained unfulfilled. No schools taught languages at that time; moreover, he did not have enough money to hire a tutor or to purchase books. He did succeed in acquiring some of the enlightenment[14] literature in Hebrew and was able to educate himself and learn arithmetic.

For a long time he worked as a Hebrew teacher, instructing young children. In 1883 he married. When he found that his expenditures were greater than his income, he taught himself to repair clocks as a supplementary source of revenue. He also began to peddle a bit. Soon he became the father of a large family, most of whom were girls.[15] Again he could not make ends meet. He then decided to study the Rabbinic law, written in both Hebrew and Arabic, so that he could work as a clerk in the court and act as a legal counsel. As a result of that he was somewhat relieved of financial pressure and began to find time to write; the present book was among his labors. In particular, his travels through Libya with Dr. Nahum Slouschz inspired him[16] to complete the present work.

These introductory remarks are followed by two standard clauses concerning copyright and publication. The first is a warning by Hakohen that no one may copy from the book without his permission. The second is an approval (haskamah) or authorization for the publication of the work by Rabbi Ḥizqiyahu Shabbetai.[17] In a final section, Hakohen explains the conventions of using Hebrew script for writing Arabic.

The following autobiographical information is provided in a footnote concerning the ransom of Jews from pirates in Tripoli during the reign of Yusef Qaramanli (Section 38, Note 34, ms. p. 66b).

Among the captives who settled in Tripoli was my grandfather, Mordechai (Marco), son of Avraham Israel Hakohen. He fled from the land of his birth, the city of Genoa, during the confusion caused by the wars of Napoleon Bonaparte, who mixed and stirred Europe like a stew. Mordechai left so he would not be forced to profane the Sabbath as a result of the war, but at sea he was taken captive by pirates. One of his relatives, from the family of Sangonetti,[18] ransomed him for good money, and also paid his passage back to Italy. On this voyage, the ship encountered a violent gale and was forced to return to Tripoli, where he disembarked for a few days, waiting for the sea to calm.

In those days, Tripoli carried on no trade with Europe, except for the city of Leghorn, and the customs house in Tripoli needed a translator who spoke Italian. Mordechai knew Hebrew, which is related to Arabic. He quickly learned Arabic and was then appointed translator in the customs house. Not long after, he received other high appointments there. In the month of Iyyar, 1814, he married my grandmother, Ḥaviva, daughter of Rabbi Yehudah 'Aton. In 1837, he died during a plague, leaving two girls and two boys. The elder was my uncle, Avraham, and the younger, my father, Yehudah, who was then about eleven years old.

NOTES

1. September 25, 1856.
2. Literally: "I was not able to overcome the desire." But the language used by Hakohen indicates passionate physical desire.
3. Literally: "whose small finger is wider than my waist" (I Kings XII:10).
4. Literally: "house of study" (*bet midrash*).
5. The son of Avraham Adadi (see below and Editor's Introduction); he was active in the field of religious education (Zuaretz *et al.* 1960:82–83).
6. See the Editor's Introduction, n. 4.
7. See Toledano (1911). It appears that Hakohen was waiting for someone to send him a copy of this book. He eventually received one from a colleague in Tunis.
8. On the importance of precision in copying names, see Goldberg (1972a:43–44).
9. This is in contrast to the normal requirement of a copyist, namely that he be faithful to the written word and not depend on his own judgment.
10. Hebrew letters are also used as numerals, particularly in dates.
11. Hakohen uses the Hebrew *muḥammadani,* which appears interchangeably with the term *muslimi.*
12. Talmud Torah (see Kahalon 1972).
13. Hakohen had two sisters and no brothers.
14. The Haskalah; see the Editor's Introduction, IV.
15. Hakohen had thirteen children, four boys and nine girls.
16. Literally: "a lamp unto my feet."
17. See the Editor's Introduction, n. 20.
18. The family name in Genoa was Sangonetti, meaning a "true-blood" Kohen, *i.e.* claiming descent from Aaron, the high priest. According to Hakohen's daughters, municipal files in Genoa still maintain a record of the family.

CHAPTER ONE

Jebel Nefusa: The Setting of the Jewish Community

Editor's Foreword

Hakohen begins his account of the Jews in the villages by sketching a general portrait of the Jebel Nefusa region. He begins with a geographic and historical description and then depicts the status of the Jews among the Berber tribesmen. The middle section of what we have translated here is actually a lengthy footnote (number 17, ms. p. 23a *et seq.*), discussing the Berbers of Yefren. While the note covers some of the information given in the geographical section, it contains other material as well. This footnote shows that Hakohen, like other ethnographers, was concerned with describing a society before the imposition of out-side—in this case Turkish—rule.

The inhabitants of the Jebel Nefusa resisted the establishment of Turkish authority. They were led by the rebel chief, Ghoma, whose revolt is described at length in Sections 42 through 46. We have not included that account here because it is primarily a political chronicle, and in any case the story has been presented by others (Slouschz 1908a; Féraud 1927:376–412; Rossi 1968:297–312; see the Editor's Introduction, XI). Hakohen does include some ethnographic details not found elsewhere; perhaps these were gained by interviewing one of Ghoma's lieutenants, Milud al-Jebali (see Section 1, Note 2, ms. p. 1b; Cachia 1945:36; al-Misurati 1960:179–181). Slouschz emphasizes the effect of the rebellion on the Jews of the region, basing his account on Hakohen's material.

Earlier, we discussed the thesis of the Judaized Berbers. Hakohen cities the claims of local oral history that the Jews were once numerous in the area, and surface archaeological remains appear to support that view. In the eleventh century El-Bekri mentions the large Jewish quarters in Jado. From the eighth century onward, the Nefusa had been inhabited by followers of the Ibadi Muslim sect, whose beliefs were heretical from the point of view of Sunni Islam. The interaction of these various groups is illuminated in Lowick's discussion (1974) of the inscriptions on an ancient mosque in Sharwas (also written Sharus, Serus, etc.). In particular, he remarks on the following verse from the Koran, which appears on a keystone arch:

> We believe in God and that which hath been sent down to us, and that which hath been sent to Abraham, and Ishmael, and Isaac, and Jacob, and the tribes, and that which was delivered unto Moses, and Jesus, and that which was delivered unto the prophets from their Lord; we make no distinction between any of them, and unto God we are resigned [II:130].

Lowick reminds us (p. 15) that "if the builders of the mosque at Sharwas saw fit to accord such public recognition to the claims of the Jews and the Christians it was probably because, even in the 10th century or later, there subsisted a strong Christian/Jewish element in the population, with which the Ibadi majority was anxious to remain on good terms."

It thus seems fairly certain that in past centuries the Jewish population of Jebel Nefusa and other areas of the Tripolitanian interior was larger than it is today. This does not mean, however, that the Jews once "ruled the land," as suggested by Slouschz (1927:66, 135, 179). It is possible that the large number of archaeological sites attesting to former Jewish habitation simply reflects the insecurity of life in the interior, and the movement of populations from place to place, and does not point to a large community dominating the area at a single period (Goldberg 1971).

Hakohen's contribution is not, however, to the consideration of these larger historical problems, but rather to an understanding of the Jews' situation in Tripolitania in his day, and in the recent past. The status of the Jewish minority in Moslem North Africa is a subject that has recently been discussed by a number of authors,[1] and the picture they present is complex. Some of the data show the Jews as a tolerated but protected minority, clearly separated from and subordinate to the Moslem majority, while other data suggest that in daily intercourse with Moslems Jews were perceived and related to in terms of their own personal and social characteristics rather than a pervasive stereotype that cast its shadow on all Moslem-Jewish interaction. Most of this documentation comes from Morocco, which provides us with the best (but by no means sufficient) data available. We will therefore make use

of the Moroccan studies in working toward an understanding of Hakohen's material, for there is little directly comparable information from
Libya.

We may sort out the arguments into two basic positions. One main-
tains that the Jews made up a distinct religious category which was
understood as being secondary to, and deserving the protection of, Islam—but that day-to-day relationships frequently ignored religious distinctions, and the disadvantages and oppressions suffered by the Jews
were also shared by many poorer Moslems. The other position states
that there were instances of political security, economic well-being, and
man-to-man relations between Jews and Moslems, *but* that the Jews
were basically weak and dependent and therefore most vulnerable in
times of trouble, so that their special status easily surfaced when general
conditions were unstable. All observers agree that the individual was not
perceived only in terms of his Jewishness, but that other attributes, such
as wealth, shared neighborhood, commercial ties, and personal honesty,
influenced the non-Jews' perception of the Jews in their midst. What
seems to be at issue is the extent to which a man's religion guided his
behavior in other areas. Was it one feature among many other features
or was it the dominant factor; or, to use Dumont's terms (1970), was it
encompassing rather than encompassed? And if it *was* encompassing,
can we describe the interrelationship between the layers of characteristics that determined a man's place in society?

The same questions can be posed in other ways. For example, we
could speak of "ethnic group" rather than "religion" as a possible encompassing factor. We have been cautioned against using the former term
in referring to Moslems and Jews since this misleadingly identifies the
North African sociological reality with that familiar from European countries or the United States (Rosen 1972; Geertz in World Jewish Congress
1975:32). Although this caution may be wise, it would be equally fool-
hardy to ignore any collective identification that does take place. In the
pages that follow, a number of different theories of the status of Jews in
North Africa will be considered and examined in the context of Hakohen's data. However, several warnings should be registered.

First, although our discussion is phrased in terms of Jews and Moslems, it is important to realize that the Jews are not the only people
included in the Moslems' category *ahl al-dhimma* (people of protection).
This classification applies to Christians and Zoroastrians as well. However, Zoroastrians were never important in the Maghreb, and native
Christianity eventually disappeared. Christians living in North Africa in
modern times were usually associated with the European powers, so a
discussion of their position must take this into account. In Libya, therefore, Jews were the preeminent *dhimmi*s. There is room for discussion,
however, in considering the extent to which Moslem-Jewish interaction

is related to the special characteristics of Judaism *per se*, or to what extent it would apply to other non-Moslem "people of the Scriptures."

Second, it would be useful to compare the Jews with other dependent and protected categories of people. A number of social classifications appear in Hakohen's narrative: Moslem/Jew, Turk/Arab, Arab/ Berber, city dweller/peasant, wealthy/poor, and slave/freeman. Except for the first, none is singled out for sustained examination. Peters (1977) describes a range of categories of dependence in the tribal situation in eastern Libya, of which there is hardly a suggestion in Hakohen's work. This probably reflects his inattention to these matters, but it may also stem from the Turks' successful suppression of tribal organization in the middle of the last century. In any case, these comparisons cannot be made here.

Third is the acknowledgment that the following discussion is not firmly anchored in space and time. We begin by considering the situation in a mountainous tribal area, far from the center of government power, and gradually encompass the communities closer to Tripoli until we reach the city itself. In a similar fashion, the facts cited range over a period of time in which there was a considerable shift in power—the gradual reestablishment of Ottoman rule throughout Tripolitania, followed by the increasing presence of and pressure from European settlers and representatives of their governments. Despite these shifts in the distribution of power and in the official relationship of Jews to their Moslem neighbors, the cultural definition of the Jews' place in society remains stable. This definition appears to have been uniform throughout the region. It is precisely because the official relationships come under stress and exhibit change that the underlying definitions become explicit, no longer taken for granted and escaping comment. With this perspective in mind, we can consider a number of different interpretations of the status of Jews in North African society.

In discussing the Jebel Nefusa, Hakohen uses the surprising term *'eved*, Hebrew for slave or servant, in describing the tie of a Jew to a Berber lord. Despois (1935), who studied the same region over forty years ago, referred to the Jews as *serfs*, while Maher (1974), in her study of a Berber area in southern Morocco, sees the Jews as one of four *estates*. Probably the most common usage is that of *patron and client* (Stillman 1975; Brown 1977), which Peters (1977) has shown to be a phrase now stretched to cover a bewildering variety of relationships. Still another designation, this time in an urban Moroccan context, is that of *foreigners* or *strangers* (Le Tourneau 1949:186). Unfortunately, none of these studies has taken the most direct line, that of exploring the traditional Islamic notion governing Moslem-Jewish relations—*dhimma*, or contract—in its conceptual and normative dimensions. This is a point that we shall discuss later.

Besides the term *'eved* (slave or servant) referring to the Jews, Hakohen uses the term *'adon* (master or lord) for the Berber protector in the Jebel Nefusa. Hakohen was not capricious in his use of language, so we may assume that he was impressed either with the power of the Berber chief or with the limitations of freedom placed upon the Jews. However, this is not an arrangement that he observed firsthand, and he appears to rely in part on Adadi's report from the middle of the last century. Adadi (1865:47b; quoted in n. 4 to Section 91) states that one Berber lord could sell a Jew to another. Hakohen adds that the Jewish *'eved* was passed on as an inheritance, and that an heir could sell his share in the Jew which he had received from his father. One may claim that this is simply an exaggerated description of a patron-client relationship, continued between families over generations, as Rosen (1968) has reported in Morocco. But Hakohen clearly indicates the existence of deeds of manumission certifying that a Jew had paid his lord and therefore had gone free.

Hakohen's account does not seem exaggerated if we broaden our perspective. Reports on the situation of the Jews in Kurdistan (Benjamin 1859; Brauer 1947:185–189) in the nineteenth century show the far-reaching power of the Aghas over "their" Jews. There, too, the Agha could receive money for transferring a Jew under his protection. The Agha also exercised some control on movement in and out of his territory, thereby restricting the mobility which is often critical to people in client status (Peters 1977). One clear expression of the Agha's control is that he collected a large part of the bride price paid for a woman from his territory when she married a Jewish man from another region.

There may have been similar restrictions on the movement of the Jews in the Jebel Nefusa. After quoting from Adadi, Hakohen states: "Whereas the Jews taken captive in Jebel Yefren were enslaved by difficult masters, they had no power to leave their territory and contact their brethren in Jebel Nefusa, or to go to Tripoli" (Section 11, ms. p. 24b). The time period Hakohen refers to is uncertain, but the ability of a tribal chief to limit the movement of the Jews in his territory is quite clear.

Even if these conditions definitely prevailed in the Jebel Nefusa, the term *slave* would not adequately describe the status of the Jews there. It is important to note that the tie of a Jew to his lord did not involve uprooting him (Finley 1968). The Jew retained his traditional ties to his family and community. Indeed, Hakohen's summary statement about the Jews of Tripolitania at the time of the Moslem conquests may be relevant here: "Even though the gentiles ruled over the bodies of the Jews, they did not rule over their wives, and they did not intermarry with one another" (ms. p. 31b). This is a very different situation from that of the African slaves who are briefly mentioned in his description of

Moslem marriage (Section 5, ms. p. 8b): "He who marries his maidservant, purchased by money, has no legal burden. For one who buys a male or female slave is like one who buys an animal. He cannot be punished in court for any reason." Thus the deeds of manumission involving Jews may have been different from those relating to legal slavery (*cf.* Martin 1978). The Ottoman insistence that the Jews need not pay their Berber lords was very likely an assertion of Turkish sovereignty (*cf.* Goitein 1941:31–32)—indicating that the government alone had the right to the poll tax paid by *dhimmis*—rather than an abrogation of slavery in a strict sense of the term.

The far-reaching power of the tribal leaders may have led Despois (1935) to call the Jews *serfs*, a usage that is understandable if there were any restrictions of movement. His selection of that term may be related to Goguyer's (1895) discussion of *servage* in southern Tunisia and DeAmbroggio's (1902:266–267) mention of serfdom in the Jebel Nefusa. Another label taken from European history is that of *estates* (Maher 1974). These two notions are usually said to be very different, or even opposed to one another—the first indicating a status defined by a personal tie, and the second placing a man in a broad social category. Considering them together, however, may help us interpret the situation of the Jews. The use of *estate*, or *status* in the Weberian sense, means that a person's position in society is assigned by a mechanism other than the market. In these terms, the *dhimmi* category places one in an estate. Being a *dhimmi*, however, does not determine precisely with whom a person can contract social ties, or the content of those ties (Rosen 1972). What this status does determine is that, more than other people, the *dhimmi* needs person-to-person ties to afford him protection. These individual ties do not ignore the categorical distinction of status; rather, the latter is the precondition of the former.

If being a Jew, or *dhimmi*, automatically defined a person as requiring protection, certain occupations made patronage even more imperative (Waterbury 1972:88–92). In the traditional situation, Jewish peddlers could hardly think of going out into the countryside unless they were under the protection of a strong Moslem (Brown 1977:314, 321). It is hard to assess how consistent or effective this form of protection was. Hakohen says that the Jews dwelt "in security," but also describes cases in which the system broke down. There are a number of instances, reported from different tribal areas in the Middle East, in which this type of patronage was applied in a dramatic fashion (*e.g.* Goitein 1947:34–37; Brauer 1947:185–189). In the case of Aby-Serour (Semach 1928:392; Bazin 1923:23–34), it appears to have saved his life, but not his money. Geertz (1973:7*ff.*) stresses that in defending his client, the patron promoted his own honor. Maher sums up the situation (1974:15): "In the last analysis a Berber afforded protection to a Jew as a concession to an individual which barely affected his own political situation except to mark him as a man of honour. But his participation in the segmentary organization was the condition of his political existence and he would readily sacrifice the Jewish connection to the latter.''

As noted, the most common way of referring to individual Moslem-Jewish ties is to call them patron-client relationships. Peters' (1977) analysis of these ties among the Bedouin of Cyrenaica also sheds light on the position of the Jews. Patrons sometimes claim, according to Peters, that they are prepared to defend their clients with their lives. However, this ethic is not the essence of the relationship, but merely part of a general morality which is extended to any resident. Patrons are also usually wealthier than clients, but this is not necessarily the case. A client can achieve more wealth than his patron, but this wealth is not based on rights to land. What this means is that, lacking the base in land, a client cannot convert his wealth into political power.

In both of these respects, the Jew can be said to have a client status. There is a moral code obliging a Berber protector to defend the Jews dependent on him. The word *moral* is important here because this obligation, backed in Morocco by a conditional curse (Westermarck 1916:90–100) that a Jew placed on his Moslem protector, was not a legal norm linked to explicit sanctions. It is interesting to note that in describing the situation in Tripolitania Hakohen asserts that the Jews "dwelt in security" under the Berber lords before he discusses the *'eved* relationship. We do not know whether the written document itself stipulated the obligation of protection (see the document reproduced in De Foucauld 1939). Like other clients, the Jew might be wealthier than his patron, but, as we have said, this wealth could not be converted into power. Hakohen puts this quite plainly in his description of the town of Zawia (Section 104):

> Many Mohammedans are dependent on the Jews who lend them money. Yet despite this, the Jews live among them only through cunning and by humbling themselves before the honor-seeking Mo-hammedans. Even so, many Jews have been murdered, and their blood cries out for justice.

The position of the Jews with regard to land is worthy of further discussion. Unlike the situation which prevailed in feudal Europe, the Jews were not legally debarred from owning land (see, however, Streicker 1970:13). Hakohen gives several examples of Jews farming and owning land. Still, the Jews clearly specialized in crafts and trade, and any wealth they had was not based on landowning. Hakohen's account of the Ghuryan (Section 103) suggests a reason for this situation. The Jews "know how to plow and reap. However, they refrain from working the soil because of the strong religious hatred of the inhabitants, who steal the fruit of their crops and their labors, leaving them only a pittance to reap." It seems, then, that the protection extended to the Jew is somewhat conditioned by the extent to which he is directly competing with the Moslem majority. The ideal of protection is put into practice when he is a peddler traveling around the countryside rather than when he is engaged in farming and holds land that his neighbors covet.

Hakohen also mentions the Moslem encroachment upon Jewish land belonging to cemeteries and synagogues, but here the situation is quite complex. There seems to be a notion that the Jews have a spiritual closeness to the land. The Berbers encourage their water-spilling play on the festival of Shavuot because they see it as a good omen for a year of rain (Section 97). This is in accordance with Turner's notion (1969; *cf.* Goldberg 1978a) of the "power of the weak," in which groups that are politically weak may be viewed by the dominant population as possessing spiritual power over rain and fertility. We also note here the belief that the Jews were the first to settle the land (Section 90), and the reverence that Berbers sometimes hold for ancient synagogues, even when they have been destroyed (Section 96).

These general sentiments also have their normative counterpart. Hakohen reports several incidents in which Moslems wished to encroach upon the Jews' ownership of a synagogue, but the Jews' rights were upheld by law, on the basis of deeds testifying to their longstanding ownership. It has been noted that stories of ancient synagogues are widespread in Middle Eastern history (Baron 1942:164), and this has been seen as a means of circumventing the "Pact of 'Omar," which provides that the Jews may not build new synagogues but may repair old ones. What is interesting here is that all these cases substantiate the protection of the Jews' communal rights, tied to their religious worship. There is one case in which their right to water is upheld (Section 94), but here too the basis is communal. There are no reported instances in which, despite unfavorable circumstances, the rights of the individual Jew are upheld in his dealing with a Moslem. If, as has been suggested for Morocco (Rosen 1972), the categorization of a Jew *as* a Jew is something that recedes into the background, and each Jew is related to primarily on the basis of his individual characteristics, it is puzzling that the established power has granted legitimacy to the Jew's communal status while his individual rights seem most vulnerable.

To state this another way, Rosen asserts that in Morocco "Moslem social organization seems to center around the relations between pairs of individuals, each of whom is perceived as a concatenation of particular social ties which are differently weighted and apportioned from one individual to another" (1972:443), and that the way Moslems "view and act toward the Jews in their midst can be seen as an only partially modified extension of the ways in which they perceive and relate to their fellow Moslems" (p. 445). Still, we must take into account the fact that the notion of "the individual," and the way the individual's social actions are given meaning in a cultural context, are not necessarily the same among these people as they are in everyday European thought.

In the West, it is commonly assumed that if a number of people are wealthy on an individual basis they are free to form a corporate association to further their wealth, or to use their wealth as a basis of influence and power. This was not possible in the case of the Tripolitanian Jews, where the tacit, and sometimes very explicit, understanding is that individual wealth will not affect the honor of the collectivity. Thus the Jews, having achieved a high position individually, *may not* convert it into resources which enhance the status or power of the group.

Rosen recognizes this when he states (p. 444) that the Jew stands outside the common pool of social resources and that "he does not enter into relationships that involve the same sort of social competition as that which characterizes the relations between two Moslems." This exclusion from social competition may even act to the economic benefit of the Jew. Hakohen gives an example (Section 92) in the case of the Jewish peddlers who are free to enter Moslem houses and trade with the women; this kind of contact would be forbidden to other Moslems. This is not to say, as Rosen does, that religious identification provides only "minimal and partial" (p. 446) information on the kinds of individual ties that can be established. Instead, this identification provides the overarching context for individual relationships, and it is to the advantage of the Moslems that this context remains an unspoken assumption. The fact that the situation goes unquestioned helps make the factor of individual choice, and the development of personal ties, appear more prominent than they would if the assumption of Moslem dominance were not taken for granted (*cf.* Bourdieu 1977, Chapter 4).

Moreover, in the case of Tripolitania, it would be an oversimplification to state that the Jews "stand outside the sociological pool," and therefore outside the Moslem arena of competition. The Jews are not viewed simply as a different cultural group who just happen to live in the region. Rather, Hakohen's material suggests that there is very intense competition between the world-embracing claims of Judaism and Islam, together with an *agreement* to keep this dispute hidden so that people can get on with their daily affairs. The Jews may be viewed as strangers (Pitt-Rivers 1968) who are opposed to Islam. As in the case of other strangers, there are institutionalized mechanisms for including them in society and rendering them harmless. This is accomplished by having the Jews assume *dhimmi* status, which "does not eliminate the conflict altogether, but places it in abeyance and prohibits its expression" (Pitt-

Rivers 1968:25). By agreeing to be *dhimmi*s, Jews are free to pursue their own welfare, and Moslems are free to enter into relationships with Jews, so long as there are no activities that openly challenge the superiority of Islam and the subordinate position of the Jews.

These points of view are fairly explicit in Hakohen's material, as in the following passage from Section 5 (ms. pp. 10a–11b), in which he discusses religion in Tripoli:

> Most of them [the Moslems of Tripoli] are eager to argue about matters of religion, but this is not done justly, for the sake of determining the truth. They deeply believe that their religion is the most holy and the most felicitous, compared to all other religions, and they do not accept rational argument. If a Jew bests them in a dispute, they will hold a deep resentment toward him,[2] especially if his honor is offended in the argument. They are astounded at the Jews and Christians who appear to wear blinders, keeping them from seeking and choosing the felicitous Mohammedan religion, which gives its believers great joy and concubines in paradise hereafter. The learned and the notables, however, do not involve themselves in disputes.[3]
>
> The Mohammedans of the district have a hatred of Jews and Christians implanted in their hearts, but the Jews succeed in minimizing that hatred; they humble themselves before the Mohammedans, the lords of the land. The Jews, and the Christians too, bear animosity toward the Mohammedans, and are wont to say, "As in water, face answers face, so the heart of man to man."[4] During the reign of Yusef Pasha Qaramanli, a marabout from the Mohammedans of Wadday came to Tripoli and preached vilification of the Jews, and sowed hatred, as recorded in Section 38.[5]
>
> The Turks are not so committed to religious hatred, but after being here some time, some of them have learned the ways of the Arabs. In former times, if someone from another religion so much as uttered a word that suggested belief in Mohammed, prophet of the Ishmaelites, he became trapped like a bird in a snare. It was impossible for him to return to the religion of his fathers unless he succeeded in fleeing to another city where he was not known, where he could return to his people and to his God.
>
> A person who accepts the Mohammedan religion is viewed as a saint. He will be surrounded by many new friends, who honor the religion and receive blessing through him. They will donate money to him in great and small amounts, each man according to his means. At present, however, the officials of the Turkish government have realized that the converts who enter the Mohammedan religion are usually not upright people. It is not that they love the Moslem religion more than the religion into which they were born, but that for some reason they wish to use the religion, and as soon as possible they will return to their former faith.[6] Therefore, the officials have

decided not to accept converts except after thorough investigation, so that the religion will not be trifled with.

The Mohammedans of the villages do not have religious hatred toward the Jews, but they are still very proud. They will not allow a Jew to pass in front of them, mounted on an animal, nor will they permit him to carry a weapon.[7] The Jews lower themselves and accord honor to the Mohammedans, the lords of the land. Even so, when the Mohammedans have the opportunity to rob and oppress, then the wealth of the Jew becomes like ownerless property because he does not believe in the Mohammedan religion and he has no weapon to defend himself against attackers.

The Mohammedans of the villages are unstinting in following one of their customs: they desire to honor their guests by preparing them an elegant meal and gladly bring them everything they need in a generous manner. If something is lacking in the house, they will borrow from another in order to properly honor their guests. In particular, if a mounted warrior comes to their house, or even an ordinary Jew, they earn a good name by honoring him greatly. This is so even if they follow the law of blood vengeance, pursuing a murderer to avenge him a life for a life, as described in Section 11, Note 17 [reproduced in this chapter]. If the murderer is in the avenger's house, the avenger will not harm him so long as he is under his protection.

In the small communities outside Tripoli, there were conventions concerning how a Jew should act in the presence of a Moslem. Upon meeting in the street, a Jew must greet a Moslem first (Goldberg 1975). A Jew calls a Moslem *sīdī* (Sections 110, 114), while the Moslem calls the Jew by his first name. People often simply accepted these customs and did not give them much thought. However, intertwined with the accepted, seemingly thoughtless, everyday behavior were threads of challenge and debate by which the Jews symbolically refused to acknowledge the place assigned to them in Moslem society.

Consider, for example, the custom of wearing a black headdress. Hakohen clearly recognizes (Section 94) that this practice had its origin as a sign of separation and degradation. Some old men in Israel continue to wear the headdress, but Jews there to whom I have spoken say that it commemorates the destruction of the Temple of Jerusalem. This interpretation, by giving the custom a special symbolism to Jews, takes the cutting edge off the original intent and disguises the official meaning given to it by Moslems. Moreover, Jews do not remember the destruction of the Temple only because it is a tragic event in their history, but because they await its ultimate restoration. The fast day of the Ninth of Av, on which the destruction is mourned every year, is also understood to be the day on which the Messiah was born, or the day on which he will appear. This same idea is reflected in a story concerning Rabbi Akiva, who laughed when he saw a fox running through the ruins of the Temple. Akiva explained his strange behavior by saying that because the prophecies of destruction had been fulfilled he was certain that the prophecies of redemption would also come true, and therefore he could laugh at the same sight that made his colleagues cry (Babylonian Talmud, *Makkot* 24b). Mourning the Temple, then, implicitly states the belief in its rebuilding, so that wearing the black headdress not only hides the original intention of the custom, but may be seen as a *retort* to the Moslems, and a profession of faith that the Jews' subjugated status will someday come to an end.

The main audience for this veiled repartee is, of course, the Jews themselves. A more direct statement of the Jewish claim to deliverance from exile and an end to their current status could be viewed as direct opposition to the dominant Moslems. On the other hand, there may have been some subtle processes of communication whereby these symbolically coded messages crossed conventional religious boundaries (Goldberg 1978a). Such a possibility was envisioned by Rabbi Ḥazzan (see the Editor's Introduction) in the custom of "burning Haman" on the holiday of Purim. When the Jewish children gleefully burnt Haman, the biblical archetype of enmity toward the Jewish people, they could easily be seen as burning other Haman-like characters, past, present, and future. Rabbi Hazzan tried to suppress this custom, for fear that it might arouse resentment in non-Jews who could understand its meaning. The dangers of this kind of cross-religious understanding, or misunderstanding, are illustrated in the incident described in Note 90 (Chapter Five).

From this it can be seen that acceptance of the prevailing situation was not total, and certainly not among the Jewish population. These customs indicated, and even contributed to, an awareness of their situation and the possibility that it could be otherwise. When the conventional arrangements between Jews and Moslems began to be questioned, this awareness was heightened throughout the population.

This leads us back to the incidents concerning the synagogues, and in particular two accounts that appear in the narrative. One takes place in the village of Zawia at the end of the eighteenth century. It is summarized in Section 104 and presented at somewhat greater length in Sections 32 and 36. The second incident, involving the successful intervention of the Alliance Israélite Universelle on behalf of the Jews of Zliten, takes place in 1867–68. Hakohen describes this affair in Section 108, and there is a parallel account in Féraud's book (1927:420) which contains details not mentioned by Hakohen.[8] The two versions appear complementary. Féraud indicates that pressure was brought to bear by the Alliance in Paris, through the consul in Tripoli, concerning some "curious practices" in the villages. Apparently, the Jews, upon receiving permission to build a synagogue, had been boisterous in their celebration when the building was started. This gaiety offended the Moslems, and was also said to have offended the shade of the marabout Sidi 'Abd es-Salem, whose tomb was in the vicinity (Cesàro 1933:60ff.). The Moslems claimed that the marabout miraculously caused the conflagration in the synagogue because of the offense on the part of the Jews. However, investigation by the French consulate revealed that two brothers were responsible for the arson. These brothers, according to Féraud, had hoped to rid the area of Jews and thereby eliminate their competition in commerce. Burning the synagogue, they reasoned, would make it impossible for the Jews to live there, and they would be forced to leave the town.

There are systematic parallels in the stories of the synagogues at Zliten and Zawia. In both cases, the Jews are resented by local notables. While it is not made explicit in the Zawia story, the Zliten case clearly indicates that the Jews are successfully competing against aspiring Moslem merchants. In both cases, pressure against the Jews is exerted in the form of pressure against the synagogue. In both instances, overt signs of Jewish communal well-being and success are seen, almost by definition, as offensive and threatening to the Moslems. Thus the Qadi (Section 104) explicitly tells Yusef Pasha that by building the synagogue the Jews are diminishing the strength of the government (in Sections 32 and 36 the phrase "weakens the strength of the Mohammedans" is used). The Moslems understand that Jewish communal, and hence individual, life is predicated on the existence of a synagogue. However, the Jewish dependence on the synagogue has different effects in the two stories. In Zawia, the Moslems prevent the building of the synagogue and the Jews combat this by leaving the town demonstrating that Jewish presence is required for the economic well-being of the region. In the Zliten story, the Moslems burn the synagogue, hoping to force the Jews to leave the town so that they can then move into the Jews' economic niche. In both cases, the Jews are clearly a group with a well-defined subordinate religious and social status, and an equally well-defined economic role.

Let us introduce yet another term into the discussion, one taken from a different region—namely, caste. Superficially, one could point to parallels between the structure of Moslem-Jewish relationships in Tripolitania and the caste system. Here, the Jews would appear as a group, specializing in trading and crafts, which is ritually and socially separated from the Moslems, who specialize in agriculture. Together they form an interlocking system. The link between ritual notions and economic function could be developed even further. The Jews are noncombatants, not being allowed to carry arms. Yet in their role as smiths, they are responsible for making and repairing arms. In Section 42, Hakohen describes how they served in this manner for the rebel Ghoma (Slouschz

1927:192–193). As tradesmen and gunsmiths, they met economic needs which were not easily filled by the tribesmen themselves. The protection extended to the Jewish peddler may thus play the same role as the market peace (Benet 1957) which enabled one Berber group to trade in the same market as another. Similarly, it may be argued that by giving the Jews a marked status and having them specialize in certain crafts, including gunsmithing, the tribesmen protected these vital activities and ensured their continuous operation.

However, even if this functional reconstruction is plausible, the resemblance between caste and the situation in Tripolitania is superficial because caste, *in principle*, is irrevocably assigned by birth and is rooted in the immutable categories of pure and impure. This is not the case in Islam or Judaism, where it is theoretically possible for an individual to move from one category to another. This characteristic may be related to two other cultural features—the emphasis on the individual as a locus of social structure (as stressed in Rosen's analysis) and the concept of contract in establishing the framework for Moslem-Jewish interaction. But the notion of caste, as interpreted by Dumont (1970), may be useful in suggesting that the daily ties between Moslems and Jews, no matter how they must be understood in economic and political terms, ultimately take place in a cultural context defined by accepted religious beliefs.

For example, one could argue that religious considerations are secondary in the synagogue stories, and are being manipulated for economic ends. But it is precisely the form of this manipulation that is worthy of attention. One cannot get rid of Jewish competitors just because they are competitors and are successful, but one can get rid of *religious* competitors who do not know how to keep their place. Conversely, the Jewish propensity for and skill at trade are seen as secondary to religious considerations. Even though the Jews profit from their monopoly of trade in the area, it can be assumed that they will not live in a town unless they are allowed to worship according to their religion.

What is interesting is that these understandings are the subject of a social "contract," again setting the situation off from the Hindu case. Stillman (in World Jewish Congress 1975:73) notes that the regulations restricting the activities of the Jews are not usually known by the term "Pact of 'Omar," but as *dhimma*, or contract. In the story of Zawia, the notables put in writing the conditions of the Jews' return to the town. Moslem-Jewish relationships, therefore, are culturally conceived as an agreement between two parties which, in principle, is voluntary, although obviously it is grounded in the political reality of the weakness of the Jewish community.

Several points should be raised concerning this view. One is the question of the "Pact of 'Omar," the classic document in Islam which sets forth the regulations concerning Jewish existence. It has been noted (Cahen 1965; Udovitch in World Jewish Congress 1975:68–69) that there are difficulties in using this document as a reference because there is no single text known as the "Pact of 'Omar," and the contents of parallel texts vary in different times and places. Gerber (1975), who surveys Moslem-Jewish relations in the city of Fez according to the "terms" of the pact, states that the document is never referred to by name. Similarly, Hakohen does not mention any specific written code.

Important as the question of historical documentation may be, it should not obscure the significance of another equally weighty consideration, namely the *cultural definition* of the place of the Jews in the society in question. The definition of this relationship from the point of view of the Moslems, as it appears in Hakohen's work, appears to be as follows: (1) Islam has superseded Judaism through God's revelation to Mohammed. (2) Judaism and Islam are in competition. (3) Moslems have conquered Jews—a fact that fits into the notion of Islamic superiority— and this is the proper state of affairs in the world. (4) Moslems will protect the rights of the subordinate Jews if, in exchange, Jews will pay homage to the Moslems (and by implication to Islam) and refrain from actions which appear to challenge the foregoing assumptions. These underlying understandings may be expressed both in the formulation of legal documents and also in proverbs, folk tales, and day-to-day intercourse. In other words, the presence or absence of a specific "pact" is a different, though obviously related matter from the presence or absence of daily behavior patterns based on underlying attitudes. What we want to stress is that these cultural understandings are symbolically coded notions which define the very nature of reality. In this way, they are different from the institutionalized beliefs which more directly organize day-to-day interaction; they are part of the unspoken assumptions in which such norms are grounded.[9]

In other words, the cultural definition of the situation is that there is an agreement or contract between the Moslems and the Jews. However, the social reality in which these assumptions operate is that the power of the Moslems is much greater than that of the Jews. This means that the burden of the contract falls upon the Jews, who have to be more meticulous in observing its terms. The Moslems, by contrast, are freer to act in a casual manner, and can be either stricter or more lax in its observance. This fits in with Stillman's findings (1975:26) that Moslem images concerning Jews, as represented in oral lore, are more stereotyped than Jewish images of Moslems. The Jew is forced to observe closely and distinguish between Moslem and Moslem. The Moslem *may* do so with the Jews (Rosen 1972; Geertz in World Jewish Congress 1975:32–33), but may also choose not to. The Jew has little choice.

There are two ways of deviating from the terms of a contract—by not living up to its terms or by being overzealous in its interpretation. When the Jew does the former, he risks retaliation against the whole Jewish community. When he does the latter, he further restricts his access to socially valued goods and, presumably, through self-effacement and denial, pays the psychic cost. The Moslem too can be overly strict or overly lenient. When he is strict, he can claim that he is acting in the name of religious standards. If he violates the rights of the Jews, he may be punished,[10] but his actions do not endanger the Moslem community. If a Moslem is lenient in adhering to the terms of the agreement, he *may* be verbally chastised by a religious leader (*cf.* Goldberg 1977b, which quotes from Section 38; Rossi 1936:170ff.). On the other hand, he may be commended for his largesse and his humanity.

We must do more than simply ascertain to what extent, historically, the more restrictive legislation placed on *dhimmi*s was put into practice or ignored. It is also important to realize that the option itself derives directly from cultural premises. These premises can stress either the brotherhood of mankind (Goitein 1971)[11] or the special status of the Jews (Goldberg 1977b). It thus does not matter whether at any specific period more or less restrictive legislation is enacted, or whether conformity to the rules is meticulous or casual. In either case, there is no formal alteration of the basic categories and values which define and justify the place of Jews in Moslem society. Practice is not divorced from cultural premises; it realizes the variety of options implied by the traditional assumptions.[12] These assumptions limit the options of the Jews, while giving Moslems much greater leeway.

The Jews' consciousness of this situation is clearly expressed in Hakohen's narrative. In Section 17 (ms. p. 31a), he speaks briefly of the effect of the Moslem conquest of North Africa:

> They also pressed the Jews to enter the covenant of the Moslem religion. Many Jews bravely chose death. Some of them accepted under the threat of force, but only outwardly. These, however, were gradually assimilated. Others left the region, abandoning their wealth and property, and scattered to the ends of the earth. Many stood by their faith, but bore an iron yoke on their necks. They lowered themselves to the dust before the Moslems, lords of the land, and accepted a life of woe—carrying no weapons, never mounting an animal in the presence of a Moslem, not wearing a red headdress, and following other laws that signalled their degradation.

Hakohen sees this situation continuing up to the time of the Turkish conquest of Libya. While he distinguishes between the "haughtiness" of the villagers and their "religious hatred," his accounts show how easily these two matters become intertwined. Thus the Jewish peddler, though presumably enjoying the protection of his Berber patron, has to be very careful not to pass in front of a Berber who is praying lest he forfeit his life (Section 92).

This consciousness is even further heightened when there is a possibility for an improvement in status that is not fully realized. Hakohen quotes at length the case of the Jews in Benghazi who are accused of purposely mocking the Christian religion (Chapter Six, Note 90). Some of these Jews were citizens of European countries, but their situation differed from that of European Jews in Morocco, as described by Bowie (1976). In Morocco, some wealthy Jews abused the protection of European countries by inhumanely prosecuting poor Moslem debtors. In remote Benghazi, the desire for the protection of the consuls is clear, but this has not been fully established, and the Jews are thus required to engage in complicated maneuvers. While trying to obtain the rights guaranteed them by law, they must at the same time appeal to the honor and pride of the ruler.

Still another example of the consciousness of the agreement concerning status appears when the situation is temporarily reversed. After the Italian conquest of Tripoli, some Jews were quick to grab the "chance of revenging themselves for numberless slights and injuries endured at Arab hands" (McClure 1913:278). They did this by serving as translators for the Italian authorities, deliberately giving misleading interpretations in order to prejudice the Italians against individual Arabs or Arabs in general (Section 112 and Section 114, n. 1). While some of these translators may have sought financial gain, it seems clear that a vindication of status is the dominant motive involved.

These last several examples also show us that a discussion of Moslem-Jewish relations cannot ignore the broad historical context. Even though it was the Moslem Turks who initiated reforms giving greater rights to the Jews of Tripolitania in the nineteenth century, it is clear that the Turks had to take into account the pressure of the European powers. Thus it is quite reasonable to argue that the data from the past century are not "typical," but represent a situation in which the Moslem world is being threatened, both spiritually and politically (Cahen 1965; Stillman 1975:73). The anti-Jewish incidents in Tripolitanian coastal towns during the last century may reflect an unstable situation in which the tribal system of protection was no longer operative and the rule of the Turks still not fully established. Outbreaks against synagogues in these localities (for another instance, in Misurata, see el-Hachaichi 1903:267–268) would thus also represent opposition to the Turkish regime and the new order that did not distinguish between Moslem and Jew. Rosen has suggested (1972:447) that one test of strength for the individual-based social structure he sees in Morocco is how well it fares

under social or political strain. Viewed from this perspective, the number of cases that Hakohen reports in which Jews were attacked with
impunity, synagogues sacked, or Torah scrolls torn and burned may be
seen as a measure of the fragility of these social ties. In comparing the
rate of these incidents with those elsewhere, we should also note that
Rosen's assertion (p. 447) that "attacks were . . . invariably directed
against the property of the Jews rather than against their persons"
would be misleading for Tripolitania.

Finally, we return to the question: to what extent were these actions
directed toward Jews as Jews? At times of an interregnum (Sections 111
and 112) the Jews might be attacked, but these attacks could easily be
extended to the other sections of the population. Perhaps the Jews
should be seen simply as one example of an entire category of vulnerable persons? Hakohen seems to have a view of these matters, although
he states it in the course of describing a much earlier period than the one
discussed here (Section 17, ms. p. 33a):

> Throughout the days of Byzantine rule, from the time Libya was
> taken in Justinian's conquest of North Africa, and also during the
> terrible wars of the Mohammedans' rise to power, the land of Libya
> was never at rest. And during every troubled time, the Jews of
> Tripoli and its surrounding areas were the scapegoats, the first to
> suffer captivity, looting, death, and destruction along with their
> brethren elsewhere in North Africa.

One could argue that although the Jews may have been first, they
were, in principle, no different from other weak groups. However,
differences in quantity and differences in quality are often linked. If
the Jews are not distinguished from other groups, why consistently
attack them first? The sequence of the narrative in Section 111 suggests an answer. The Jewish shops in Tripoli were looted by the
peasants outside the town; they then planned to attack the Jews themselves and rape the women. The Moslems of the city were well aware
that these attacks might eventually be extended to them, and they
pressed for a truce to stop the fighting. The order of these incidents
has a definite logic. The government is least likely to stop looting
against the Jews. Indeed, the narrative shows that the policemen appeared to encourage the peasants ("Take what you can; it is better
that you should have it than that a Christian infidel should benefit").
Having succeeded in this, the looters could attempt something more
daring, an attack on the Jewish quarter. If they met with further
success against the Jews, the Moslems of the city were presumably
the next target. On the other hand, if the Jews were being protected,
then it follows that the rest of the population was protected as well,

and further forays were not advisable. Hakohen describes such a sequence when the Jews of some eastern communities (Zliten, Khoms, and Mesallata) were beset by the followers of the rebel chief 'Abd-a-jalil in 1839 (Section 46):

> First the wealth of the Jews was plundered because they are well-suited to be the scapegoat who receives the first injury; from childhood, the law forbids them to carry arms, that their hands [might] learn battle and their fingers war [Psalms CXLIV:1]. Instead, they are as sheep, who go dumb to the shearing [Isaiah XLIII:7]. The booty of the Jews gave the troops strength, and afterwards they plundered the wealth of the Moslems too.

Thus a culturally defined distinction is expressed in action in quantitative differences, but this does not mean that the underlying categorical differences are not important.

There are other examples of the social implications of this logic. Toward the end of the last century, the Ottoman governors in Tripoli tried to implement various reforms, including conscription of local Moslems and reorganization of the system of taxation. Part of this effort was a plan to require the citizens of Tripoli either to serve in the army or to pay an exemption tax. In furthering this plan in the first half of this century, Hafez Pasha, Husni Effendi Pasha, and Rajeb Pasha used an interesting tactic. They pressured the Jewish community *first*, knowing that if the Jews agreed either to bear arms or to accept a tax in place of military service, the Moslems would not have any grounds to argue against these laws. Hakohen, who appears generally to have been sympathetic to the reforms introduced by the Turks, became directly involved in resisting the application of the new rules to the Jews (Sections 61–64). What is important for our discussion is the logic linking Moslems and Jews, which was understood by all. The Jews, for their part, argued that if the Moslems would accept the new laws, they too would have no choice but to accept. But putting the Jews first, they claimed, would only increase the resentment against them.

We have already mentioned that the continued Turkish pressure for reform produced a "backlash" against the Jewish community. In the fall of 1908, the new government of the Young Turks announced parliamentary elections for representatives to be sent from Tripoli to Istanbul. Jews had the same formal rights as other citizens, but, in Hakohen's terms, "because religious hatred was on the rise, the elections were not carried out justly, and not one Jew was elected throughout the whole region" (Section 65). While one Jew was elected as an alternate delegate, the results of this selection process may be contrasted to those in

1911, when conscription finally was instituted. Out of 142 conscripts from within the walled city and its immediate environs, 59 (or 41.5 percent) were Jewish.

The direct connection between Ottoman reform and local treatment of the Jews is shown in another incident. In 1900 and 1901, Hafez Pasha attempted to pressure the peasants into accepting a new form of land tax. This attempt was first focused on the village of Tajura, not far from Tripoli. After some negotiation and maneuvering, the people decided to resist the Pasha. "They heaped scorn haughtily on the Pasha; they vilified his actions. They chose to forget his abilities; only his failings crossed their minds. They decided to incite all the thugs to commit outrages—robbery and plunder—in order to keep the Pasha from accomplishing his purpose" (Section 59; see Goldberg 1980).

This decision on the part of the peasants took the form of a raid on the neighboring town of 'Amrus during the Friday market. Hakohen says that all the money and merchandise belonging to the traders in the market was stolen. In the next paragraph, he indicates that these merchants were mostly, and perhaps exclusively, Jewish. The merchants appealed to Hafez Pasha, who took strong measures against the thugs, and eventually the villagers were forced to repay the merchants for their losses.

In this account, Hakohen alternately speaks of the merchants and the Jews in referring to the victims of the attack. One could argue that this indicates that Jewishness is not the central factor, that the plunder of the merchants was most important. However, one might also remember that it is not necessary to specify that the merchants were Jewish, since this is presumed by all. Just as it is not necessary to say that the peasants are Moslem, so it is understood that merchants are Jews. *Merchant,* in addition to its generic meaning, may also be an unmarked phrase meaning *Jewish* merchant (Greenberg 1966).

Furthermore, just as it is taken for granted that merchants are Jews, so it is taken for granted that they are vulnerable. Looting them is thus a direct test of the Pasha's strength and resolve, and a statement of the peasants' basic objection to the reform he represents. While Jews came to enjoy greater security under Turkish rule, they were still viewed by the local populace as a community which was there only conditionally. Just as, earlier, the treatment of the Jew could test the honor and strength of rival tribal chiefs, so the protection of the Jews is a test of power between the reforming Ottomans with their new laws (including the guarantee of "freedom of religion") and the local inhabitants. The latter are not only trying to resist taxation; they also want to preserve their whole way of life, a way of life in which Moslem and *dhimmi* are clearly separated. The position of the Jews in their midst is an inverse indicator of their own situation (Goldberg 1977b).

Finally, it may be that in separating the Jew-as-a-Jew from the Jew-as-a-merchant or the Jew in his other social roles, we are exhibiting our own social-science tendencies to sort things out into analytical categories—categories that may not reflect the way the society in question perceives itself. This can be seen, once again, in the case of trade. Waterbury (1972:89–92) has stressed the necessity for traders to have patrons or protectors, whatever the religious affiliation of the men in question. This association of trade and protection receives curious anthropological confirmation from alternate translations given to the *mizrag* relationship in Morocco. Brown (1977) says *mizrag* refers to a patron-client tie while Geertz (1973:7) calls it a trade pact. Both of them mention *mizrag* while describing itinerant Jewish commerce. It appears that in the traditional Moroccan situation trade, need of protection, and Jewishness were part of a single cultural bundle. We now appreciate that French ethnologists made artificial distinctions between the religious and political authority of the sultan of Morocco (Burke 1972).[13] So we suggest here that it is somewhat forced to separate the religious status of the Jew from other social roles that he may have had. The difference between one cultural milieu and another lies in the fact that ideas which seem to be separate in one tradition are concomitant in a second (Hocart 1970). Thus, if a Moslem trades, works, chats, or dines with a Jew (and Hakohen's text shows that all these activities went on), it is not only because the religious difference is forgotten, but very often because the *dhimmi* status enters directly into framing, or providing the context for, the relationship between the two men.

NOTES

1. See, for example, Rosen (1968, 1972), Gerber (1975), Stillman (1975), Bowie (1976), and Goldberg (1977b, 1978a).

2. Here Hakohen inserts Note 8, translated in the Editor's Introduction.

3. Here Hakohen inserts Note 9, as follows: "I was in the town of Yefren. The governor, Rajeb Pasha, had a broken watch, and no one there could fix it. He invited me to the government palace and did me the honor of asking me to fix it. While I was there, a Berber notable entered, donned a cloak of zealousness, and said, 'Filthy Jews! Why do they not believe in the Mohammedan religion?' I answered him, saying, 'Have you come to argue with me? I only argue with learned people.' The Berber glared at me in anger, his eyes sharp as daggers, and said: 'See what gall! He belittles me in front of the *mutaṣarrif* (governor). Has the Jew become so important that he can determine my knowledge and say that I am not learned?' I answered him, saying, 'Calm your zeal. The words of the wise are spoken in quiet [Ecclesiastes IX:17]. One can already determine

that you are not learned, for it is written in your Koran, 'Do not dispute with the Peoples of Scripture, except in the best fashion' [Sura XXIX:46]. If you had learned that, I should not assume that you would directly oppose Mohammed's dictum, beginning your dispute in an angry manner and saying that the Jews are filthy.' At this the governor said, 'The Jewish sage is correct; one must only argue with pleasant words.'"

4. The saying is an almost direct citation of Proverbs XXVII:19, meaning just as a face is reflected in water, so one man's feeling toward another reflects the other's feeling toward him.

5. Part of Section 38 is translated in Goldberg (1977b).

6. In Section 48, Hakohen describes such an incident, which led to a confrontation between Tripoli and France in 1852.

7. In a Note in Section 101, Hakohen mentions that he carried a revolver, which presumably he could do easily under Turkish rule.

8. Further details are found in a document translated by Littman (1975).

9. On the distinction between the normative and the cultural, see Schneider (1976).

10. Jason (1975) has studied folk tales of intercommunal conflict and interreligious rivalry. From a Jewish point of view, these are usually resolved in one of three ways: (a) by a fair-minded Moslem (*e.g.*, a King or Qadi), (b) through Jewish cleverness, or (c) through supernatural intervention. The prominence of the latter type of story might be seen as an inverse indicator of the strength and consistency of secular protection. (See Noy 1967 on Jewish folk tales from Libya.)

11. An expression of this concept of mankind is found in Hakohen's account of the Moslem festivals (Section 5, ms. p. 9a): "Their [the Moslem] New Year falls on the New Moon of the month of Muharram. On the tenth of that month, many of them fast. Pious Moslems reckon how much they have profited during the past year and take from that a tithe as charity to the poor. The Holy One, blessed be He, gives every creature his due; may he bless the work of their hands." The phrase "gives every creature his due" (literally, "does not withhold the reward of any creature") may have a double meaning here, referring both to the religious reward due to the pious Moslems and to the fact that the needy are provided for. In the former context, the implication may be that "even the undeserving should be rewarded for good deeds," based on the usage in the Babylonian Talmud (*Nazir* 23b).

12. This view is analytically parallel to the approach taken by Schneider (1968) in *American Kinship*. The observed variation in whether some affinally related individuals are treated like and called cousins is not just the failure of practice to conform to standard usage, but stems from the basic definition of kinship in American culture.

13. See the two versions of the story of the synagogue in Zawia, in which the terms *government* and *religion* appear interchangeably. In Section 83, while enumerating the synagogues in Tripoli, Hakohen states: "As the Mohammedans have a tradition that when the Jews have many synagogues the strength of the Mohammedan government is weakened, they do not allow the Jews to build a new synagogue except by legal evasion and great effort, after which they may receive a permit to build."

The Geographic and Historical Setting

(SECTION 90)

In the Atlas Mountains[1] of Tripoli, there is a broad region called Jebel (Mt.) Nefusa.* The Berbers who reside there are called Nefusa. Formerly the land was inhabited by Jews, who were great in number and powerful. The whole area from the land of Taghermin, which is now called Zentan, to Jebel Nalut near Tunisia was a single district that included Rejban, Fassato, Rehibat, Haraba, Serus, and so forth.

Zentan is approximately a seven-hour walk southwest of Jebel Yefren. Formerly it was inhabited by Berbers, but now it is inhabited by Arabs. They are proud and lazy. Their dwellings are clay houses; actually they are four-sided excavations that one reaches by descending a slope in which cave-like rooms have been dug out, similar to those in the land of Ghuryan[4] (see Section 102 for details).

Rain water for drinking is stored in carved-out water cisterns, but springs can be found nearby. In a place called Riaina there is a spring that flows constantly, but without force; between the place called Bugal[5] and the place called Zentan, there is another flowing spring called Wad (Valley) Afilau.[6] Between Zentan and Rejban to the southwest there is a flowing spring called Wadi (Valley) Metlala. In the place called Brahama there is a flowing spring called Wad li-Brahama. In a place called Zamla, near Wad Metlala, there is a hill called Qil'at (Hill of) Kammun.[7] The local inhabitants believe that it belonged to a Jew named Kammun and that the inhabitants of the hill were all Jews. Even now, there are ancient caves in that place that served as granaries, and the local residents believe that these caves were dug by Jews.

The village known by the name of Rejban is a three-hour walk to the southwest of the Hill of Kammun. Nearby is the town Ulad 'Atiya (the sons of 'Atiya). This town belonged to the Jewish family 'Atiya. The ruins of a synagogue, as well as those of a Jewish cemetery, can be found there. The local inhabitants say that many Jews lived in the city.

Three hours' walk to the southwest of Rejban lies a district named Fassato.[8] The government fortress is located in a town named Jado. At the foot of the mountain near this town there are fresh-water wells; the water in some of them is mixed with mineral water. From the wells, it is a flat journey to the village of Zawia al-Gharbia, west of Tripoli. The people from the village get their water from these wells.

*In a Moslem book called *Ta'arīkh Ṭrablus al-Gharb* (*The History of Western Tripoli*),[2] I found (page 56) the following: "Mt. Nefusa is a three-day walk to the south of Tripoli. Its length is a seven-day walk eastward of Jebel Mesallata. It is settled by a people called Hawara as far as Misurata and Baraqa. This mountain was called the land of the Hawara, the Nefusa, and the Luata. After the destruction of Zawilah, the Hawara went to the Fezzan and settled there. They ruled there until Qaraqush came and captured the area. . . . "[3]

THE JEBEL NEFUSA

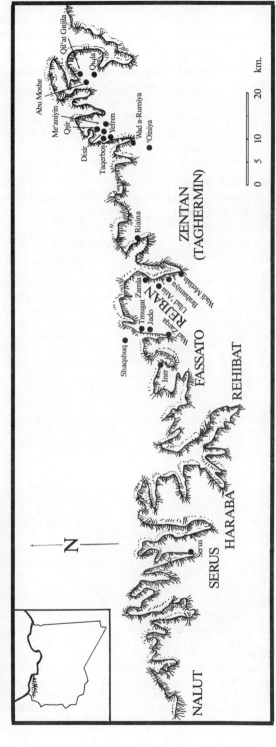

N

mountain escarpment

NALUT

SERUS

HARABA

REHIBAT

FASSATO

ZENTAN
(TAGHERMIN)

Serus

Iner

Shaqshuq

Jado
Zamla
Imugat

Ual 'Ala
Wad Zarga

REIRAN

Betamiya
Wad Mafaala

Riaina

Wad a-Rumiya
'Oimiya

Yefren
Taqerboss
Qsir
Disir
Me'aniyin

Abu Moshe

Qili'at Gujila
Oujla

km.

0 5 10   20

Once the Jews were numerous in this district, preceding the Berbers, who also dwelt in the land and who lived with the Jews in love and brotherhood. They had neither ruler nor judge; every tribe was a government unto itself.

At the present time, there are no Jewish inhabitants, except for two Jews and their families who came from Jebel Yefren because of difficult economic circumstances. There are many hills with ruined cities, and an air of antiquity hovers over them. However, the extent of destruction testifies to the size of the former settlement. There is still a ruined cave in Jado, and local tradition holds that it was once the synagogue of the Jews. Jewish cemeteries* can also be found there,[9] but now most of them are farmed by the Berbers.

*In the year 1906, I traveled there with my friend, the scholar Dr. Nahum Slouschz. We excavated one of the Jewish cemeteries on a hill and found, deep in the earth, a square gravestone made of rock, about one handspan thick and three handspans square. Arabic letters were engraved on it, but without the customary markings of Arabic writing. Four Hebrew letters, חסנא , the word Hasna (the name of a woman), were carved at the end of the Arabic letters. The Arabic letters were unadorned and this was their form: חסנא هاد القبر لحسنا The Arabic letters without embellishments are *had al qbar liḥasna* ("this is the grave of Hasna"), and the Hebrew word is spelled ḤSNA. This is the proper name of a Jewish woman (see Section 73, letter Ḥ). But every feminine name similar in form to Rivka, for example, should be written with the ה , not א at the end, whether it is a Hebrew or an Arabic name. Therefore, this word on the gravestone should have been written لحسنـة in Arabic and חסנה in Hebrew. After intensive study, I saw in a scraped-off section an Arabic word in Hebrew letters, שנה (year). The other letters were very thin and I could not reconstruct them, so the matter remained an unsolved riddle. Perhaps, in those days, the Jews of the district were forced to convert and by this clever subterfuge of writing the Hebrew name on the stone were able to indicate that this was the grave of a Jewish woman.

I met there with some Berber elders, headed by a venerated man named ‘Omar Ḥashad, who was a local historian. He told us that their tradition speaks of the courage of the Jews in those early days. Once, enemies made a surprise attack on the Berbers of Fassato on a Friday afternoon at a time when all the Berber warriors were unarmed in the mosque. When this became known to the Jews of Fassato, they summoned their courage and went out ready for war against the enemy. They worked wonders, for the enemy was smitten with a mighty scourge before the Berbers themselves could enter the battle. I asked these elders if their tradition has anything to say about the date of the beginning of Jewish settlement in the area, and what was the Jews' situation, and when they were exiled from this district. Their answer was that the time of settlement was not known to them. ‘Omar Ḥashad answered: "It is not clear to us when the Jews were exiled because our forefathers were not accustomed to write down their history, but we do know from ancient legal documents that in the year 900 (according to the Moslem calendar, or 1495 A.D.) there were in the town of Jado 80 silversmith shops owned by Jewish artisans, and many more Jews were there in those days." The rest of the elders said that there is no answer to the question of the origin of Jewish settlement because "Our tradition says that Jews were

The inhabitants there are Berbers. They are not religious fanatics like the other Moslems of Tripolitania; they honor the Jews who come to peddle there.

The Mohammedan religion reigns in the country, but it is divided into four systems: the Maliki, Hanafi, Shafi'i, and Hanbali. But the Berbers adopted a different system,[11] a mixed system called *Khamasi* (fifth) because it is a combination of the four Moslem systems plus the Hebrew system.[12] The Berbers accepted the Mohammedan religion of their own free will, without coercion, on the strength of the rumor that the religion was successful. They also adopted from the Jews some ethical commandments and special customs, for example, the practices of *leqet, shikhehah,* and *pe'ah*[13] that are written in the Law of Moses. They also adopted, among others, the commandment "When you shake the fruit from your olive trees, do not go over them again."[14] They also eat from the meat slaughtered by the Jews, and they avoid even numbers. For instance, if a man eats two figs he is told to eat a third for fear of the consequences (we have found caution in the Talmud with regard to the use of even numbers).[15] The women wear a silver bracelet on their left arm, for they say that the left side is harsh, and silver is soft and merciful. This custom is taken from the wisdom of the Kabbalah,[16] which softens the law with mercy.

the first in the land; they resided here before our forefathers, the Berbers, came here. They received our forefathers with love and said: 'Come, for the land stretches out before you, and we shall live together in security.' After that, a Berber tribe called Hawara was banished from here and settled in the land of Fezzan.

"The Jews were industrious in harvesting and in all manner of work in the house and in the field. From childhood, their hands were trained for battle and their fingers for war, so that they could stand up against those who rose against them. If an enemy approached them, the Jews and the Berbers would unite as one man, with sword and spear, so as not to let the aggressor encroach upon their land. They accepted the yoke of neither ruler nor judge. Instead, each tribe was a political unit unto itself, and the head of each tribe was the leader and the conciliator between a man and his fellow. But when a difficult case arose, the elders would gather in council."

I also asked why there was no religious enmity between the two groups. They answered: "Remember that all we have said is not written in books but passed on as tradition; according to what we have heard, the first Berbers were not so orthodox in the observance of the tenets of their religion."

In the area, some tombstones with Hebrew engraving can be found, most of them dating from the fifth millenium. I have not seen a tombstone dated later than 5270. It is possible that when Tripoli was captured by the Spaniards in the year 1510, as recorded in Section 19, the Mohammedans fled to the countryside. It appears that a large number of them went to Jebel Nefusa and displaced the Jews. But this is only a supposition, for we have no evidence to support it. Perhaps other engraved stones will be found from that period that will disprove this hypothesis.

They have adopted another custom: that a bride, before entering the house of her groom for the first time, shall take a hen's egg from her bosom and toss it against the wall of the house in order to soil it. This custom is widely practiced among the Jews of Tripoli as a sign of mourning over the destruction of the Holy Temple (Section 89). Even in Jerba, which was once part of the district of Tripoli,[17] Jews practice this custom. But I do not know how the Berbers acquired this practice and what connection they could have to the mourning over the destruction of the Temple. We might say that they were originally a sect of Jews that assimilated in the course of time, or that the Berbers adopted this custom for some other reason.

The residents of the district do not work their land industriously. They exert themselves only during the grain harvest and the season for gathering olives, figs, and grapes, at which time they work with understanding and good judgment. The quality of the land is uneven, and there are only a few flowing rivers. They suffer greatly from famine in drought years, when they must import bread on the backs of camels. During the summers of dry years, they also suffer thirst, for then the mountain springs that flow down from the crevices of the rocks are sparse and feeble. There is an arroyo there called Wad Tmugat. Another is called Wad Shinsha; it comes down from the mountain. Yet another is called Wad Zarqa, after a Jew whose name is Zarqa (see Section 73, letter Z). Once I saw in a geography book from Palestine, in a passage concerning desert regions, that *Wad Zarqa*[18] was translated into Hebrew as "blue river." Anyone who knows Arabic and Hebrew will see that this translation does not follow the rules of grammar. If *zarqa* is used as an adjective indicating that the river is blue (*zraq* in Arabic), it should have been called *wad al-zraq,* which is the correct masculine form with the definite article *al* at the beginning of the word, like the definite article *he'* in Hebrew. For example, the Black Sea in Arabic is *baḥr al-swad.* Therefore, it is more plausible to assume that *zarqa* is a personal noun which does not take the definite article *al* in Arabic.

About a five-hour walk south of Jado is a village named Rehibat. A flowing spring can be found there between Iyur[19] and Jimar, and also a group of five towns called Ḥrab a-Sabbata[20] (the Sabbath ruins) because these towns were inhabited by Jews who observed the Sabbath. Now they are inhabited by Arabs, not Berbers. There is a ritual bath that catches the rain water and has a capacity of forty s'ah.[21] Jewish cemeteries, also found there, are considered sacred by the local Arabs. Gradually, however, the Arabs are expanding their fields and sowing and reaping in the cemeteries. Deep in the earth one can always find tombstones with engraved Hebrew script, bearing the dates of many generations; the Arabs break some of them and bury others,* but some are still in the hands of the local inhabitants.

About five hours' walk from Hrab-a-Sabbata is a village called Haraba, and close to it a village called Serus. According to local tradition, all these villages once belonged to Jews. Even now, there are remnants of many silversmith shops, and tradition has it that they all belonged to Jews. There are also synagogues and Jewish cemeteries which are considered sacred by the local inhabitants. Many Hebrew inscriptions, both engraved and in relief, but unadorned, can be found on tombstones and elsewhere.

In the mountains of that district there are many hills of differing colors, containing precious, shiny, metallic stones. Perhaps lead, gold, and silver are also to be found in those hills.

A Jewish silversmith named Ḥaim Da'dush took a nugget from that district, refined it in a furnace, and extracted a bit of silver. He found that his expenses were greater than his profit because the cost of the coals was greater than the value of the silver he obtained. Still, he did not want to tell me where he had found the stone.

The local inhabitants are reluctant to give information about these places of interest because they fear that the Turkish government will find wily ways of expropriating these useful lands. They also fear that the government will impose a corvée upon the population.

In 1902, a man from Riaina brought [to Tripoli] a nugget that came from the hills to the southwest. A Mohammedan scholar named al-Ḥaj Ḥasin Jibara gained access to it. He performed experiments on the nug-

---

*In 1906, I visited this village and found four Jewish peddlers engaged in trade. They return home only in the months of Nisan and Tishrei, to celebrate the festivals with their families. They pounced upon me with joy, for they craved meat but were not authorized to slaughter. They quickly brought me a goat; I slaughtered it for them, and they roasted and ate it eagerly. I asked them if they had found any tombstones with Hebrew engravings. They said: "We have found several from time to time and, thank God, we were privileged to bury them deep in the earth (as is their custom). However, there is one unburied stone still here." (Mr. Slouschz made a copy of this stone.) We went to the Jewish cemeteries and found only fragments of stones, so broken by the plow that, though they were engraved with Hebrew characters, I was unable to decipher them.

These same four Jews told me that recently a subterranean cave had been discovered and a copper Hanukkah lamp found in it; the lamp is now in Yefren. They also told me about a stone in the wall that is engraved in Assyrian[22] script with the name of the Jew who owned the cave, Aharon ben Aharon, and about a poem concerning his heroic deeds that was written in a Hebrew script.[23] I tried very hard to get the stone, and the four Jews also begged the Arab owner of the cave to take money and show us the stone. The owner, however, denied knowing its whereabouts. He apparently was worried that the government would force him to say that the cave was not his but belonged to a Jew named Aharon ben Aharon.

get and found that it contained lead. As was customary, he wrote a
report to the governor, Hafez Pasha. Hafez Pasha sent the nugget to
Istanbul and received an order to set up a guard around those hills.
However, the local inhabitants would not disclose which hills they were,
nor the whereabouts of the man who had found the nugget. To this day,
it is not known whether he is alive or dead.

This same al-Ḥaj Ḥasin also went to Shaqshuq to see if there was
coal to be found. He found a rock that contained a fossil and showed it
to his colleagues, demonstrating that it was once a plant and it had
become petrified.[24]

NOTES

1. Geographers do not include the Jebel Nefusa in the Atlas range, which
ends in western Tunisia. However, Schulmann (1877:99) does call the Nefusa
range part of the Atlas, adding further weight to the belief that his work was of
special significance to Hakohen. The most thorough social study of the Jebel
Nefusa is that of Despois (1935).

2. See the Editor's Introduction, n. 33.

3. The footnote continues in the Hebrew text as follows: "And Alstad
said . . . When he traveled to this mountain . . . It extends from the ocean
(circumferential sea) of Thither Sus until it reaches . . . (see Section 13, Note
20)." The manuscript of *Ta'arīkh Ṭrablus al-Gharb* translated by Rossi (1936)
has different pagination from the book cited by Hakohen (see the Editor's Introduction). A parallel passage to the section quoted here may be found in Ibn
Khaldun (1925, I:280–281).

The Hawara Berbers of Tripolitania helped establish the Ibadi Rustamid state
at Tahirt in the eighth century. Hawara warriors attacked Tripoli in 811, after
which the authority of the Rustamids in the Maghreb was acknowledged outside
of the regions in Tunisia and Algeria controlled by the Aghlabids (Abun-Nasr
1971:75). Qaraqush was an Armenian, supported by Saladin, who conquered
Tripoli in 1172 and ruled it for several decades, extending his sway to the
Fezzan. The term "circumferential sea" reflects a medieval view in which all the
land in the world is surrounded by an ocean (see the description of *bazīn* in
Section 93).

4. The houses of the region are described by Despois (1935:184–206).

5. Perhaps this is Ouad el-Bagoul, recorded in Calassanti-Motylinski
(1898:80).

6. I have been unable to identify this place on a map or in any other
geographical account.

7. Again, I am unable to identify the place.

8. The social structure of Fassato is discussed by Sahli (1970).

9. The Jewish quarter of ancient Jado, including the Jewish cemetery, is
identified by Despois (1935:245).

10. El-Bekri (eleventh century) mentions the large Jewish population of Jado
(1913:25).

11. The Nefusa Berbers are Ibadis (Lewicki 1971). See Norris (1977:55–56) on the term *khawāmis*.

12. Ibn Khaldun (1925, I:208) states that the Nefusa were one of the tribes that adopted Judaism. The whole problem of the Judaized Berbers has been reviewed by Hirschberg (1963). See also Goldberg (1972b).

13. These terms refer to verses enjoining the farmer to leave a portion of his land to be harvested by the poor (Leviticus XIX:9 and Deuteronomy XXIV:19).

14. Deuteronomy XXIV:20.

15. Babylonian Talmud, Tractate *Pesaḥim* 109b.

16. See, for example, the Zohar on Exodus XXV:3. There, silver is associated with the Day of Atonement, during which Israel is forgiven for its sins, in contrast to gold, which represents Rosh Hashanah, the Day of Judgment.

17. See Despois (1965).

18. Possibly Wadi Zarqa in Jordan, which empties into the Dead Sea.

19. Possibly Iner on maps.

20. I am unable to identify the place.

21. A *s'ah* is a measure of volume. A ritual bath (*miqweh tahorah*) must contain at least forty *s'ah*.

22. The standard Hebrew script, as distinguished from the ancient, pre-exilic, script.

23. An old informant who comes from Yefren told me that he had seen this stone but said that he did not know how to read it.

24. See Rossi (1968:315) on an incident concerning a carbon fossil.

Political Organization of the Berbers

(NOTE 17)

Mt. Yefren is about a three-day walk from Tripoli. It lies atop a high mountain range, and can be reached only through great toil and effort. Winding roads rise among the boulders like a spiral staircase, while narrow paths are hewn between the rocks. Only those who go by foot, or on the back of an animal, can twist through, because a cart cannot gain enough momentum. The traveler on those paths can easily make a fateful stumble if he does not pay attention to these dangers; his legs will take him to his death. The outsider who climbs up the mountains will become weary of the difficult traps that his feet encounter. He will feel as if he is marching in a wild land, and his legs are taking him into hell. But the inhabitants of the region skip barefoot through the mountains and leap over the hills with heavy loads on their shoulders, without any effort.

Every road is not the same, however, for there are short stretches of plateau. It is a place neither of grain nor of fruit trees, but a place of thirst, where the empty wilderness wails. Where there is habitation, the land is fruitful, yielding shrubs and grass aplenty, olive and fig trees wherever one goes. Date palms are found in the wadis and where springs emerge from rocky cliffs. Few garden crops are grown there. Snow and hail appear infrequently. Rain usually pours down in torrents, toppling many of the olive trees, which are not replenished.

In 1885, a torrential rain swept away the land and all that was in it—the mountain, its trees and its tents, man and beast and the land on which they stood—like a ship at sea, without any casualties. The whole mountain came to rest an arrow shot away in a place called Wad al-Ghezaz. Anyone who passes there cannot cease to wonder at the workings of nature.

Wild beasts and dangerous snakes are few. The Berbers who inhabit the land, upon seeing a snake, are obligated to chase after it and smash its head, according to the verse in the Scriptures: "I will put enmity between you and the woman . . . " (Genesis III, verse 15).

Among those mountains are black hills, and others spotted with various colors. Some are pure marble, others appear to have coal ore, and some contain minerals. In 1911, European researchers, sent by the Turkish government, passed through there to investigate the natural resources hidden in the mountains.

Sometimes precious stones with seal designs are found. Armored clothes belonging to earlier generations, worn for defense during battle, are also found there. Ostriches were formerly abundant in the region and were hunted by the inhabitants, who sold their feathers to the Jewish merchants of Tripoli. But in the middle of the nineteenth century, the ostriches migrated southward to central Africa.

Most of the inhabitants of the district are Berbers, but some are Mohammedan Arabs. The Mohammedan religion reigns there. The Berbers speak a Berber vernacular mixed with Arabic. However, the language is becoming extinct because it is not written down. The Berbers write only in Arabic, which is sacred to them; they learn it as a second language. They are polygamous, marrying more than one woman, and pay a full bride price for each. Whoever takes a woman takes her as he purchases an animal, and if he divorces her he forfeits his money.

The whole district is becoming impoverished because of the indolence of the inhabitants. They are not lacking in intelligence and knowledge, but they also have an excessive measure of pride. They rejoice in extending hospitality. They fulfill the request of any stranger who comes under their protection and extend him a helping hand, but Christians are absolutely despised by them. If a Jewish traveler happens to pass through to seek contributions from the wealthy, and he is wearing a European headdress, it is incumbent upon him to wear a Turkish hat.[1] If he does not, he cannot be sure that they will not mistakenly suspect him of being a Christian.

Even though they are bound by a pact of friendship, the Berbers still harbor deep hatred for one another, each man trying secretly to trip up his fellow. They wallow in indolence, gathering together in groups, with hands folded, engaging in idle talk. But in the season of plowing and reaping, and at similar times, they are moved to action; even the weak proclaims, "I am strong enough to provide for my family." At reaping time, they observe the commandments of *leqeṭ, shikheḥah,* and *pe'ah*[2] for the poor, as written in the Torah of Moses. The same holds true for the commandment "When you shake the fruit from your olive trees, do not go over them again."[3] In lean years they bring home food, purchased for cash in Tripoli, on the backs of camels.

If a man's camel becomes sick and seems likely to die, the notables of the city gather and stab the throat of the animal before it perishes. They eat camel meat as a delicacy, but avoid eating animals which have not been slaughtered. They distribute the camel among the inhabitants of the town, according to the size of each family. Afterwards, they gather money from each family to equal the price of the camel so that the owner can replace his animal and continue his work.

In the district as a whole there are more men than women.

The Berbers shame easily. There are no bandits among them, but there are a few men who specialize in robbery at night. Particularly in years of drought, they tunnel under the walls of a house in order to steal what they need. If the thief is discovered, the owner normally will not kill him in his house,[4] because the rules of blood revenge apply there, even toward him who slays a thief. Rather, the owner fires a pistol in the air to summon a crowd. Sometimes the thief does not flee but melts into the crowd, claiming that he just arrived.

Complex interconnected caverns stretch out underneath the ground. These are the ruins of old towns, enveloped in an aura of antiquity; there is no trace of them above the ground. Only the network of caverns remains, excavated by former generations as a protection against the dangers of the night. At that time, the whole district had neither prince nor ruler. Even now, when no one is looking, each one does what is right in his own eyes. A man does not go out of his house at night; and if he does go out, his life is in his own hands. If one family has to borrow something from another at night, they go through the network of caves.

In earlier days, when a corpse was found in the fields, and it was known who killed him, the following rules applied: The elders of the town gather together and investigate thoroughly to find out the truth; then they banish the murderer for up to ten days. When he returns, they pressure him to slaughter a camel, to burn his house, or to make payment to the blood avenger, according to the amount decided. If he cannot raise the amount of blood money that has been set, then he must be banned from the community, to wander among the mountains and over the hills, seeking contributions so that he can pay his debt to the avenger.

If the blood avenger refuses to accept money, but instead awaits an opportunity for vengeance, then the murderer goes into the house of the avenger, accompanied by his companions. He goes in great humility, with his hands tied behind him and a funeral shroud over his head, and says, "I have sinned exceedingly before you. Slay me, if you so desire, as atonement for the life of the deceased." If the blood avenger accepts his gesture and forgives his wicked deed, they then arrange a feast to celebrate both the forgiveness of the debt and the establishment of a pact of friendship and peace. But if the avenging kinsman refuses to be placated by money and continues to hate the murderer, seeking a life for a life, he may not slay the murderer in his house. The murderer flees from there. He then knows definitely that he is being hunted and must always carry his weapon with him, ready in his hands, to save himself from the blood avenger. He can also flee to another city and live there. (Even today, the people believe in the rules of vengeance, if the murderer is not punished under Turkish law.)

If the killer is a brave warrior, then his companions accompany and assist him. They gird their loins and consecrate a war—camp against camp—and victims from both sides fall dead on the battlefield. If a chief is slain in combat, those drunken with victory sever the joints of his hands and disgrace his supporters by beating them upon a drum, singing songs of mockery at their opponents. Then the battle gains momentum and hatred flows like brimstone until the mighty subdue the weak and destroy them, or until the notables of the surrounding towns gather to mediate. Sometimes wars would break out over the Jews, who were the servants; he who humiliates a Jewish servant humiliates his master.

The Berbers' houses are built low and are unadorned. They have narrow rooms without windows. The doors to the houses and rooms are made of twisted olive-wood planks, but they are thick and strong and last up to four hundred years.

The keys are not made of metal, nor do they open and close like the keys that we use. Instead, the keys are made of olive wood and are used only for opening, whether from the inside or from the outside. What follows is an account of the lock that lies inside the handles which are fastened to the door:

A hole in the doorpost matches up with a bolt which can go in and out of it. When the bolt closes, a set of holes in its upper surface receive wooden pegs from the door handle. These move freely until they fall into the bolt, preventing it from coming out of the hole in the doorpost. There is a slit in the bolt that receives the key on the inside. The key is made of wood and matches the slit. On the key are wooden pegs that exactly match the surface of the bolt into which the loose pegs that secure the bolt have fallen. In the door is one hole, an arm thickness wide. When a person closes the door from the outside, he inserts his hand in the hole, pushing the bolt into the hole of the door post so that the free pegs fall from the door handle and keep the bolt from moving until the pegs are lifted again. When a person comes to open the door from the inside, he places his right hand on the door handle and grasps the key in his left hand, inserting it into the slit, and lifting the loose pegs by means of the fastened pegs. Afterwards, the bolt can be drawn out of the hole. He who wishes to open the door from the outside puts his arm through the hole, up to his armpit, and opens the door with the key.

We may therefore conclude that this key is called *mafteaḥ* because it is used only for opening,[5] and that is why the ancients also called it *mafteaḥ*. It seems that this was the key that the early generations used, before the building of the First Temple. We can thus understand the meaning of the Scriptures in the case of Ehud (Judges III, verses 23–25), where it is written, "And he closed the door to the upper chambers behind him and locked it . . . and they took the key and opened it up, and lo their master was dead." Apparently Ehud closed the upper chamber on the dead man without a key. Instead, he inserted his hand in the hole. The phrase "he closed the door to the upper chambers" means that he pushed in the bolt because it is written "they took *the* key," using the definite article.

Similarly we can understand the phrasing of the verse (Song of Songs V, verse 4), "My beloved thrust his hand from the hole. . . ." For he who opens from the outside puts his hand through the hole to pull out the bolt, and he who opens from the inside places his hands on the door handle.

In the days of the Second Temple they also used the same kind of key, for it is written in the Tractate *Tamid*, Chapter 3, Mishnah 3: "There were two keys. One reaching the armpit, and the other opening directly." (For other customs of Yefren, discussed at length, see Sections 91–101.)

NOTES

1. Other travelers and adventurers have been warned not to wear European ("Christian") clothing in the interior of Tripolitania (*e.g.* Osther 1912:31–33).

2. These terms refer to verses enjoining a farmer to leave a portion of his land to be harvested by the poor (Leviticus XIX:9 and Deuteronomy XXIV:19).

3. Deuteronomy XXIV:20.

4. Here there is an implicit comparison to the biblical law which does not penalize a man for slaying a thief who has tunneled into his house (Exodus XXII:1).

5. The Hebrew verbal stem FTḤ, meaning "open."

The Jewish Community

In the region of the Atlas Mountains there is a district called a-Jebel al-Gharbi (the western mountain) that is also known by the name Ye-fren, after the head of a Berber family called Yefren (see Section 11 and Note 17). Even though its population today includes only about two thousand Jews,[1] the earliest traditions claim that once there was a larger Jewish population there. Because they were unaccustomed to keeping written historical records, we have no details concerning where they went or how their numbers dwindled to such an extent. Perhaps they were assimilated or were destroyed by the sword, or perhaps there is another explanation still unknown to us.

The Berbers, who are the owners of the land, do not show great hatred towards the Jews; instead, the Jews belittle themselves before the Berbers, who are constantly demanding homage, even though the Jews themselves are the pillars of the society, the craftsmen and merchants.

Even before the conquest of the land by the Turks, when the region was governed by neither ruler nor judge, the Jews lived in security, for every Jew had a Berber lord who championed his cause in any quarrel. When a wrong was done to a Jew and his lord let it pass in silence, this was considered to be a disgrace to the lord who had not protected his servant, the Jew. There were even times when the tribes went to battle in matters concerning a Jew.

The Berber lord passed his Hebrew servant[2] down to his children as an inheritance. If the Berber lord had many sons, each inherited a share in the servant. Each could also sell his share in the servant. But the law was not precisely that of the Canaanite slave: "what a slave purchases his master possesses."[3] For if the Hebrew servant met his obligation in giving homage to his lord and was able to acquire money, he could redeem himself by paying a sum agreeable to both parties. With this money he could acquire a deed of manumission for that portion of the rights held by the seller.

Even today, some Jews have certificates of emancipation stating that Lord So-and-So received in good faith from his servant Such-and-Such a sum of silver weights and in return that servant was released from bondage. (Since there was no government, there was also no legal tender and all trade was done in weights or by barter.) When the land was conquered by the Turks, a law was enacted that all Jewish servants were to be freed.[4] Not only the masters but also the Jews were allowed to wear the red hat of the Muslims without anyone objecting. By now, even those families who could not buy their freedom have all been released from servitude. But in such cases the lord calls upon them by name[5] to

treat him with respect, and in return the lord will assist them to overcome any injury inflicted by other Berbers.

Today the Jews of Yefren dwell in three villages in the following
manner:

O

O

O

One is called al-Qṣir, the second Me'aniyin, and they are separated by
only a three-minute walk; the third is called Disir,[6] and it is separated
from the other two by a walk of approximately twenty-five minutes. In
all three villages, Jews and Berbers live together.[7] Their homes are
built on all parts of the mountain—the peak, the slope, and the foot.
All the houses are windowless and have narrow, simple rooms without
flooring; the crooked ceilings are covered with roofs made of olive
branches.

In the other places near Yefren there was once a large number of
Jewish inhabitants, but now there is no trace of them, except for their
cemeteries or place names.

An hour's walk to the south of these three villages is another village
in which a spring gushes continuously from the crevices of the rocks. It
is called Wad a-Rumiya (Valley of the Romans); the place is gloomy and
bears the danger of tuberculosis. Another hour's walk to the south
brings one to a flat valley with wells, most of them not deep enough to
yield sweet, pure water. This place is called al-'Oiniya. Among the wells
there is one traditionally called al-Yehudiya (the Jewess), for it was used
as a bath for ritual purification after menstruation, and the women
reached it by descending a staircase. The entire surrounding area was
inhabited by Jews.

About a four-hour walk north of Yefren there is a village called
Qiqla. Here too the majority of the settlers in the early days were Jews.
In old deeds of purchase it is recorded that the lands were bought from
Jews. The boundary markers also indicate lands belonging to Jews.

Among the various places in the area there is a town called abu-
Moshe.[8] Near it is a hill called Qil'at (the hill of) Gujila. The local
Berbers believe that there was a palace there named *Qaṣr* (Fortress)
Gujila where a one-eyed Jewish governor lived for forty years.

Near Yefren there is a flat area with fertile soil called a-Dahar and a
village planted with figs and grapes called Kohen. According to tradition, all of the land belonged to the head of a Jewish family named
Kohen. When this family saw that the rule of armed might had displaced the previous social order and the Berber leaders did not demand
justice for the Jews, the Kohen family went into exile and left their
land.

NOTES

1. I think this is a high estimate, although it is clear that many Jews later left the Jebel as a result of the fighting there against the Italians (see Goldberg 1971:257).

2. Hakohen uses the word *'eved*, which is normally translated as "slave" or "servant." (See the Editor's Foreword to this chapter.)

3. Babylonian Talmud: *Pesaḥim* (88b). Jewish law distinguishes between a Hebrew slave (*cf*. Exodus XXI:2–6), whose indenture is not permanent (Leviticus XXV:39–46), and a Canaanite slave, who is his master's "money" (Exodus XXI:21).

4. The following account is given by Adadi (1865:47b): "I have heard from the elders that there is a tradition that Fanjar, King of the Ishmaelites (see *Midrash Rabbah* to Lamentations I:32) is the one who brought our ancestors from the captivity of Jerusalem to a mountain in this region, a two-day distance from Tripoli, and sold them to the local Ishmaelites. From there, they reached this town, and to this very day, in that mountain, there is no Israelite family without an Ishmaelite master to whom the Israelite must make a token payment every year. The Ishmaelite may sell him to another, and this arrangement persisted until only six or seven years ago, when the Ottoman rulers took the area from the Arabs." Hakohen quotes this passage in Section 11 (ms. p. 24b). See also Zuaretz *et al*. (1960:17–18) for the testimony of an old informant who remembers such a deed of manumission.

5. See Goldberg (1972b) on Berber-Jewish names, and the Editor's Introduction.

6. The identification of places on maps is often complicated. Not only are the Berber and Arab names sometimes different, but the Jewish dialect shows variations too. Me'aniyin appears as al-Gusbat on maps, and Disir as a-Shegarna (Goldberg 1971:248–249).

7. Despois (1935:219) calls these "coupled quarters."

8. This appears on official maps as *Bu-musa*. Hakohen formalizes the prefix, making it *Abu*, and Hebraicizes *musa* to *mosheh*.

CHAPTER TWO

Economy and Language

Editor's Foreword

After providing a general description of the region, Hakohen turns to an account of the occupations of the Jews and their economic role. Some general remarks on the small Jewish communities in Tripolitania will help to place his narrative in perspective.[1] The Jews appear to have occupied a well-defined niche in the Tripolitanian economy. Italian census data from the 1930s show that about eighty-five percent of the Jews were engaged in crafts and commerce, while about eighty-five percent of the Moslems worked in agriculture, herding, and related occupations. There is every reason to believe that a similar situation existed in the Turkish period as well.

If one makes a list of all the Jewish communities mentioned by Hakohen and another list of the major towns in the Tripolitanian hinterland, the two will be almost identical. All of these were market towns, with markets usually held several times a week. Smaller local markets met once a week, and apparently there was a coordination of market days among the different centers in a region. Many of these centers seemed to be "vacant" towns, with only a few permanent residents, which would fill up with people on market days. For this reason, the Jews often formed a high percentage of the permanent population of these settlements. It appears that in the older towns there was an established Jewish residential area, while in some of the newer towns[2] Jewish dwellings were likely to be interspersed among those of the Moslems.

The Jewish presence in these towns was also fluid since the pattern of itinerant hawking in the Nefusa region was common throughout Tripolitania. Some crafts were also carried out on an itinerant basis. The name for these tradesmen in Tripolitanian Arabic was *tawwāf* (the plural is *tawwāfa*), from a stem meaning "to go around." This semantic asso-

ciation has a parallel in biblical Hebrew, where the root SHR means "to
go around in a circle" and also "merchant."

The village[3] Jews thus occupied an intermediate position in the flow
of goods, in both directions, from the most local level up to that of
regional commerce. The artisan who was paid in cash at harvest time
implicitly extended credit to the peasants. The peddler would barter in
trifling amounts with the women of the village. The eggs a woman had to
sell might eventually make their way to Tripoli, as seen in one of Hakohen's autobiographical notes in Section 92. More commonly, a two-step
process was involved. The few well-to-do merchants would bring goods
from Tripoli to the regional towns and from there the goods would be
distributed throughout the area by the poorer peddlers. It seems probable that the economic crisis Hakohen describes is linked to the decline
of the trans-Saharan trade, which had once brought money and goods
into the whole region.

The Jews, although they were formally residents of the towns and
were occupationally specialized, had a good familiarity with the remote
villages and their customs. As in other cases of trade between different
or opposed cultural groups, economic relationships were made possible
by recognized social ties. An individual Jew would often be linked to a
Moslem "friend," *ma'arūf* (or *saheb* in some communities), a relationship that might continue between families over the generations. It is
possible that with the greater security offered by Turkish rule, some of
the earlier patron-client ties turned into ties of "friendship" (*cf.* Brown
1977:314).

Another social (and political) factor in commerce was the fact that
Jewish communities were located near Turkish forts, where they enjoyed the greatest protection. They were thus ready-made intermediaries, both socially and commercially linking the dominant outside
power with the local population—and also keeping them apart. Jewish
merchants served as suppliers to the military not only under European
rule (Goldberg 1972a), but also under the Turks and during the reign of
the rebel chief Ghoma (Slouschz 1927:192–193). The status of the Jews,
which linked them only conditionally to the established center of power,
whether central government or tribal chief, gave them the maneuverabil-
ity needed for trade. This was less feasible for the Moslems, who were
more firmly locked into the existing social structures. At some time in
the historical past, there may have been significant numbers of Jews
owning land and working in agriculture. However, the traditional social
and political arrangement appears to have pressured Jews out of agriculture and landowning and encouraged their specialization in trade.

Several times, Hakohen mentions that the Berbers and other Moslems had lately begun to engage in trade, so that it was no longer a
Jewish monopoly. It has been noted before that Berbers from Ibadi

areas of North Africa were quick to seize opportunities for trade.[4] However, the phenomenon is more general, and has been the subject of a study in Morocco (Waterbury 1972). It is interesting to speculate on whether there was any organized Jewish resistance to these attempts to "encroach" upon their domain by withholding wholesale goods, not providing information, or the like. No suggestion of this emerges from Hakohen's account.

In distributing goods throughout the region, the Jew was a cultural merchant as well. Former peddlers have told me that when they came to a village and stayed at the home of a *ma'arūf*, or village sheikh, they would be expected to provide entertainment by telling stories. Presumably they also spread news and ideas. Loeb (1976), who has discussed this role in the context of Iranian society, argues that the degraded status of Iranian Jews acted as a brake to the potential flow of information. New ideas could be discounted, if necessary, because they were associated with the despised *dhimmi*. This may have been more characteristic of Shi'ite areas, like Iran, which maintain a stronger ritual distinction between Moslems and nonbelievers. In Tripolitania, the flow of ideas, even if only through debate, appears to have been quite free.

The subject of cultural interchange leads naturally to that of language (Goldberg 1974b). The first language of the Jews of Jebel Nefusa was Arabic. In Tripolitania, unlike some regions of Morocco, there were no Jews whose "mother tongue" was a Berber language, although many members of the Yefren community were fluent in Berber as a result of their commercial activities. In the city of Tripoli, there was a Jewish dialect of Arabic that was distinguished from the Moslem dialect by some phonological and grammatical features, as well as a considerable number of lexical items. Although more study needs to be done, it appears probable that the Arabic of the city of Tripoli was (and is) undergoing a process of "ruralization" in which it increasingly resembles the spoken language in the countryside. If this is correct, the Arabic of the Jews of Tripoli probably represents an older form of urban speech. This interpretation fits in with the fact that Jewish speech in some of the villages appears to resemble Moslem speech more than it does in the city (Goldberg 1974b). Thus, among the Jews of Jebel Nefusa, the Arabic /t/ is pronounced [t], and not [č], as is common in Jewish speech in Tripoli itself. This is not at all surprising in view of the small size of the Jewish communities in the interior, and the daily contact between Jews and Moslems there.

In fact, the survival of any special features in Jewish villagers' speech would seem to require some explanation. The Jews of the villages had both direct and indirect contact with the Jews of Tripoli (see Chapter Three), and this contact worked to preserve the Jewish dialect among them. But there is no evidence that Italian, which was spoken by merchants in Tripoli since at least the middle of the last century (Goldberg *et al.* 1980), penetrated to the interior before the Italian occupation, although individual words of Italian origin may have diffused inland.

The Jews' situation as intermediaries would appear to have some bearing on the "language of the peddlers" that Hakohen describes. This is probably a merchants' argot, although Slouschz, who considered and rejected this view (1926), sees it as the preservation of an ancient tongue. Intermediaries, in bringing together and manipulating goods and money, bring together and manipulate information as well. Here, and particularly in situations where there is only partial trust, withholding information can be as important as passing it on. It is not surprising, therefore, to find that the Jewish merchants have an argot; in fact, parallels have been reported from Tunis and Algiers (Section 94, n. 15). The social situation does not create the argot. Given the fact, however, that there is a ready-made vocabulary not understood by local Moslems, the social situation encourages the continued use of a code unknown to outsiders. This vocabulary consists of Hebrew, or Hebrew-Aramaic, which is derived from the literary language found in the classic religious texts.

The merchants' argot was known in other villages outside the Nefusa region. While most of the people I have interviewed were aware of the existence of this "language," none was able to say much more about it. Hakohen himself noted that it was beginning to become extinct. If the social factor is in fact important in understanding the maintenance of this argot, we may surmise that its disappearance is linked to the greater security brought by the Turks in the last century. There does not seem to have been any change in the extent to which Jews engaged in commerce, and their knowledge of Hebrew, if anything, was probably on the increase.

Hebrew, of course, was taught in synagogue school, which young boys began to attend at an early age.[5] Most of them learned to read the Hebrew text of the prayer book, and those portions of the Bible which were incorporated into the liturgy. An understanding of the text was taught through the recitation of a standard translation in Judaeo-Arabic (*sharah*), the Arabic language written in Hebrew characters. For most boys this translation was probably learned by rote and did not entail serious study of the meaning of the Hebrew original. Others, however, seemed to be able to extract the principles of meaning embedded in this exercise and develop an understanding of Hebrew which they could then use in a creative fashion. We have already indicated (see the Editor's Introduction) that there were reforms in Hebrew education in the city of Tripoli toward the end of the last century (Kahalon 1972). Hakohen shows that innovation and change also took place in the villages.

NOTES

1. See Goldberg (1971, 1974a, 1974c).
2. See the Editor's Foreword to Chapter Five.
3. We will use the terms "village" and "town" interchangeably in referring to these communities. In absolute size, they could easily be called villages, but when they are considered as market centers, "towns" is a more appropriate word.
4. See Alport (1954) and Stone (1974).
5. See Goitein (1953) and Zafrani (1972) for descriptions of Jewish education in other Middle Eastern communities.

Commerce and Crafts

(SECTION 92)

Merchandise is brought from Tripoli on the backs of camels: pepper, cumin, coriander seeds, ginger, sweet calamus, and all sorts of spices— honey, sugar, tea, coffee, and tobacco; the flower of the rose, the flower of the myrtle, spikenard, saffron, cassia, and cinnamon; buds of perfume,[1] powders, pure frankincense, incense, and women's cosmetics[2]— antimony powder to darken their eyes, the bark of nut trees to paint their lips like a scarlet thread, henna plants to redden their arms and legs; mirrors, hair combs, glass and coral beads, matches, threads and needles; and other kinds of merchandise too numerous to mention.

All the Jews are tradespeople who scatter throughout the region with sacks on their shoulders, or on their donkeys, to sell their merchandise to the Berbers and the Arabs in exchange for grain, olives, olive oil, figs, butter, sheep's wool, goat's hair, silver, eggs, and so forth.[3]

There are those who return home each evening and others who travel so far that they are gone from home six days of the week and return only on the Sabbath eve. There are others who travel so far that they are gone from the Feast of Tabernacles until Passover and from Passover to the New Year, when they return to wash their clothes and to participate in the joy of the festival with their families, with meat, wine, whisky, beans, and potatoes, all of which heighten the pleasure of the feast. They have no greater pleasure than to be with their families, before them a cup of wine and a full table spread with large chunks of goat's meat, roasted or half-boiled; then no pleasure is lacking, for they have never gotten used to luxury and they do not know what real pleasure is.

All the Jews know how to butcher meat. This skill is special to the Jews and not to the Berbers, for the Berbers eat meat slaughtered by Jews without reservation, not like the other Mohammedans of Tripoli.

A Mohammedan stranger[4] in the area who slaughters one or two sheep on market day will find no customers. Not so with the Jews, who slaughter ten sheep or goats at once and are immediately mobbed by customers. Sometimes the Rabbinic emissary from Palestine[5] will forbid slaughtering if the Jews do not give him the amount of money assessed them. If, then, the Berbers slaughter by themselves on the market day, usually their meat is declared unfit. They often slit the animal's throat at the top ring of the windpipe, and if the matter becomes known, their Qadi will declare the animal unfit for eating because it wasn't properly slaughtered.

Sundays and Thursdays are market days. Active trading begins as a large crowd gathers near the government palace, which is a half-hour walk from the Jewish neighborhoods. (In the early days, the market was held inside the town of al-Qṣir,[6] where the Jews dwelt.) Buying and selling take place under the open skies, but most Jewish merchants set up goat-hair tents. Originally, there were no open shops in the area, for fear of night robbers, and the Jews did their selling from their homes. Only recently have they established a few outdoor stalls. They also built warehouses in the city next to the government palace. These establishments made it possible to conduct trade on days other than market days.

Originally, all trade was in the hands of Jews and no one could compete with them, for commerce requires planning and talent, for which the Jews are well adapted. Recently the Berbers have begun to undertake trading and many have been successful. But in peddling and bartering with the women, no one can enter the Jews' reserve; it is a Moslem rule that Arab or Berber men may not look upon their own women, for it may lead to evil thoughts, but Jewish men can look upon them freely.[7]

Besides commerce, the Jews engage in agriculture. They are also active in smithing, for when the season is not right for commerce they work as artisans. Some make combs for wool, others make bracelets, and still others are shoemakers or blacksmiths.

This is how they manufacture combs for wool: Thin iron wires are cut into bent bristles, which are set into a square piece of skin covered with thick paper. About one finger-length square, this skin is stretched flat onto a square piece of wood with a handle, and attached with nails. A pair of combs is sold in the summer for about one and a half francs and during the rest of the year for about one franc.

The bracelets are made from goat's horns. They are embellished with strands of tin shaped in lines and circles and dots. A pair of bracelets is sold for about half a franc.

Shoes are made simply but elegantly, with a fine embroidery of silver and silk threads.

Blacksmiths fan charcoal fires and create useful tools: hammers, axes, hatchets, scythes, plows, and all the other tools required by the people of the region. They also repair weapons. These artisans' workshops are in the entrances to their homes. The Berber who needs any tool will bring the metal and charcoal to the Jew's house, assist him in fanning the flame, and even pound the hammer on the anvil together with the Jewish artisan. The artisan is paid not in cash but in produce: wheat, figs, olives, grapes, butter, and so forth. The price for a set of horseshoes is one sheep. All the artisans who work in this way are called *maʿārfa* and the produce that they get in payment is called *wehāba*.[8]

The Jews lend money and fruit by verbal agreement. They also enter into partnerships in the ownership of animals, and in business and even in real estate without any written agreements. There are some, however, who write witnessed deeds. If a man dies owing a debt contracted by verbal agreement, his heirs honor the debt. Recently, though, cheating and deceit have become widespread, even among the Jews. But if someone acquires the reputation of being a cheater he will be ostracized and called despicable and hateful.

Formerly, stone weights for the scales were stored in the merchant's pockets,* but now the merchants have begun to use metal weights, and the leading merchants have a special box in which to store them.

The entire area is facing a crisis[9] because a great deal of merchandise is imported from Tripoli and the only items exported are barley, figs, olive oil, butter, sheep, cattle, goat's hair and skins, eggs, linen, and mats made by the women according to an African pattern.

There is no great wealth, except among those who have obtained positions in the courts. The wealthiest of the Jews have assets in livestock, real estate, and chattel worth about eighty thousand francs. Even a man who is worth a thousand francs is considered to be wealthy, for he has no expenses and needs no luxuries.

The rest of the people are poor and in want. Some own only about ten francs' worth of goods in the peddler's packs on their shoulders. With the profit that this small amount of capital yields, the peddler must keep hunger from his door and also buy clothing. Even so, there is no

---

*In the year 1886, I saw a Jew, selling onions, take two weights out of his pocket. They were close in size but not exactly the same. He weighed half a liter for one customer with one of them and a whole liter for a second customer with both. I said to him, "The two stones appear to be unequal and at first you weighed half a liter with one of them." He answered, "One is larger than the other, but together they equal one liter." I rebuked him, saying, "Scriptures (Deuteronomy XXV, verse 13) refer to you in the passage, 'You shall not have in your pouch alternate measures, larger and smaller,' for sometimes you may err and use the smaller to weigh a half liter." He then sought to excuse himself, saying, "Even if I err, I am not stealing, because this side of the scale is heavier to make up for the deficiency in the weight."

community charity fund, for he who receives charity cannot hold his head up in public* or erase his shame; how much more so a poor person who begs from door to door.

Even though the Ottoman government has given the Jews freedom and equal rights—insisting there be no differentiation among peoples, so that a Jew can even ride a donkey in public with no one objecting—the Jews have not dared to ride on their donkeys in front of the Berbers, who are the lords of the land. For they are proud and powerful and make fun of the government, and violence is deeply rooted in them.[13]

When a Berber is praying by the roadside a Jew cannot pass him by, but must stand still and honor him until his prayers are finished. If a Jew dared to disobey this rule his blood would be on his own head. Because of our sins,[14] several people have died under the yoke of this oppression, and their blood cries out for retribution.[15]

NOTES

1. Song of Songs IV:4.
2. Esther II:12. The use of these biblical verses raises the question of whether each and every item mentioned was actually found in the local trade.
3. See Goldberg (1971) for an analysis of the pattern of itinerant trading.
4. The Hebrew *ger*. The word could also be read *gar*, in which case the phrase would translate: "A Mohammedan who resides in the area. . . ." The former sense seems correct, since it contrasts a Mohammedan outsider whose meat is not purchased and a local Jew whose slaughter is preferred. Griffin (1924:112, 203), a British doctor who resided in Yefren during the Italian-Turkish war, engaged a Jew to slaughter meat when entertaining Moslems.
5. See Section 95.
6. He may mean that the market was formerly at Taqerboṣ, near the fort at Yefren, and was later moved (see ms. p. 216a and Despois 1935:317).
7. The familiar phenomenon of a lower status person being permitted intimacies with a superior, intimacies that a person who is a status rival would not be allowed. See Antoun (1968) on gypsies in a Jordanian village.
8. See Goldberg (1971:251). The use of the term *ma'arūf* (singular) for this

*In the year 1886, in the month of Av, I introduced egg trading there, buying eighty eggs for one franc and selling them to the merchants of Tripoli for three francs. Before that, no one had thought of bringing chicken eggs to Tripoli in crates packed on the backs of camels. A woman had been abandoned by her young husband who, because of financial difficulties, had gone out into the world to try his luck.[10] It was the Sabbath eve and she did not have enough to prepare three Sabbath meals[11] for her children, but she would not take charity. I cleverly called the woman and said, "I have packed my eggs but am short of forty or more eggs to fill my last crate. Here are two francs; can you supply me with eighty eggs?" "Yes," said the woman, and she quickly went and purchased eighty eggs for one franc and brought them to me. With the remaining franc she bought barley and olive oil for the Sabbath meals.[12]

type of "trading partner" relationship is apparently quite old and very widespread. It is mentioned by Katz (1961:34n, 58–59) in connection with early Ashkenazic Jewry.

    9. Perhaps an indirect result of the decline of trans-Saharan trade.

    10. A local proverb states that "He who travels, brings."

    11. The Sabbath is distinguished in Jewish law by three full meals instead of the customary two.

    12.. Hakohen's tactics here are in accord with Maimonides' ranking of the various forms of charity—the highest is not to give alms but to help the poor rehabilitate themselves by lending money, taking them into partnership, or providing them with work. See his *Mishneh Torah*, *Sefer Zera'im*, Laws of Charity 10:7.

    13. The mention of this topic here probably reflects the dangers involved in peddling throughout the countryside.

    14. The Hebrew *ba'awon* is an elliptic formula bemoaning the condition of exile in which the Jews are vulnerable to all manner of suffering.

    15. The Hebrew reads: "their blood cries out *El neqamot*," meaning "God of retribution." The phrase is taken from Psalms XCIV:1–2:

O God of retribution, Lord,
O God of retribution shine forth.
Raise up Thyself, Judge of the earth,
Render to the haughty their desert.

God's retribution is judgment, so the sentence might also be translated, "their blood cries out for justice."

Food

(SECTION 93)

    The villagers gain their livelihood easily. They can get grain and eggs, firewood for cooking and baking, and wash their clothes at no cost (as discussed at length in Section 100).

    At harvest time, they gather in grain, olive oil, and figs in large or small amounts, produced on their land, or from portions of the plowed fields owned in partnership with the Berbers. Some do all their plowing and harvesting by themselves. In addition, they receive fresh produce, including olive oil and figs, in exchange for merchandise. Grapes for wine are sold cheaply, but most of the wine is made from figs.

    Their clothes are made mostly from ewe's wool, which is woven by their womenfolk. Other materials, such as cotton, and pepper and other spices, are purchased with cash from the merchants who bring goods from Tripoli.

They eat two meals a day, one in the morning and one at night. Their meals consist of barley bread, baked in an oven that opens from the top, dipped in gravy mixed with spiced olive oil and hot pepper. This gravy is cooked in a ceramic pot, black with the smoke of wood and straw.

All the men eat together around a large wooden bowl, sitting on the ground with their legs folded beneath them. They have no need for either spoon or fork, using only one utensil to take food from the pot and put it into the bowl.

After the men finish, the women, in seclusion, eat the leftovers, for it is shameful and disgusting for the women to eat with the men, or before the men have eaten.

They do not eat fruits after dinner, but occasionally they sweeten their diet with dried figs, or with grapes or watermelon in the summer. They also eat *zumīṭa*[1] (parched grain), sometimes called *suwīqa*, which is slightly roasted in an iron tube and afterwards ground very fine. Before it is eaten, it is kneaded with water and sprinkled with a bit of olive oil. This mixture is called *taṣmīṭ*.* It is customary for the harvesters working on the threshing floor to eat *zumīṭa* because it slackens thirst.

They also eat couscous, although infrequently. And this is how the couscous is prepared: Groats are dipped in water and rubbed in a bowl until they form small kernels. Afterwards, they are placed in a ceramic vessel with a porous bottom called a *kaskās*. A pot of soup is put on the fire, and on top of it the couscous pot. The lips are sealed with dough around the edges of the *kaskās* so that the heat entering through the pores of the pot to cook the couscous grains will not escape. After the couscous is cooked, it is placed in a bowl, and soup from the pot is poured over it. This is, for them, a very special dish.

But the most important dish for a main meal is *bazīn*,†[5] which is made in the following manner: A measure of grain is cooked into a

---

*Perhaps this explains the passage (in Ruth II, verse 14): "*vayiṣbaṭ* her roasted grain and she ate it." Rashi[2] explains "*vayiṣbaṭ* means 'he extended' and it has no parallel in Scripture." See also the commentary of Ibn 'Ezra.[3] Accordingly, *vayiṣbaṭ* may mean "he kneaded," even though the root is ṢBṬ and that of *zumīṭa* is ṢMṬ;[4] we know that the letters BWMF are likely to be substituted for one another.

†A European tourist, on seeing the manner in which *bazīn* is eaten, was seized with a desire to try it. He ordered a woman to make him *bazīn*, in its authentic form, served in a large wooden bowl. As soon as the food was ready, he began to twist it in the soup with his hand inside the bowl, as was customary. But he made a small error, for he changed the format that the Arab wise men decreed as necessary for eating *bazīn*. He sat on a chair and placed the bowl on a table, as is the custom in Europe, and since he was heavy handed in twisting the *bazīn*, he overturned the bowl, which fell off the table and soiled his clothes. The *bazīn* became hateful to him, and he said, "I cannot manage this because I have never tried it before."[6]

cake-like shape in a pot, which is set to boil until smoke rises. After it has been well cooked, and while it is boiling over the fire, the round cake is beaten well with a wooden utensil that has been specially prepared for this purpose. Afterwards, it is placed in a large wooden bowl, and soup is poured over the *bazīn* so that the ball of *bazīn* in the bowl looks like the world and the soup surrounding it like the ocean. Then everyone gathers together on the floor around the bowl, each with a cup of water before him from which to drink. Everyone tears a piece off the ball and twists it in his hand while it is still hot, rolling it up and down his arm as far as the elbow. He thereby saturates it with the soup, and then takes it with dirty hands and eats it with immense pleasure. A single mouthful weighs two hundred grams. After eating, they lick off the soup that is stuck to their arms.

The Arabs and the Berbers go one step further than the Jews when it comes to eating *bazīn*.[7] If the soup includes a meat and butter sauce, they will pay no attention to it, smearing this material over their face and hands. No matter that it goes to waste, the important thing is that anyone coming close to them will know that they have eaten meat.* Sometimes they will wash their hands in the same bowl from which they have eaten, or in another vessel.

It is now customary throughout the district to drink olive oil, for it is said that this will make a man more vigorous, add strength to his vision,[8] and also brighten his face. (Perhaps this explains the figure of speech in Psalms CIV, verse 15: "And wine will make glad the heart of man and brighten the face more than oil.")[9]

The women are capable of preparing the food quite quickly. When a meal must be made for a guest, the woman first puts the pot on the fire to cook the soup. Then she takes grain and grinds it with nimble hands at an awesome speed. I estimated by the timepiece in my hand that in the space of one hour the dish was prepared and unleavened bread baked in the oven as well. (From this we should learn not to be surprised that when the visitors came to our father Abraham in Genesis XVIII he was able to place a meal before them in a short time.)

The villagers' souls lust after meat, but the poor among them do not eat it except on the Sabbath or on holidays. If they do manage to get some meat it will not be cooked thoroughly and will be served in large

---

*The Arabs and Berbers invite the groom and his relatives to a wedding feast and divide them into groups of approximately ten men each; in front of each group is placed a large bowl with a ball of *bazīn* weighing approximately forty kilograms, not including the soup and the meat. After eating all of it and licking their hands and the bowl, they wash their hands in the bowl itself, scrub the bowl, and then one of them will drink up the cleansing water left over in the bowl without any feeling of repulsion. Thus not a drop of the fat left in the bowl will be lost.

chunks; they will rip it with their fingers and teeth, only half chewing it. Even rotten meat is eaten as a delicacy.

On the Sabbath and on holidays there is a table, low to the ground, on which is spread a red cloth made of ewe's wool. The well-to-do place on it a loaf of wheat bread that has been baked in an open-topped oven, so that the holiday shall be honored. On these occasions, almost all of the villagers are full of wine and brandy and also palm tree juice that is called *lagbī*. (See Section 4, Note 6.)[10]

They have no toilets. That is, there is no special room set aside where they can go to void. In the early hours of the morning, they disperse in the fields in special unoccupied places where they squat and wipe themselves with stones. (This custom was also practiced in the days of the Talmud.)[11]

However, in the government palace, and in the nearby town that was founded recently for the Ottomans and Tripolitans, special rooms have been set up with toilets. In these rooms, holes are dug that lead the waste outdoors to a large pit, as is the custom in Tripoli. There they have also built new houses to match the luxurious standards of other houses in the district.

NOTES

1. Hakohen writes the term with a צ, even though it is pronounced with a *z*.

2. The famed biblical commentary known by the acronym of the author's name, Rabbi Shlomoh Yitzhaqi (1040–1105).

3. Rabbi Abraham Ibn 'Ezra, a Spanish commentator (1089–1164) who attempted to establish the literal meaning of the text through etymological and grammatical study.

4. Again Hakohen writes the term with a צ, even though it is pronounced with a *z*.

5. Here Hakohen writes the term with a ס though once more it is pronounced with a *z*.

6. The Jews of the mountain communities themselves accord humorous attention to *bazīn* in the form of word play. In the Ghuryan, Slouschz (1927:139) was told that *bazīn* is *mazon* (Hebrew for food or sustenance). The same community of Jews in Israel jokingly liken it to concrete (the Hebrew *beiton*). Hakohen is obviously impressed by the heaviness of the food.

7. Dearden (Tully 1957:108n) notes that the Libyan Arabs "call themselves *ahl el bazeen* or *bazeen* eaters."

8. The Hebrew *re'ut*. There may be an error; *rē'ot*, lungs, might be the intended word.

9. Diacritical marks in the text indicate a play on words. The intention of the verse is changed to: "For brightening the face—oil!"

10. Part of the footnote in Section 4 reads as follows: "In addition to the other uses of the tree, the palm, while still standing, will yield, with man's intervention, a drink called *lagbī* which is white as milk and sweet as honey. It is

better than the juice of the coconut for strengthening the body and as a laxative for the stomach. (Perhaps it is the "palm juice" mentioned in the Tractate *Shabbat*, Chapter 14, Mishnah 1.) When left to stand, it ferments and is as intoxicating as wine.

"This is how *lagbi* is made: First the leaves and branches are cut off the tree. Afterwards, a large cuplike hole is dug out at the top of the palm, into which all the liquid gathers. Then a slit is scooped out on top so that the liquid flows into the jugs which are hung at the top of the palm. The flow of the liquid lasts about two months. Afterwards, the palm tree itself grows new branches and bears fruit."

11. Babylonian Talmud, Tractate *Shabbat* (82a).

Clothing and Language
(SECTION 94)

The woman's garment, covering the entire body, is made of one four-sided sheet that requires no sewing, wrapped around the body from below the knee. Its length is three times the width and it is made of ewe's wool, woven by the women themselves. There are some made of cotton, spun in a European style but with an African weave. This sheet is called *rda*.[1] It is wrapped around the body and fastened by a stone or a pin. Most of the women do not wear tunics—their arms are bare and sunburned—but it is a rule that a bride must wear a tunic. The wearing of pantalettes by a woman is unheard of; it is considered a great disgrace for a woman to wear them.* Nonetheless, these are modest women and not loose.[2]

They cover the entire head above the forehead with a band called 'aṣaba (headdress). There are those who make the band out of ewe's wool, but in recent times they have begun to make silk head scarves. Silk is currently used by the rich for the sheet (*rda*) and the tunic as well, for they are worn on the Sabbath and on holidays. The women also wear shoes when necessary.

For jewelry, the women wear silver bracelets with seal engravings and flower designs. A pair of bracelets weighs about half a kilogram. They hang rings of silver from their ears by bands. A pair of earrings

---

*When a European tourist expressed his attraction to a certain woman, she fastened on him an angry gaze, for his behavior was despicable. He apologized, trying to exonerate himself. Once he asked her (laughingly) why the women here will not wear pantalettes as European women do. Her answer to him was, "The European women are ill-bred, and perhaps because they wear pantalettes they are tempted to carnal behavior. Not so the Jewish women of Yefren. Even without pantalettes they are not tempted."

weighs about three hundred grams. There are beads on their necks and small silver chains. As part of their jewelry, they hang silver on their breasts, and also coral and glass. In addition, they have rings and bangles threaded through the hair on their heads.

As for the men's clothing, the rich cannot be distinguished from the poor.[3] A man will cover his entire body, including his legs, midsection, and head, with one four-sided piece of material made of white ewe's wool, whose length is three times its width. At night he also covers himself with it. He carries loads with it by throwing them over his shoulder into the end of the sheet. This form of carrying is called *mishimelha fi shelamtu*;* the load is put on the man's shoulder. Some of them will wrap their bodies in a burnous (cape) which is also made of ewe's wool.

All of the people in the district dress alike. A stranger cannot tell the difference between a Jew and a non-Jew except for the fact that most Jews wrap a turban or a head scarf around the hats on their heads. They may also wear a burnous.[5] They despise drawers. No one has the courage to endure the disgrace of wearing drawers, for he will be called foolish and vulgar. But the Berbers who have posts in the government palaces have begun to wear them.

Some of the villagers wear, covering the whole foot, a shoe in which the leather is treated by an African process. Others wear a piece of leather on the sole of the foot, with a strap coming out between the second toe and the big toe. This is stretched over the top of the foot and tied with two cords around the heel in order to tighten the shoe so that it will not fall off.

At one time, the men, like the women, did not wear pants, only a gown made of ewe's wool. The groom at the time of his wedding had the right to wear a white cotton gown, but after the wedding he stored it away for his son and his grandson to use at their own weddings. Now, however, times have changed; cotton cloth is brought from Tripoli, and all the men manage to obtain a gown and a pair of pants. But they are not clean; they are laundered only once every three months or on holidays.

In former days, the Jewish men wore black hats as a sign of their low status,[6] but when the country was conquered by the Ottomans, each man was given the right to dress as he saw fit.

As for their religious ways, the Jews believe in the immortality of the soul and in reward and punishment; they await the resurrection of the

---

*It seems that this is the dress mentioned in the passage in Exodus XII, verse 34, "Kneading bowls wrapped in their cloaks upon their shoulders," and also in Exodus XXII, verse 25, "If you take your neighbor's garment (*salmah*) in pledge . . . the sole covering (*simlah*) of his skin, in what shall he sleep?" How is it that the text opens with *salmah* and ends with *simlah* unless we say that the sheet is called *salmah* when used during the day and *simlah* when used at night?[4]

dead and the day of salvation. They keep themselves from marrying non-Jews and do not allow non-Jews to touch their wine.[7] The Jews will not eat non-Jewish cooked food unless a Jew throws a splinter of wood into the oven before the bread is baked.[8] They also do not permit themselves to eat the meat of an animal that has not been ritually slaughtered, neither the meat of the hindquarters that contains the sinew,[9] nor meat in milk. They do not use cloth containing a mixture of wool and linen,[10] and they otherwise keep traditional precepts. Because their towns are not walled, they do not carry anything in their hands on the Sabbath.[11] They also believe with a perfect faith in evil spirits, demons and nocturnal ghosts, witchcraft, incantations, amulets, dreams, and the evil eye.

Even though they have family names based on the founder of the family line, they use only the given name of the father—for example, Jacob son of Isaac, or Isaac son of Abraham. But in a written deed or other legal document they mention also the family name, *i.e.* the name of the family line. No Kohanim or Levites[12] are found there. But there is one village named Kohen, and there is a tradition that the Kohanim, who were the owners of the village, all went into exile and left their land. (See Section 91.)

The extant family lines are 'Atiya, Guweta', Megidish, Maimon, Raḥum, Balulu, Ba'dash, and 'Ovadiah. The family of 'Ovadiah, however, began only in 1860. Then a man from the Guweta' family, whose name was 'Ovadiah, had a son whose name was Moses and he gave his own name to his grandsons instead of the name Guweta'.[13]

Intelligence and knowledge are not foreign to them. They absorb skills as if from the air, solely by observing them. If they were to find a decent teacher there is not doubt that, with the help of their pure spirit, their potential would be realized. They would excel in their studies, rising above the heads of their brethren in the city.

In former days, when the teachers taught the pronunciation of vowels, it was not customary to give names to the vowel symbols as is done in Tripoli—*ḥiriq, ṣiri,* etc.—but, for example, they would call a *ṣiri* "two dots lying down," a *patah* "a line lying down," and so forth. Recently, however, they have become used to giving them names, as is customary among the Jews of Tripoli.

The fire of religion burns within them. Some send their sons to Tripoli and spend a great deal of money on the study of the Torah.

The Berbers have a language of their own,[14] which they use when necessary, but most of the Jews know it too. And the Jews, even though they do not know Hebrew, also have a language of their own that they use among themselves, when necessary; they call it the "*ṭawwāfa* holy tongue," the Hebrew of the peddlers, because it is used mostly by peddlers. It has influenced the language of the Jews of Tripoli, where it is called the "*'aṭṭāra* holy tongue" (the Hebrew of the spice merchants) because when the village Jews come to Tripoli most of their trade is with the Jewish spice merchants.[15]

This language is gradually weakening because it is unwritten. Some words are ordinary Hebrew and some words, though they seem to have originated in Hebrew, have now been slightly changed.[16] Other words appear to be descended from Aramaic, with slight modification, and some words seem to be from Greek.[17] I here present to you, dear reader, some unusual words that scholars may find interesting. But first peruse the section at the beginning of the book after the author's introduction which discusses the pronunciation of letters.[18] There is no need to write at length about every verb in first, second, and third person; singular and plural; past, present, and future; etc. I will clarify the verb once, and from this you will understand the other forms. Most of the verbs follow the Arab forms with regard to past, present, and future, and also in singular and plural.[19]

Jewish term	*Translation*
ḥiṭṭīn [H]	wheat
bərīn	dates
mākhīr	knife[20]
fəjra	silver[21]
'atōn [H]	donkey
'atōnā [H]	she-donkey
qōfālā	head
kōhīn	bribery[22]
bīghed	deed
zōzīm [H]	money
pāḥ	penny (small coin)
mishkāḥā	prostitute
neshāmā [H: soul]	mirror
binshamtō	respected person
ḥinnā [H]	here
'arōr [H: cursed]	bandit
mekattīl	thief
kettell	he stole
zefarnā	sack
zefarnā	satchel
'əllāi	The fast of the Ninth of Av[23]
'abad [H]	died
ḥarīmī	Berber[24]
ḥarīmeyā	Berber women
ḥarīmiyā	Berbers
'ōtō [H: him]	Muhammad
mizōnā [H: food]	bread

Jewish term	Translation
shelat [H: of?]	utensil, instrument
shelāt-layīsh	pistol[25]
shelāt-yad	bracelet
shelāt-reghel	shoe[26]
riglāimō	his feet[27]
riglāimek	your feet
riglāimī	my feet
riglāimehem	their feet
yidāimō	his hands
'īnāimō	his eyes
'iznāimō	his ears
shellōyā	my [mine][28]
shellōk	yours
shellōh	his
shellōkem	yours
shellōna	ours
shellōhem	theirs
yəqātī	he will bring[29]
təqātī	you [sing.] will bring
nəqātī	I will bring
yəqātíu	they will bring
təqātíu	you [pl.] will bring
nəqātíu	we will bring
qātā́	he brought
qātáu	they brought
qātītó	you [pl.] brought
qātīnā	we brought
təqátā	he came
nitqātā	I will come
ḥazzer	see
təqātā	come [imp.][30]
yitsōref	go to hell
bīṣī 'adama [H: eggs of the earth]	potatoes
ləvōnā	roasted grain
milbosha [H: clothing]	kerchief
'ōrā	wardrobe
gōi [H]	Mohammedan
mə'āyīṭ [H]	little
bōshā [H: shame]	a non-Jewish holiday
'abārā	Hebrew[31]
adermekh	he lay down
rōkhev [H]	ride
shāti' [H]	he drank
shātī [H]	drinks
mizbānā	sale[32]
tərassā	quiet [imp.]

Jewish term	Translation
leyīkh [H]	go [imp.]
məṣā'ā	sat[33]
məṣā'ī	sits
fartell	fled
'emmōyā [H]	by me [*chez moi*]
'emmōk [H]	by you
'emmōh [H]	by him
təshabber	was killed[34]
shellāt mayim [H: water utensil]	gourd
qiyaitā	lintel
shə'ōrīm [H]	barley
rəkhōsh [H]	merchandise
'arel [H: uncircumcised]	Christian
shimmah	there is[35]
mekhkhél	he ate
mákhkhel	eat [imp.]

NOTES

1. The various meanings of this term in different communities are discussed in Goldberg (1974a).

2. The following incident is related by Hakohen earlier in the manuscript (Section 6, ms. p. 13b): "In former days, no woman wore pantalettes, for it was a great shame to them. Instead, they draped a sheet halfway down the thigh. The notable Shlomoh Khalfon was the first to break with tradition. In the year 1752, he included pantalettes in the dowry of his daughter, Miss 'Aziza, and it was an innovation and an example. Then this custom began to spread, and women can now wear pantalettes if they wish. However, when they launder them, they do not dry them publicly in the sun, but in the innermost rooms." See Goldberg (1973a) for a modern comparison.

3. Griffin (1924:232) also notes that the rich dress like the poor.

4. Hakohen notices the reversal of positions of the L and M both in the biblical terms and in the local Arabic expression.

5. Generally an older man or another person entitled to respect would wear a burnous.

6. Tripolitanian Israelis have told me that the black turbans symbolized mourning over the destruction of the Temple. What is initially a mark of low status (see Lyon 1821:7) is thus reinterpreted from the Jewish point of view, perhaps obscuring its original intention as a sign of discrimination.

7. Katz (1961:24–47) analyzes the social implications of this and similar restrictions in Jewish-Gentile relationships among early Ashkenazic Jews.

8. The gesture of putting a piece of wood in the fire involves the Jew in the preparation of the food, thereby circumventing the prohibition against eating food cooked by a gentile (Babylonian Talmud *'Avodah Zarah* 38).

9. Genesis XXXII:33.

10. Leviticus XIX:19; Deuteronomy XXII:11.

11. Carrying an object more than four cubits in the public domain is one of the categories of work forbidden on the Sabbath.

12. The descendants of Aaron, Moses' brother, are the Kohanim, while the Levites are the descendants of the tribe of Levi. Kohanim and Levites continue to have special ritual privileges, despite the fact that their main ritual tasks and rights, associated with the Temple worship, are not in force today.

13. See Goldberg (1972b) for a discussion of this case.

14. The language of the Nefusa Berbers is the subject of two monographs. Calassanti-Motylinski (1898) provides a narration from Yefren, and Bequinot (1942) gives a description of the Fassato dialect.

15. This "language" is better seen as a peddler's argot rather than as an independent language (Goldberg 1974a). Similar argots were found in Algiers (M. Cohen 1912:404–408) and in Tunis (D. Cohen 1964:114–115). Hakohen notes the social conditions of its usage—when it is "necessary" for an outsider not to understand.

16. See some of the items in the list and in my notes 25, 27, and 28 below.

17. Hakohen may have taken the notion of Greek origin from Slouschz (1927:195). The Aramaic referred to is the Aramaic of traditional Hebrew works, the Talmud and the Midrash. See my notes 20, 29, 31, and 32 below.

18. The dialect does not distinguish between "o" and "u." In transcribing, I have used "o," following Hakohen's orthography, although in most instances the spoken form is probably "u." No attempt has been made to evaluate the accuracy of the author's transcription. Long vowels correspond to his use of א, י, and ו.

19. In the list that follows I have indicated a word of clear Hebrew origin with a bracketed H and have added the translation of the original Hebrew meaning when the argotic meaning represents an extension of the original. Other explanations appear in footnotes. These explanations are illustrative; there has been no attempt to provide an exhaustive treatment of the subject.

20. Of Aramaic origin (Jastrow 1950:738).

21. This word has become standard among the Jews of Tripoli (Goldberg 1974a).

22. Slouschz (1927:290) interprets the fact that the word *kohen* means bribery as evidence of an earlier period when the Kohanim (pl.), rather than the Rabbis, held the leadership of North African Jewry. One need not engage in guesswork about earlier historical periods in order to find a plausible explanation for this meaning. In a standard ritual based on Exodus XIII:13, every first-born male must be redeemed by his father with the payment of five *sela'im* to a Kohen. In Tripoli and elsewhere, this practice customarily takes the form of mock bargaining, in which the Kohen tries to "extort" more money from the father and the father tries to pay as little as possible. Eventually, the Kohen agrees to accept money for quitting an obligation that he must perform anyway, hence "bribery." Also, the Kohen profits handsomely in the case of the redemption of a first-born animal. See Section 98 and Hirschberg (1974:163–165).

23. Derived from the Midrash Rabbah on Lamentations I:16.

24. The Hebrew *harim* means "mountains." *Harīmī* is thus the equivalent of *jebali* (mountaineer), the local Arabic term referring to the Berbers (Despois 1935:150).

25. Perhaps this means "no-man instrument": *shelat* (the argotic word for "instrument") plus *lā* (the Arabic "no") plus *ish* (the Hebrew "man").

26. Literally, "a foot instrument": *shelat* (the argotic word for "instrument") plus *reghel* ("foot").

27. The Hebrew "feet," *raglāim,* with the *a* of the first syllable becoming *i* plus *o,* the pronominal suffix. See D. Cohen (1964:114–115).

28. The Hebrew "his," *shello,* plus *ya* (the Arabic first person singular pronominal suffix).

29. In this and the following items a common talmudic Aramaic term, *qa' 'ata* (he came) is combined into a single root and conjugated according to the local Arabic dialect. Tripolitanian Arabic is described in Stumme (1898) and Cesàro (1939).

30. Possibly from the Hebrew root SRF, meaning "burn."

31. The Moslems called this Jewish argot *'abriya* or *'abrani.*

32. From the Aramaic ZBN, meaning "sell."

33. Possibly of Aramaic derivation (Jastrow 1950:1293).

34. From the Hebrew root ShBR, meaning "break."

35. This may be from the dialect of the Jews of the city, in which the /t/ of the Moslems is spoken as /č/ by the Jews, so that the term *timma* ("there is") becomes *čimma.* The Jews of Yefren do not have this communally marked feature in their normal nonargotic pronunciation of Arabic (Goldberg 1974a).

CHAPTER THREE

Communal Life and Festivals

Editor's Foreword

Various scholarly images have been projected on the Jews of rural North Africa. We say projected, since these images appear to reflect the preconceived concerns of researchers as much as they reflect the data at hand. As we have seen, Slouschz tended to view the communities of rural Tripolitania as the last remnants of an earlier stage in Jewish history when the Kohanim (priests) ruled over Jewish tribes, before the authority of Rabbinic Judaism was established. While he does give descriptions of these communities as he met them, and while he recognizes that they have been touched by more recent developments, it is the hints of a remote past that fire Slouschz' scholarly imagination. Alas, this theory is based on hardly any evidence at all, even though Hirschberg does it the courtesy of mentioning it (1974:163–165). Speculation about origins is not a forbidden activity (Needham, in Hocart 1969: ix), but Slouschz goes about it in a way that totally outreaches the available data. Keeping this in mind, we have suggested some reconstructionist interpretations of particular matters but have not attempted sweeping statements concerning historical periods.

A second set of scholarly images comes from the sociology of modernization, the dominant perspective in the study of the absorption of immigrants in Israel during the 1950s. The modernizationists paid little attention to variations in culture and history. Instead, and in some ways reminiscent of Slouschz, they embraced, by implication, an evolutionary scheme which labeled immigrants as traditional, transitional, or modern (Goldberg 1976, 1977a). Among the traditional groups were the small communities from the rural and usually mountainous areas of the Middle East—Kurdistan, Yemen, and rural North Africa. Included in the last category were some of the communities of Tripolitania.

The notion of a traditional society carried with it a list of other attributes. Two of these were particularism (as opposed to universalism) and the importance of an oral tradition (as opposed to a written tradition). Neither of these concepts is very useful in characterizing the communities described by Hakohen. True, individuals have strong family loyalties, and family status and pride are values that emerge in the narrative. At the same time, there is a strong sense of the community, within which individual families are bound to one another. Indeed, they gain and demonstrate their prestige by contributing to it. For its part, the community is defined in terms of religious values and in specific acts of ritual, worship, and communal duty such as the upkeep of the synagogue, the cemetery, and the ritual bath. There is no evidence that these structures (in either the physical or the cultural sense) were used to reinforce corporate patronymic groups in opposition to one another (Goldberg 1972a). The prayer leader, the slaughterer, and the circumcisor serve all the members of the community; even as they and their families attain prestige, they earn universal religious merit.

While undoubtedly there was a great deal of oral lore that both expressed and directed the actions of the community, Hakohen constantly reminds us that its major orientation was provided by standard religious texts. The festivals described in Section 97 are the same as those celebrated in every traditional Jewish community. These are based on classic Jewish writings such as the Bible and the Talmud. The posttalmudic academies of Babylonia (contemporary Iraq) also directly influenced North African Jewry (Hirschberg 1974:300*ff*). The writings of the Spanish exiles in the fifteenth century, including the code of Joseph Caro[1] and the Lurianic school of mysticism in Safed, are among the major forces shaping Maghreb Jewry, just as they affected the Jews in Europe. Thus, although Rabbinic scholars were not found in the village communities, the influence and authority of central Jewish traditions were still clearly recognized.

The relationship between the standard religious law and local organization and practice is not only a historical link, but one that requires constant renewal. Hakohen gives ample evidence that this continued contact took place. It is significant that his discussion of the spiritual life of the community begins by describing ties to other Jewish communities (Section 95). Torah scrolls written by practiced scribes probably were brought from Tripoli. A man planning to serve as a circumcisor or slaughterer was expected to spend some time in the city of Tripoli in order to study the law and be certified there. Many of the teachers in the outlying communities came from Tripoli, or at least had studied there, while Hakohen mentions that the wealthy Jews of Yefren sent their sons to Tripoli to study the Torah. Rabbis would often visit the district, particularly to collect funds. The most prestigious of these were the emissaries from Palestine. Of course, their visits were not everyday occurrences, and the importance Hakohen gives to these infrequent stays indicates how significant they were to the villagers. On a more secular plane, it should be noted that seven or eight years after the founding of the Alliance Israélite Universelle, it was called upon for assistance by the Jews of Zliten (Section 108 and Littman 1975:69).[2]

Domestic life also required a connection with the centers of Judaism. A marriage could be performed locally, but a divorce, which is a complex matter in Rabbinic law, could take place only in the court in Tripoli (Section 103). In Section 100, we learn that the Rabbinic court became concerned with the weekly domestic routine of the women in the Nefusa because collecting firewood took them, unprotected, far from their homes. The women did not accept the Tripolitan Rabbis' attempt to restrict them, but their refusal was not phrased in terms of any autonomous legal tradition. Of course, these varied religious links were not separate from the fabric of everyday life, since the hinterland was linked commercially to the city of Tripoli. In addition, commercial contacts sometimes led to marriages between communities, giving families ties of kinship in the city or in other rural towns.

The demonstration that these "remote" communities were socially and culturally involved with an urban center does not necessarily negate the image of the poor, provincial, semi-literate peddler with few concerns beyond those stemming from his daily activities and contacts. In fact, these different images are complementary. In order for the community to function, it was not necessary that every member visit the city frequently, be well informed on current affairs and familiar with the traditional literature. In fact, only a few individuals needed to fit this cosmopolitan image, as long as they held central positions and status within the community as a whole. This pattern was true of a Tripolitanian community which migrated to, and settled in, Israel, and which appears to show a continuation of the original communal structure (Goldberg 1972a). Hakohen's material suggests that the pattern existed throughout the region.

This contact with other Jewish communities should be juxtaposed with another source of cultural influence, the non-Jewish environment. As we will see in the next chapter, this influence is pervasive, but it is also selective and complex. Some of the customs described in Section 97 had their origins in the non-Jewish environment, but, having become popular within the Jewish community, were invested with meanings taken from Jewish tradition. We also find practices which first appeared as Ashkenazic customs (Zimmels 1958) and later became part and parcel of Jewish ritual in the Sephardic world, including North Africa. An understanding of this sort of cultural flow into Tripolitania requires a subtle assessment of which periods were characterized by close contact with other areas, and which by relative isolation. For this reason, the study of origins requires disciplined speculation based on a knowledge of local non-Jewish practice, Jewish practices in many different areas, and the ways that customs can be transformed and reinterpreted.

The long parenthetical account of the *waqf* arrangements (Section 96) also raises questions about local influences. The *waqf* is an Islamic institution that allows property to be given in perpetuity as a pious foundation for the upkeep of a mosque, an orphanage, or the like. There are differences in the legal forms that a *waqf* can take, as Hakohen indicates. In one form, property is kept in a man's family for many generations, protected against alienation and division, before it is given over to its ultimate charitable purpose. The history of the institution and some of its uses are surveyed by Heffening (1929).

The reason Hakohen includes this discussion in his narrative is unclear. *Waqf* arrangements were presumably common elsewhere in Tripolitania, not only in the Nefusa. Were there some special features in the Ibadi laws that he wanted to emphasize? Are these *waqf* lands used for different communal purposes than elsewhere? Perhaps Hakohen sees a parallel between a synagogue's ownership of an olive grove and the institution of *waqf*? Synagogues did own property elsewhere (Goldberg 1974a), but the usual way of providing for the upkeep of a synagogue was through regular contributions by individuals, rather than through ownership at the communal level. Another possibility is that Hakohen thinks this sort of arrangement worthy of emulation. Whatever the reason, the juxtaposition of this account to his discussion of the synagogues indicates that Hakohen was fully conscious of the parallels in values and institutions between Jewish and Islamic society.

NOTES

1. The *Beit Yosef* and *Shulḥan 'Arukh*. See *Encyclopaedia Judaica,* vol. 5, pp. 194–200.

2. The Alliance's concern with the Tripolitanian Jewish communities is first found in its *Bulletin* in 1864 (premier trimestre, October, p. 4), in an entry on the town of Misurata.

Emissaries from the Land of Israel

(SECTION 95)

Even though they are not scholars of the Torah, the Jews of Nefusa still respect and study the Law and take great care to keep the commandments. The *miṣwah*[1] of hospitality is especially dear to them. When a stranger arrives, both Jews and non-Jews stare at him, especially if he is dressed in European clothes. But he must wear a Turkish hat;[2] otherwise, he will be suspected of being a Christian and his life may be in danger.

When a Jewish visitor comes to solicit from his generous brethren, he will wear a Turkish hat and a wide robe, as is customary among the Rabbis. Even if the visitor is an ignorant man, he can establish a reputation by the size of this garment, and the entire town will resound: "A wise man has come; a wise man has come." They greet him with rejoicing and extend to him the hand of friendship. Even though there is no place to purchase a loaf of bread, or an inn with rooms to rent, the Jews receive him. They make him flat wheat bread that is baked on the side of an open-topped oven. They fry eggs with salted meat to place in the flat, thin bread. They offer him sweet brandy. Throughout the time he stays with them, all his needs will be met wholeheartedly. There is an established order in which hospitality is arranged, with everyone taking his turn at receiving the guest. On the Sabbath, in each of the three villages [of Yefren], people pledge donations in the synagogue, every man according to his will. Donations, both large and small, are collected for the visitor on Monday. When he leaves, he is escorted out of the village, and the camel driver is ordered to protect him on his way.

When a *shaliah kollel* from the Land of Israel[3] comes, the community pays the camel driver who brings him. He is given a special room, which thereby receives a blessing. He is given great honor, for in the eyes of the community he is like a messenger of God.[4] They swerve neither to the right nor the left in fulfilling his requests. They pay him according to the standard amount imposed upon them for every *shaliah kollel*. This sum is proportionate to the size of the head tax paid to the government treasury, in which everyone pays according to his means. For instance, if the tax on the Jewish community is five hundred francs and the allocation to the *shaliah kollel* is two hundred francs, then the person who is taxed five francs will give the *shaliah kollel* two francs.

No one dares to deduct from the amount that has been assigned to him. And if a jealous spirit comes over a person so that he challenges the sum and does not wish to pay the money, then the *shaliah kollel* will pour out his fury upon him. He will ban the man from communal life; then no Jew has the right to speak with him until he humiliates himself before the emissary and begs him to lift the decree. After that, he will not deduct even one cent from the money that has been levied. And all the people will hear and take heed, and will never dare to hold back from giving their contributions willingly.

Every emissary that comes there sets up a collection box with a hole cut in its door; he places the box in the hands of a trustworthy man, who strives to collect vows and contributions on the day before the Day of Atonement and Purim, and also on other days of the year. He persuades people to gather funds and to put money in the box until the time when the emissary arrives; then the money is delivered and counted into the hands of the emissary by the trustee, and the emissary will pour out blessings upon the trustee for his work.

When the emissary goes away, the villagers give him provisions for the journey and accompany him for about an hour's walk in order to obtain the farewell blessing. The emissary also pours his blessing on the sheikh (head) of the Jews, a double and redoubled blessing for his efforts to collect contributions.[5]

The sheikh (head) will also collect the head tax from the Jews and hand it over to the state treasury. He receives no salary for this task but is exempted from paying the head tax himself. Even so, people will spend a great deal of money in an attempt to be chosen for this job because it bestows much status; it also includes the power to imprison and to grant reprieves. In addition, he who collects the head tax is granted a place among the local leaders in the council and generally can wield considerable influence.

In the year 1907, the Ottoman government allocated permanent dwellings for army personnel in the three villages where the Jews live in order to safeguard them and to protect them from the oppression of unscrupulous Berbers.

NOTES

1. A religious commandment; also the act of fulfilling a religious obligation, particularly one of benevolence or charity.

2. A "fez." For similar experiences, see Griffin (1924:10–11) and Osther (1912:31–33).

3. A *shaliah kollel* was an emissary from a religious institution in Palestine. Traditional communities in Palestine that devoted themselves to the study of the Torah and prayer would send emissaries abroad to collect funds for their support.

4. Ben Zvi (1964) provides an account of a Rabbinic emissary's visit to Tripolitania in the middle of the last century, one very different from that presented here. In the community of Misurata, all the Jews fled from the emissary, probably fearing the financial burden he would impose on them. The emissary says that he stood in the center of town, all alone, and in great dismay.

5. Various aspects of the preceding account could be discussed in terms of "the stranger and laws of hospitality" (Pitt-Rivers 1968).

Synagogues and Communal Organization
(SECTION 96)

Most of the people recite the afternoon, evening, and morning prayers. The *hazzan* (prayer leader) and the *shofar*-sounder[1] do not receive wages, only the reward of performing a *miṣwah*. Even so, there is always competition for these posts because they bring honor to the holder.

Synagogues, both new and old, are found there. Formerly, in the town of Disir, there was no synagogue, and the people had to walk about a half-hour to pray in a synagogue called al-Ghrība,[2] which is a six-minute walk from Me'aniyin.

In the year 1714, there was a Jew from the town of Disir named Moshe Ben Shim'on who purchased a plot of land at the edge of the city and built a synagogue on it. After some time, his heirs sold a large part of this property and the Berber purchaser claimed that the synagogue belonged to him. The stormy litigation between the Jews and the buyer continued for a long time until Khalifa Ben 'Omar, a rich Jew from the Guweta' family, redeemed his brother's land from the heirs of the Berber who had originally purchased it.

In the year 1904, the Jews wanted to extend this synagogue, but the Berbers again arose as adversaries and said that all the land adjacent to the synagogue belonged to them. Then the son of Khalifa Ben 'Omar showed the government officials the records of his father's purchase. The officials decided in his favor, and his claim was honored; the boundary of the synagogue was extended against the will of the Berbers.

A pit excavated there collects rain water and is used as a ritual bath. In the summer, the waters of the ritual bath are smelly and foul, and their odor spreads over a wide area.

A synagogue called al-Ghrība can be found between the village of al-Me'aniyin and the village of al-Qṣir. It is also known by the name al-Qabliya (the southern). I asked the elders there whether there was another ancient synagogue in the place, for if they gave it the name "the southern" there must have been another synagogue located in a different direction. They answered, "Yes, there was once also a synagogue called Ṣlat-a-Zqaq, which is not far from the southern synagogue." At present, in ruins, it is used as an orchard by the Berbers, except for one cave, which had been used as the ark for the Torah scrolls and is holy in the eyes of the Berbers as well. At present, Jews and Berbers offer prayers and light candles there.

The southern synagogue was originally only a single cave that was used as a synagogue. In the year 1742, the cave was sealed, and on top of it the present synagogue was built at ground level. The Jews own an old manuscript, written on parchment, which clearly states that the synagogue was founded by a Jew whose name was 'Atiya. It is considered holy even by the Berbers, who make vows there and contribute alms to it. The synagogue does not have a roof covered with logs; it is merely a stone building with whitewashed plaster. Inscribed there, in plaster relief the depth of a finger, are both old and new personal names and family names in Assyrian script.[3] The inscription is unadorned.

There are no wooden benches in the synagogue, only platforms for sitting, built on the sides of the walls. Most people prefer to sit crowded in the middle of the synagogue, which can hold a large number of people close together on the ground. They spread out mats of straw in the synagogue, remove their shoes at the entrance, and enter barefoot. However, the new generation has begun to break with this tradition, for the young men enter the synagogue with their shoes on (they have learned this from the Jews of Tripoli).

The dais upon which they placed the Torah scrolls was originally made of solid stone and stood on four pillars. In 1885, they enlarged the al-Qabliya synagogue and built a dais made of wood.

The al-Qabliya synagogue owns olive trees, donated to it in olden times, so that the synagogue can be maintained by their produce. It is always lit by the oil from these consecrated trees, and all excess oil is sold. The proceeds, kept in the synagogue fund by the beadle, are to be used for public purposes. The beadle keeps not only the proceeds from the sale of oil, but also those from the sale of *'aliyot*[4] to the Torah.

In former times, neither Jew nor Berber would dare to desecrate the honor of this synagogue by stealing anything from it or by taking anything from the specially consecrated trees. But now both Jews and Berbers have begun to steal from the religious trust when possible. The Berbers sometimes even steal the mats and the oil in the lamps.

In 1910, the Berbers came and stole whatever they could and also set fire to the ark of the Torah scroll and the other books there. The Jewish leaders of Tripoli sent letters about this to the Chief Rabbi of Turkey and to the Alliance[5] in Paris. Then the government officials of Tripoli and of Yefren received orders from Istanbul to make a thorough investigation and to mete out stern punishment to those who had stolen from a holy place. They also ordered that all residents of the district contribute to the reconstruction of the ruined synagogue.

The government officials, attempting to quiet the matter, pressured the sheikh of the Jews, and other notables who sent the complaint, to sign a document against their will saying that no man was involved in the incident—a candle had been lit and a spark from it had set the ark ablaze. But before the matter was finished, the government was overthrown, Tripoli was conquered by the Italians, and the whole land was in turmoil.

The synagogue in the town of Disir, which has been mentioned previously, has no consecrated olive trees and no other means of support. It depends on the sale of *'aliyot* to the Torah, as do all other Jewish synagogues in the district.

In contrast, the prayer houses of the Moslems in all the districts are supported from the funds of the *waqf* (consecrated property), which provides for maintenance, lighting oil, the prayer leader's salary, and other expenses. It owns large amounts of land and trees that have been donated by the Mohammedans, mainly those with no sons, to be consecrated as *waqf* to a given house of prayer. The *waqf* becomes a fund in perpetuity, whose profits support a specific house of prayer.

This is the law of the *waqf*, whose rules are different from other civil laws.[6] Some Mohammedans stipulate that as soon as, or even one hour before, they pass away, a certain mosque receives rights to their property in perpetuity; these rights cannot be sold or redeemed, and the income derived from them is for the general good of the mosque, to support the prayer leader, the teacher, and so forth.

Some people who have offspring consecrate the property beginning immediately, reserving the income from it for their male descendants, but not for their wives or relatives. If an individual dies owing money or owing rent and the period of his lease has not ended, the creditor has no claim against any property consecrated to the *waqf*.

If one of the descendants dies without leaving offspring, the *waqf* is awarded full ownership, including usufruct, of his share. It may neither be sold nor redeemed.

If one of the descendants wishes to redeem and secularize his share, he may do so through a legal evasion: he may make a *munqla* (transfer). Two valid witnesses must testify before a Qadi (religious magistrate) that such and such a consecrated field is left unattended because the heirs cannot manage to plant trees on it; or that it lies in ruins and the heirs cannot manage to rebuild it; or that a parcel is ready for building but the heirs do not have the means with which to build, and that it therefore does not produce any income; and that such and such a person currently owns another parcel, yielding an income greater than that of the *waqf* property, which should become *waqf* in its stead. Then the Qadi will agree to the redemption of the land, for the exchange is to the benefit of the *waqf*, and the original parcel of land can be sold without restriction.

Sometimes the usufruct of the *waqf* property can be sold so that the purchaser will pay a monthly rent to the *waqf*. With his own means, he then builds storehouses and dwellings and takes the risk of profit or loss. He is restricted, however, by the *waqf* law in that only male descendants may inherit; if one of his descendants dies without offspring his share of the income rights reverts to the *waqf* and other relatives have no claim to it.

Some people consecrate land for the reinforcement and maintenance of city walls, but the laws concerning this type of consecrated land are more lenient.

In the town of Taqerbos, which is not far from the town where the government palace is located, there were once Jewish residents. In 1850, the Jews removed themselves from there. They left their homes, which are today in the hands of the Berbers, and chose to reside in the town of al-Me'aniyin. Formerly, on the Sabbath and on holidays, and also on Mondays and Thursdays,[7] they would pray in the al-Qabliya synagogue, and the afternoon and evening prayers were recited in a certain room in the town of Taqerboṣ. This room is now in the hands of the Berbers and the surrounding area is planted with orchards and gardens; the Berbers have left no access road to it. The room itself is holy in the eyes of the Berbers and they, giving honor to its name, even light candles there. All the walls of this room and the ceiling are constructed of plaster, covered with unadorned Assyrian letters in plaster relief. Here are written the given names of Jews and of their fathers (for they did not trace descent to the name of the original head of the family). I saw on the right, as one walks in, an intact inscription of a given name dating from the year 1812.

The family of 'Atiya[8] that live in the town al-Qṣir have inherited the duty of serving as beadles. They are responsible for the produce of the olive trees consecrated to the al-Qabliya synagogue, a duty that has been entrusted to them from the earliest generations. In 1902, they purchased a small plot of land with the funds of the treasury. In 1904, in al-Qṣir, they excavated and built a cave-like shelter for reciting the afternoon, evening, and also the morning prayers on those days when a scroll of the Torah is not needed. They also dug out a ritual bath for rain water so women who finish menstruating will no longer have to immerse themselves in the ritual bath in the al-Qabliya synagogue. They also built a room to be used in the early morning for studying the Zohar[9] and a room to serve as an inn for guests, who can thereby have a special place to rest.

NOTES

1. The *shofar* is the ram's horn used at the time of the Solemn New Year (Rosh Hashanah).

2. The term *ghrība* means "strange," "solitary," or "wondrous," and is applied to a number of venerated synagogues in the Maghreb (D. Cohen 1964:89). The *ghrība* at Yefren was apparently a place of pilgrimage in the middle of the last century (Benjamin 1859:290).

3. The standard Hebrew script.

4. The *miṣwah* of being "called up" (*'aliyah* means ascent) to recite a blessing over the Torah when it is publicly read. This privilege is auctioned to individuals when the Torah is taken from the ark for reading.

5. The Alliance Israélite Universelle, known in Hebrew as KlaKH, an acronym of the phrase "All Israel are brethren." See Chouraqui (1965) and *Encyclopaedia Judaica*, vol. 2, pp. 647–654.

6. The details of the Ibadi *waqf* law are presented by Mercier (1927).

7. The Torah is read publicly on the Sabbath during the morning and afternoon services, and also on Mondays and Thursdays during the morning service.

8. Here, as elsewhere, Hakohen specifically mentions the name of the family involved in building or maintaining a synagogue. Contributing to communal and synagogue life was one of the main ways of gaining religious merit. At the same time, it was also a way to gain prestige within the community, or to legitimate prestige based on wealth.

9. The Zohar is the most well-known book of the Kabbalah (the mystical tradition). Reading portions of the Zohar on specified occasions has been standard practice throughout Judaism since the sixteenth century (Scholem 1946:285). Sessions of reading the Zohar are described by Stahl (1979).

The Festivals and Fasts[1]
(SECTION 97)

All the Jews who scatter for the purpose of trade and barter gather during holidays and festivals to rejoice with members of their households and to wash their filthy clothes.

On the eve[2] of Rosh Hashanah[3] they slaughter a fowl for each person: a cock for each male, and a hen for each female. The bones of the bird must be buried. On the two days of Rosh Hashanah, no stranger may set foot in their homes and no one may benefit from their possessions.

The *'amidah*[4] prayer of the Solemn Holidays[5] is not recited in a whisper but in a loud voice, with the entire congregation reciting together and the prayer leader repeating it afterwards. I asked them the meaning of this custom and they answered me that in the early days they had no printed Solemn Holidays prayer books[6] and the congregants were not expert enough to know the prayers by heart.[7] Therefore they decided to teach the prayers out loud so that the entire congregation might participate.

The morning prayers are stretched out so they last until two hours after noontime. In the evening, they walk to the wells to conduct the *tashlikh*[8] ceremony. On the eve of the Day of Atonement, they slaughter other fowls[9] and there are those who look especially for a white[10] chicken.

Before the day ends, they pay up all the dues they have pledged to the Land of Israel fund and other funds, and afterwards they immerse themselves in the ritual bath of forty *s'ah*.[11] They also receive stripes[12] on the flesh of their shoulders, forty strokes with a whip made of oxhide and donkey leather.

Every male brings an olive oil lamp to the synagogue.

On the Sabbath and on holidays the males do not eat on the floor. Instead, a table is set up, a finger length off the ground, and covered with a red woolen cloth.

The pre-fast meal is eaten in broad daylight while the sun is high in the sky. Even the nine-year-old boys are taught to fast. All of them walk barefoot. On the night of the Day of Atonement while the Torah scroll is on the dais, they recite a memorial prayer, reciting the names of the Tannaim, the Amoraim, the Geonim, and the early and latter-day scholars.[13] (See Section 86, Note 66.)

They stretch out the evening prayer until three hours after the setting of the sun and do not return to their homes until the stars come out at the end of the Day of Atonement.

On the eve of Sukkot[14] everyone makes a *sukkah* in his house thatched with date palm branches.[15] They eat and sleep in the *sukkah* all the days of the holiday. They import the citron, willow, and myrtle[16] from Tripoli.

Everyone fattens sheep. On the night of Hosha‘na Rabbah[17] the slaughterer is brought to the house to slaughter the fattened sheep; even a man of limited means will slaughter at least one lamb. (In the Tractate *Ḥulin*, Chapter V, Mishnah 3 it is written, "Four times during the year a person who sells an animal must inform the purchaser 'I have sold its mother to be slaughtered' . . . [one is] the eve of the last festive day of Sukkot.")[18]

On the night of Hosha‘na Rabbah,[19] in his *sukkah*, everyone reads the following scriptures: "And this is the blessing"[20] and "In the beginning" until the verse "which God had created in order to make it."[21] Then they sanctify the holiday over a glass of wine, reciting the *qiddush*[22] for festivals. Then they read the *hafṭarah*[23]: "And it came to be after the death of Moses."[24] Afterwards they eat the roast liver and lungs of the slaughtered sheep.[25] The rest of the meat is used for the holiday repast and whatever is left over is spread out and made into dried salted meat. If any man has not honored his pledge, the sheikh of the Jews will issue an order that no slaughterer may slaughter for him until he pays his debt or gives security for it.

During morning prayers on the day of Hosha‘na Rabbah they recite *Nishmat Kol Ḥai*[26] as on other holidays, and during the *'amidah* prayer they recite *Zokhreinu Leḥaim* as on the Ten Days of Repentance.[27] When they leave the synagogue they recite *qiddush* over wine, as they do on other holidays before eating the festive meal. Then they eat and drink a great deal.

On Simḥat Torah,[28] while singing spiritedly, they take all the Torah scrolls into the synagogue yard. The Berbers come to give honor to the scrolls of the Torah and present gifts of figs and olive oil to the Jews in honor of the Torah scrolls.

Everyone lights a Hanukkah[29] lamp in his home, and an additional candle is lit on the lamp of the synagogue, as is the custom in Tripoli. On the days of Hanukkah every fiancé sends cakes fried in olive oil to his betrothed.

Purim.[30] On the thirteenth day of the month of Adar, the boys gather together with their teacher, each boy bearing in his hands an effigy of a man with head, hands, and legs made of cordons of olive wood. These effigies are given the name Haman.[31] They are put into a bonfire to which each woman contributes a bundle of wood in honor of her son. Many women and children, together with the boys' teacher, dance around the flames of the bonfire. With a loud voice and raucous songs, they mock the fall of Haman as the images burn. Afterwards, they examine the flames carefully to see whether any effigy remains intact. If they find one, they break it into little pieces with the axes in their hands and burn it, saying, "May all memories of Amalek be erased."[32]

All people keep the fast of Esther[33] until approximately one hour after sunset, when they gather for evening prayers, like a multitude of people attending the king, to hear the reading of the Book of Esther. On the fourteenth day, when they reach the phrase, "A Jewish man,"[34] they clap their hands. There are some who bring a sledgehammer and a piece of rock carved with the name of Haman. They swing the sledgehammer until the stone and the name of Haman are broken to bits. This practice is based on the verse, "All memory of Amalek shall be erased."

Although they are not wealthy, none of them will bear the yoke of disgrace that comes from accepting gifts to the poor;[35] only small children get honey wafers.

The treasurers of the funds for the Land of Israel will accept the gifts for the needy. Everyone is required to give a half-shekel (approximately sixty centimes).

With regard to the obligation to send gift portions, they do not send gifts to their Jewish friends, but they do send them to their Berber neighbors, and the Berbers send hen's eggs to the Jews.

The feast of Purim Day consists of flat wafers dipped in butter. In the evening, they prepare a feast consisting of a large dish made of eggs and pieces of meat fried in olive oil, which they call *tajīn*. On Purim they all become drunk until they do not know the difference between "cursed be Haman" and "blessed be Mordechai."[36] When they are saturated with brandy they pay visits to one another.

In preparation for the Passover festival, before the beginning of the month of Nisan, the women grind all they will need for fifteen days, and hide the leavened flour in such a way that it will not touch the rooms prepared for Passover.[37] Afterwards they carefully hollow out the millstones to use for grinding the Passover wheat. The eve of the new month of Nisan is called *al-halal* (the new moon). They eat *bsīsa* (see Section 67, Note 48).[38] From the beginning of the month, they scatter in the mountains to the places where there are white chalk (limestone) quarries.

They burn the limestone and crush it very fine in order to whitewash the rooms. All the rooms are cleaned so that there is not the slightest suspicion of *ḥameṣ*,[39] and they do not bring any *ḥameṣ* into the rooms. They will not sleep in the cleaned rooms until the night of Passover; until then they sleep under the open skies. They wash all their clothes in running springs.

From the time the women begin to grind the Passover wheat, they tie a scarf around their mouths and will not utter a word until the grinding is completed for fear that saliva from their mouths will spray onto the flour and cause it to ferment. On the night before Passover, near sundown, they go down to the river with their pitchers on their shoulders to draw enough water from the well for kneading throughout the days of the holiday. They bake hot *maṣah* wafers for each day of the holiday on the inner walls of an open-topped oven.

This drawn water is called *tanjīm* for it remains under the stars called *njūm*.[40] At the time of the drawing of the water, everyone breaks a ceramic utensil in which food has been leavened throughout the year. The breaking of this utensil signals the beginning of the elimination of the *ḥameṣ*.

On the eve of Passover they arrange the *maṣṣot* [pl. of *maṣah*], the bitters, the eggs,[41] and the other foods in a single basket, braided with a type of grass called *ḥalfa*.[42]

No stranger may set foot within their boundary on the first two days of Passover and no outsider may benefit from their belongings.* If an unknown Jew should chance to be found there, they will leave him to his own devices, even before the onset of the holiday in the evening. They will do no work even on the intermediate days of the holidays.

For the Shavuot[45] festival, they prepare a bagel made of well-sifted flour and also toasted corn flour. On the eve of every festival, the men ritually immerse themselves.

During morning prayers, when the Torah is read, they translate all of the Ten Commandments into Arabic,[46] along with sayings taken from the Midrash and the Aggadah.[47]

After the morning feast, each man battles his brother and his friend with a goatskin full of water, and the man who succeeds most often in pouring water on the next man is the victor, for the Torah is likened to water and it was on the day of the Shavuot festival that the Torah was given.[48]

*This custom is the opposite of the phrase, "Let all who are hungry come and eat,"[43] that is stated in the first paragraph of the Passover Haggadah.[44] However, what is said in the second paragraph, "On all other nights we may eat either *ḥameṣ* or *maṣah*," is correct because they eat *ḥameṣ* or *maṣah*. This is not true for us who, on every night, eat only *ḥameṣ*.

The Berbers watch these goings-on to prevent fights, disagreements, and hatreds from developing. But they also encourage the Jews to follow these practices, for they believe in their hearts that as long as the Jews continue to pour water the year will be rainy.[49] On every holiday, the Jews become drunk and therefore begin to squabble.

The Ninth of Av.[50] From the seventeenth of the month of Tammuz, they do not allow any children born that year to be seen under the open skies during daylight, for they believe that if a bird called *būma* (owl) smells the odor of an infant at night, the child will not escape sickness and death.

From the beginning of the month of Av, they do not eat meat except on the Sabbath. There are those who do not eat meat bought with their own money on the Sabbath, only cooked meat that is given to them by their acquaintances. On the Sabbath before the Ninth of Av, they read the additional portion of Scripture beginning with the verse, "The burden of the valley of vision."[51]

For the meal before the fast on the eve of the Ninth of Av, they prepare a dish called *shimshuma*, made of wheat and barley and lentils boiled without oil or spices. Then all of them fast and walk barefoot. After the *shimshuma* they eat roasted *zumīṭa* to quench their thirst (see Section 93). They prolong their dirges on the night of the Ninth of Av.

During the morning service of the Ninth of Av, when the congregation recites the dirges and reads at length from the Book of Lamentations, the youths ride around the fields on donkeys with great pride. They say that perhaps they will meet the Messiah,[52] who will come as a poor man riding on a donkey.[53]

NOTES

1. This section surveys the customs associated with the major holidays of the year. I am unable to give a full explanation of all the holidays and customs mentioned, but have referred the interested reader to the relevant articles in the *Encyclopaedia Judaica* (1972). Moreno's edition (n.d.) of Hakohen's work covers this topic in detail. Another good account of an ethnologically close area is D. Cohen's study of the Jews of Tunis (1964). The present text begins with the Solemn New Year, falling on the first day of the month of Tishrei, the seventh month according to the standard Hebrew calendar.

2. The Jewish day begins in the evening and runs through the following day. The "eve" of a festival refers to the daytime preceding the onset of a holiday.

3. The Solemn New Year. *Encyclopaedia Judaica*, vol. 14, p. 305.

4. Literally "standing," this refers to the central prayer of the three daily services, said in a standing position. *Encyclopaedia Judaica*, vol. 2, p. 838. The normal requirement is that each person say the prayer in a whisper (*i.e.* silently).

5. The Solemn Holidays begin with Rosh Hashanah on the first of Tishrei, and end with the Day of Atonement (*Encyclopaedia Judaica*, vol. 5, p. 1376) on

the tenth of that month. This period is also known as the Ten Days of Repentance (*Encyclopaedia Judaica*, vol. 15, p. 1001).

6. The common Hebrew word for prayer book is *siddur*; it is found in the spoken language of Jews in many countries. In the Arabic dialect of some of the Jewish communities in Tripolitania, the word *siddur* serves as a generic term for printed book. This suggests an earlier situation in which printed books were rare, and the prayer book was one of the few in the area. The term *sefer* (standard modern Hebrew for book) in the Tripolitanian Jewish (Arabic) dialect means "Torah scroll."

7. The following quote (Azulai 1864:81a) describes the Jews of Tripoli in the middle of the sixteenth century, after the city was taken from the Knights of Malta by the Ottomans: "When the Rabbi Shim'on Lavi came to Tripoli he found that they were ignorant of religious practice, not knowing even the prayers and blessings properly. He then thought that it would be better for him to draw them near to the Torah, to teach them the Law and the Fear of Heaven, than to continue his journey to the Land of Israel. He did thus and virtually succeeded in proselytizing them and spreading the knowledge of the Torah there. This was in the year 1549." Elsewhere (Goldberg 1974c), I have argued that this is not an exaggerated description of the Jews of Tripoli, and would therefore be even more plausible for the small communities in the mountains.

8. Literally: "casting away." A ceremony in which one symbolically "casts away" sins into the water. It was clearly described for the first time in the early fifteenth century by an author from central Europe and was spread through Sephardic Jewry as part of Lurianic mysticism (*Encyclopaedia Judaica*, vol. 15, p. 829).

9. The custom of slaughtering chickens as an expiation on the eve of the Day of Atonement is known as *kapparot* (*Encyclopaedia Judaica*, vol. 10, p. 756). As described above for Rosh Hashanah, a chicken is slaughtered for each person in the family, a cock for a male, a hen for a female. Before being slaughtered, the fowl is swung around the head of the individual three times and a formula is recited, in which the bird is declared to be the person's expiation (*kapparah*). While apparently quite old and very widespread, this custom has been criticized by some Rabbinical authorities as a superstition, and even pagan. One may surmise that it was initially attached to the Day of Atonement, and only secondarily to Rosh Hashanah.

10. White is associated with the Day of Atonement. There are various traditional explanations for this: white is said to represent purity; it is also said to be the color of shrouds and thus deceives the angel of death who seeks to strike the supplicant on the Day of Atonement. See Turner's exploration of the meanings of white (1962).

11. A *s'ah* is a measure of volume. A ritual bath must contain at least forty *s'ah*.

12. Forty stripes was the standard (and maximum) corporal punishment according to Mishnaic law (Babylonian Talmud, Tractate *Makkot* 22a). The stripes administered on the eve of the Day of Atonement symbolize the punishment one would have received if the laws were still in force, and are undertaken voluntarily. Of Ashkenazic origin (Zimmels 1958:239), this practice later spread to the Sephardim.

13. The different categories (and ranks) of Rabbinical sages, beginning with the period of the Mishnah and running through more recent periods (*Encyclopaedia Judaica*, vol. 2, p. 865; vol. 7, p. 315; vol. 14, p. 192; vol. 15, p. 798). In Note 66, ms. p. 185a, Hakohen gives the text of a memorial prayer in which the names of many sages are mentioned.

14. The festival of Tabernacles or Booths (*Encyclopaedia Judaica*, vol. 15, p. 495), during which one is obligated to live in a *sukkah*, or hut.

15. The holiday is known by the Tripolitanian Moslems as *'id ez-zrība* (the holiday of palm branch huts).

16. The "four species" (citron, willow, palm, and leafy bough) are discussed in *Encyclopaedia Judaica*, vol. 15, p. 498.

17. The festival of Sukkot lasts for seven days and is followed immediately by another festival on the eighth day. This day is a festival unto itself, but is also commonly viewed as the eighth day of Sukkot. The first and eighth days have a particular festive and sacred character, while the second through seventh days are known as the "intermediate days" because they are characterized by fewer ritual restrictions and have less of an air of sanctity. In communities outside Israel, each of the festive days is celebrated on two consecutive days, so that two full holidays are followed by five intermediate days, followed by two full holidays.

Throughout the first seven days of Sukkot there is a special procession known as *Hosha'na*. The seventh day, the high point in this ritual, is known as the Great Hosha'na (Hosha'na Rabbah). Hakohen's narrative shows that this day, which "officially" is an "intermediate" day, takes on the characteristics of a full festival. This shows the influence of Lurianic mysticism (Scholem 1946:285 and *Encyclopaedia Judaica*, vol. 8, p. 1026).

18. This is done to avoid violating the biblical prohibition against slaughtering both an animal and its child on the same day (Leviticus XXII:28). Hakohen seems to be seeking an ancient precedent for the custom of eating liver and lung.

19. The eighth day of the Sukkot (or the ninth outside of Israel) is known as Simḥat Torah. This holiday celebrates the completion of the annual cycle of the reading of the Five Books of Moses. At the same time, the reading begins again from the Book of Genesis. The customs included in the Hosha'na Rabbah celebration thus anticipate Simḥat Torah.

20. The last two chapters of Deuteronomy (XXXIII and XXXIV).

21. Genesis I:1 through II:3.

22. The prayer sanctifying the holiday, recited over a cup of wine (*Encyclopaedia Judaica*, vol. 10, p. 974).

23. A selection from the Prophets, normally read in the synagogue after the weekly reading from the Torah scroll (*Encyclopaedia Judaica*, vol. 16, p. 1342).

24. Joshua I:1.

25. This evening is popularly known among the Jews of Libya as "the night of liver and lung."

26. A prayer normally said only on Sabbaths and festivals, but not on the intermediate days of a festival.

27. Hosha'na Rabbah, whose meaning has been elaborated in Lurianic mysticism, is included in the period of atonement. It is the last day of the season on which one may receive remission of a decreed punishment.

28. Literally: "the rejoicing of the Torah." See *Encyclopaedia Judaica*, vol. 14, p. 1571.

29. Ḥanukkah commemorates the miraculous victory of the Maccabees over the Syrian Greeks, who sought to impose their religious worship on the Jews of Palestine.

30. The holiday instituted in commemoration of the events described in the Book of Esther (*Encyclopaedia Judaica*, vol. 13, p. 1390).

31. Haman is the villain in the Book of Esther.

32. This phrase is based on biblical verses requiring that the memory of Amalek be erased (Exodus XVII:14 and Deuteronomy XXV:19). According to tradition, Haman the Agagite (Esther III:1) was descended from Agag, king of Amalek (I Samuel, Chap. XVI). In Section 68 (ms. p. 129b), Hakohen notes a similar custom in which the children would jump over the fire. He quotes the comment of Rashi on a Talmudic passage in Tractate *Sanhedrin* (64b) as proof that such a custom existed in his day. He also states (ms. p. 130a) that in 1885 Rabbi Eliahu Ḥazzan attempted to stop the custom of burning Haman "lest at some future time it cause hatred toward the Jews."

33. The day before the holiday of Purim is a fast day (*Encyclopaedia Judaica*, vol. 6, p. 914).

34. Esther II:5, which introduces Mordechai, the hero of the story.

35. The Book of Esther declares that people should send gifts to one another and give presents to the poor to commemorate the deliverance of the Jews (IX:19, 22).

36. Based on a saying in the Babylonian Talmud, Tractate *Meghillah* (7b).

37. Passover commemorates the exodus from Egypt. During this time, Jews must not eat any leavened food; instead, they eat unleavened bread, *maṣah* (matzah). In ancient times, a paschal lamb was slaughtered and eaten, but all laws pertaining to sacrifice apply only while the Temple in Jerusalem is standing. Today, therefore, the first night of Passover (the first two nights in communities outside Israel) features a ceremony recalling the ancient ritual, which includes the story of the exodus from Egypt (*Encyclopaedia Judaica*, vol. 13, p. 163).

38. Note 48, ms. p. 126a, reads as follows: "*Bsīsa* is made of wheat, barley, coriander, and cumin which are roasted over a fire, ground, and mixed with olive oil. Apparently it is an Aramaic word, for the phrase 'its base' [*e.g.* Exodus XXXV:16] is rendered *bsiseih* in Onkelos' Aramaic translation. Here, it is customary to prepare it when beginning the foundation of a house, at the beginning of a wedding celebration, and also for a woman who has given birth to her first child. The *bsīsa* of the New Moon of Nisan, however, has an adjective appended to it: *bsīset al-marqūma*. Perhaps it is reminiscent of the tabernacle raised on the first of Nisan [see Exodus XL:2], which contained embroidery work [Hebrew: *ma'aseh roqem*] and therefore was called *al-marqūma*, because the Hebrew *roqem* is translated *mirqam* in Arabic."

39. Food which has been leavened.

40. The water for baking *maṣah* must stand overnight, and should not be taken directly from a well or a spring.

41. Other ritual items which form part of the celebration on the first night (or the first two nights) of Passover (*Encyclopaedia Judaica*, vol. 13, pp. 167, 172).

42. Esparto grass.

43. As Hakohen says, this is a very surprising custom which stands in contradiction to the normal practice of the Passover celebration. Slouschz (1926:90) believes that this may reflect a Marrano origin of these communities, and that the purpose of the custom was to keep any outsiders from seeing the secret observance of the Passover. A more plausible theory is that a Talmudic rule concerning the eating of the paschal lamb (Exodus XII) has been extended to the Passover ceremony, which commemorates the ancient sacrificial meal. This rule (Babylonian Talmud, Tractate *Pesaḥim* 61a) states that once it has been determined which family or families will partake of a given lamb (Exodus XII:4), no "outsider" may share in it. It is possible that the parallel custom of not sharing with outsiders on Rosh Hashanah is a further generalization of this practice, the origin of which has been forgotten. The continued maintenance of the custom, in contradiction to the central Passover tradition, still requires some interpretation.

44. The narrative of the exodus that is read during the Passover celebration.

45. The Feast of Weeks (*Encyclopaedia Judaica*, vol. 14, p. 1319).

46. This is the tradition of reading *'azharot* on the Feast of Weeks. These are liturgical poems based on a listing of Biblical commandments.

47. Homiletic and folkloristic sections of the Rabbinic tradition (*Encyclopaedia Judaica*, vol. 2, p. 354; vol. 11, p. 1507).

48. A very old custom in North Africa (Hirschberg 1974:170). The relating of the Torah to water is probably a secondary elaboration, not an original meaning of the practice.

49. There are similar examples of cases in which a politically weak population is believed by the dominant group to possess spiritual power over rain and fertility (*cf.* Turner 1969; Goldberg 1978a).

50. The day on which the Temple was destroyed, commemorated by fasting and lamentation (*Encyclopaedia Judaica*, vol. 3, p. 936). This holiday marks the end of a period that began with the fast of the seventeenth of Tammuz, which ushers in the mourning period of the Three Weeks (*Encyclopaedia Judaica*, vol. 15, p. 1124).

51. Isaiah XXII.

52. A midrash based on a verse in Jeremiah (XXXI:12), "I will turn their mourning into rejoicing," claims that the Messiah will come on the Ninth of Av. The belief in the Messiah coming as a poor man riding a donkey is based on Zechariah IX:9.

53. Hakohen's list omits a number of fast days (*Encyclopaedia Judaica*, vol. 6, p. 1195). One of these is the third day of the month of Tishrei, following immediately upon the two days of the Solemn New Year. The most common name for this holiday is the Fast of Gedaliah. While this name was known to some of the villagers in Tripolitania, in other cases it was called *khu kibbur* (the "brother" of the Day of Atonement) or *sruḥa* (a term derived from the Hebrew *'isru ḥag*, referring to the day following a major festival). In one community, this fast had no standard name, but was remembered by the saying, "Two days a holiday, afterwards a fast." This variation seems to suggest a situation in which the standard reason for the fast was forgotten, but not the practice of fasting itself. This would make sense if it is true that Tripolitanian Jewry was isolated from other centers at some time in its past.

CHAPTER FOUR

The Life Cycle and the Family

Editor's Foreword

The sections included here describe the traditional ceremonies that mark the stages of Jewish life—birth, circumcision, religious majority, marriage, and death. As in other peasant societies, the most elaborate of these celebrations is the wedding. Hakohen's inherent anthropological perspective is evident when, after the section on the wedding, he also gives an account of the women's household duties, supplying details about everyday life in addition to his description of the ceremonies.

While these accounts are detailed, they highlight certain standard practices; a present-day ethnographer would certainly supplement them with much more fine-grained data. Thus Hakohen's findings cannot be compared in great detail with the available descriptions of Libyan Moslem weddings,[1] several of which concern regions not adjacent to those discussed here. From a general point of view, however, the similarity in local practices between Jews and Moslems is very clear.

Anthropologists have not developed a satisfactory way to study these similarities. Some look at local practices in terms of well-established Jewish traditions. This means trying to find the origin of some custom in a talmudic passage or a Rabbinic tract. This point of view has much to recommend it; as we saw in Chapter Three, the remoteness of these communities from Jewish centers has often been exaggerated. At the same time, however, this view often ignores the compelling link between Jewish communities and the wider non-Jewish setting.

By contrast, a second approach pays full attention to the wider setting, and by doing so perhaps overestimates its influence. This point of view sees Jewish culture as if it were a sponge, absorbing, in an almost mechanical fashion, many of the traits of the surrounding culture. We see this perspective in the following remarks on North African Jewry (Patai 1971:206–207):

> Their roots were sunk deeply into the soil of the Maghrib. Their language was the local Arabic vernacular (with certain idiomatic differences); their ethos and values were those of the Maghribi Muslims; their personality traits and other characteristics were largely similar to those of their Muslim neighbors; even the Jewish and Muslim attitudes to the supernatural—with the all-pervading belief in magic, the evil eye, saints, amulets, apotropaic utterances and gestures—were practically identical, as was the personality of the God whom the Muslims called Allah and the Jews by one of his several Hebrew names.

What needs to be stressed is that, pervasive as the outside influence was, its nature was more complex than is suggested above, and should always be viewed in terms of developments within the Jewish community. In fact, it is sometimes useful simply to set aside an *a priori* judgment of what is Jewish and what is Moslem, and to focus on the processes that are involved both in the internal development and the external borrowing of cultural forms (Goldberg 1978a).

Many specific traits are found in both Moslem and Jewish weddings in any given region, but the patterns of these traits and the values that give them meaning may not be identical. In the Ghuryan region, for example, public exposure of young women's hair occurs in both Moslem and Jewish weddings. In Moslem weddings, exposure of hair occurs as a group of males stands opposite a group of females. The young men stand in a semicircle, with the groom in the middle, and opposite them is a line of nubile girls who kneel down and let their hair flow in front of their faces. They dance in this fashion, moving their hair, waists, and arms (al-Ahmar 1976:110–134). The public display of female hair is more restricted in Jewish weddings. Only the bride is involved; though her hair is let down, the only other parts of her body exposed are her fingers and toes. There is no dancing in front of men, although some women dance among themselves in the fashion described (Goldberg 1978b). A dramatization of the opposition of the male and female worlds occurs in both instances, but in the Jewish case, I would argue, this emphasis is secondary to another theme, which highlights the place of the newly created family within a moral and social community.

Differences betwen Jewish and non-Jewish weddings may stem from the unconscious (or conscious?) tendency to deny outside cultural influences. In Section 99, Hakohen indicates that, among both the Moslem Berbers and the Jews, a bride will break an egg against the wall of her new house before entering it. This can easily be taken as a sign of the end of virginity and, as Mason (1975:660n) states, a representation of fertility. He also suggests that it may symbolize the loosening of the tie between the bride and her family. Al-Ahmar's informants *(loc. cit.)* said that it helped bring harmony to the new house—perhaps the other side of the same process. Hakohen, in contrast, interprets the egg-breaking as mourning over the destroyed Temple. Perhaps one (forgotten) purpose of this interpretation is to give Jewish content to a custom obviously adopted from the surroundings.

It is possible, of course, to overinterpret symbols, and one should not assume that every detail of customary behavior will mesh with the social context in which it is found. In addition, there are certain symbols, very old and widespread, that need not be closely tied to a specific communal situation. The exposure of the bride's hair, for example, was common in talmudic times, when testimony that a woman's hair had been uncovered at her wedding was accepted as legal evidence that she had been a virgin at her marriage.[2]

What is surprising is that the notion of borrowing from the Moslem environment does not figure prominently in Hakohen's understanding of Jewish customs. Instead, he points out the traditional Jewish basis for practices observed in his day. He notes, several times, the parallels between contemporary Moslem, or better, Libyan, practices and details of the biblical narrative or the talmudic lexicon.

One wonders whether these parallels are based on an unstated belief in the theory of Berber migration from Palestine. In some cases, the Moslem influence on the Jews seems very obvious, as when the Jews of Yefren remove their shoes before entering the synagogue (Section 96). Perhaps this is so obvious that he does not think to comment upon it. Hakohen did not feel that learning about and borrowing from another culture was wrong in principle. After all, he was familiar with the Moslem religion and the Koran. When discussing belief in the evil eye, demons, cures with amulets, and so forth (Section 5, ms. p. 11b), he refers simultaneously to the Moslem and Jewish population. In his footnote on the Hebrew language (see the Editor's Introduction), he advocates the incorporation of words from Arabic to further the renaissance of Hebrew. Still, his major direction in presenting the customs of the Jews of Yefren is to link them with Jewish tradition.

Hakohen thus gives consideration to the possibility that some of the unusual practices found in the Jebel Nefusa are due to Karaite influence. The Karaites are a Jewish sect which developed in the eighth century in opposition to Rabbinic Judaism.[3] The sect claims to base religious law directly on the biblical text, in its literal meaning, rather than on the overlay of interpretations added by generations of Rabbis. Its own interpretations are often stricter than those of the Rabbis, and it is particularly severe with regard to the prohibitions concerning menstruant women. The nature of Karaite influence in North Africa is unclear (Hirschberg 1974:157-163), but evidence of it dates from the tenth century. They may have had some success among the Rabbinic Jews of Cairo at the time of Maimonides' arrival there in the twelfth century.

Maimonides' opposition to the Karaites is reflected in the letter quoted in Section 98, which mentions the Jews living between Tunis and Alexandria. Like the Karaites, they are very strict regarding contact with a menstruating woman. Hakohen finds similar strictness of observance in the Jebel Nefusa in his own day. In Section 101, he cites another rigorous observance not demanded by Rabbinic law, one apparently based on a literal understanding of the biblical text. Hakohen clearly understands why these Jews have been likened to the Karaites, but after considering inscriptions on tombstones in the region (Section 109) he concludes that the early Jewish settlers did not belong to this sect.

If Karaite influence does not explain some of the peculiarities of the Nefusa Jews, we again wonder why Hakohen does not lay more stress on environmental influence. The letter he quotes in Section 98 explicitly compares the Barbary Jews to Arab tribes, but there are not enough data on the Moslems of the Jebel Nefusa to examine this question in greater detail. It should be noted that Hakohen does not consider that customs can be shaped by social structure, although we might guess that rigid menstrual taboos would reflect a strict separation of men and women in daily life. The data in these sections do not support a hypothesis of exceedingly strict separation. We find the women of Yefren ignoring the Rabbis who want to impose greater seclusion upon them. There are also a number of instances in which men appear to have casual contact with women.[4] It is thus a complex task to judge which customs reflect environmental influences and which are rooted in the internal social structure. Without better data on Jewish and Moslem life in the same region, these matters will remain open to varying interpretations.[5]

NOTES

1. See, for example, al-Ahmar (1976), Calassanti-Motylinski (1898), Cesàro (1939:255-260), Hilal (1969), Mason (1975), Peters (1965), and Ghelli (1932).

2. Tractate *Ketubbot,* Chapter 2, Mishnah 1.

3. *Encyclopaedia Judaica,* vol. 10, pp. 761-786.

4. See Hakohen's Notes in Sections 92, 94, 101, and 103.

5. The complexity of unravelling mutual influences between Moslem and Jewish tradition on the one hand, and Rabbinic and Karaite law on the other, is amply illustrated in Goitein's (1978) detailed study of the Jewish Mediterranean family from the tenth to the thirteenth centuries.

Childbirth and Circumcision
(SECTION 98)

The men guard themselves from anything unchaste and are very careful to keep their distance from a woman during her menstrual period.* A man may not even step on the straw mat that she has walked on, nor may he look upon her face. He may speak to her only when absolutely necessary and even then as briefly as possible.[4]

When a woman conceives and gives birth to a male child, she is considered impure for seven days after the birth, and then for an additional thirty-three days. Should she give birth to a female child, she is impure for eighty days. (See Section 88.)[5]

When a male child is born, the mother's relatives gather to grind barley in a hand mill in sufficient quantity to prepare a feast of *bazīn* for the circumcision festival. They make meat, boiled beans, potatoes, and brandy for all the Jews.

On the eve of the eighth day, they follow the custom of Tripoli. (See Section 88.)[6] On the eighth day as well, before the circumcision, they follow the custom of Tripoli. They light candles and decorate the walls of the house with colorful clothes.[7]

After sunrise, the community gathers at the decorated home to chant hymns. The *sandaq*[8] sits with his buttocks on the ground, and the child to be circumcised is placed in his lap. The circumcisor bends over to perform the circumcision, which is done quickly while he is in a bent position. (I, the writer, set up a chair for them so that the *sandaq* could sit upon it, but the circumcisor said: "I won't be able to perform the circumcision in this fashion because I am not used to it.")

In the old days, the custom was that the circumcisor who performed this *miṣwah* was Ḥaim Megidish, who inherited the position from his relative Sir 'Atiya, the doctor (mentioned in Section 44).[9] No other person could encroach upon his domain. If he had to travel to one of the

---

*A letter from the RaMBaN[1] states: "You should also beware of certain people who live in the western region called al-Zirbi,[2] *i.e.* localities in the countries of Barbary, for they are dull and coarse. And you should always be extremely cautious of the people who live between Tunis and Alexandria in Egypt and who live in the mountains of Barbary, for they are more stupid in my opinion than other men, although they are very strong in faith; God is my witness and judge that in my opinion they are like the Karaites, who deny the Oral Law; they have no clear brain at all, neither for dealing with the Bible and the Talmud, nor for expounding *aggadot* and *halakhot*.[3] Some of them are judges, but their beliefs and actions in matters of ritual uncleanness are like those of the Beni Maos [sons of abomination], who are a nation among the nations dwelling in the lands of the Ishmaelites. They do not see the ritually unclean woman at all; they do not look at her figure or her clothes, they do not speak to her and avoid walking the ground on which her foot has trodden. . . ."

outlying villages, he was informed by letter about the day of the circumcision. Sometimes he was delayed in coming, and the circumcision was executed after its proper time.[10]

In the year 1891, Mordechai Hakohen (the writer) labored to insure that the Rabbinic court of Tripoli would demand that the monopoly of the circumcisor be voided: it was imperative that a new man be trained. At present, there are two circumcisors who perform the ceremony in turn. If one should be far away, then his partner does the circumcision. Even though they earn only the merit of performing the *miṣwah,* they still bicker to make sure that the rotation is kept. After the circumcision, the father of the circumcised child remains wrapped in his fringed prayer shawl until the baby urinates. He then invites all the assembled to a feast of *bazīn,* boiled beans, and brandy, and he throws the cooked meat on a tablecloth so that everyone can partake of it.

The redemption of the first-born son.[11] When a Kohen passes through on a visit, the opportunity is taken to redeem all the first-born males with an object worth five *sela'im.*[12] Afterwards, the object is in turn redeemed from the Kohen for about two or three francs. The father of the first-born son invites all those gathered to a feast of meat and plenty of brandy.

For the redemption of the first-born of a donkey, a man prepares a feast and redeems the donkey with a lamb or a kid. The lamb or kid becomes the property of the Kohen and is not redeemed from him. When the boy attains the age of observing the commandments, that is, when he has passed his thirteenth year, he puts on phylacteries on the second or fifth day of the week.[13] He is called to the Torah, and hymns are chanted, after which brandy is distributed to all those gathered in the synagogue. The youth's teacher cautions him that from now on he has reached the age when he is responsible for his own acts like the rest of the men. It is incumbent upon him to pray daily in the afternoon, evening, and morning; to keep the Sabbath with all its laws, such as not carrying an object into the public domain on that day; and to abide by the rest of the commandments. Upon their return from the synagogue, the father orders a festive meal consisting of flat *maṣah* wafers, soup, meat, or *bazīn* bread in addition to potatoes, boiled beans, and brandy.

NOTES

1. The author of this letter is Maimonides (acronym RaMBaM), and not Nachmanides (acronym RaMBaN), as stated by Hakohen. Slouschz questions Maimonides' authorship of the letter (1927:155), and this probably prompted Hakohen to suggest another source, implying the substitution of *M* for *N* as a plausible explanation for the mistake. Hakohen's version of the letter differs in some details from the one quoted and discussed by Hirschberg (1974:165–166).

2. Jerba.

3. *Aggadot* is the plural of *aggadah,* the folkloristic and homiletic material in the Talmud, while *halakhot* (plural of *halakha*) refers to the legal material.

4. Sexual contact with a menstruating woman is prohibited in Leviticus XVIII:19, but the taboos described go beyond those required by Rabbinic law.

5. The text mistakenly reads 78. Footnote 68 in Section 88, ms. p. 191b, reads as follows: "Apparently this custom was based on a misunderstanding of the verse (Leviticus XII, verse 4): 'For thirty-three . . . and in the case of a female . . . she shall not touch anything which is sanctified. . . .' This they understood to mean sexual impurity." See Zimmels (1958:198) on this extended prohibition.

6. The text mistakenly reads 78. See Moreno (1924, Chapter 13).

7. The same cloth that is used as outer dress by the women *(rda).*

8. The person who holds the child while being circumcised.

9. See Slouschz (1927:192–194).

10. Unless there is some question as to the health of the child, the law strictly requires that circumcision be performed on the eighth day after birth.

11. See Exodus XIII:2, 12–13.

12. A biblical coin.

13. Weekdays when the Torah is read publicly.

Marriage and the Wedding

(SECTION 99)

A man should fulfill his obligation to marry when he is twenty years old; a woman can do so from the age of thirteen.

Generally, the youth picks a maid at the well. Each evening, at the time for drawing water, the daughters of the town go out to a well called Ba'isi with their pitchers or leather water bottles on their shoulders. The women and girls drink from that well and draw sufficient water for all their needs.*

When a young man finds a girl to his liking, she may no longer be seen with him face to face. From the moment she is spoken for, she keeps her distance from him; she covers her face from him with the veil of shame.[1]

---

*The wells of Wadi Ba'isi are not deep. Two wells belong to the Berbers; the third has been the property of the Jews since the early days. The old deed is written on parchment and is still preserved in the hands of a Jew named Mordekhai of the 'Atiya family. In the early days, from time to time, the Berbers of the countryside rose up and brought false charges against the Jews, claiming that the water was theirs. However, the Jews won their case when they produced the ancient deed of purchase. In a dry year, when the springs are weak and thin, the water drawers must stay from dawn till night taking their turns, because the crevices of the rock are merely dripping water, and order must be maintained.

The bridegroom counts out a sum of money according to the bride price[2] of virgins, and he gives the father of the maiden the bride price and a gift. The bride price is the price of the virgin, the value being six hundred francs, or at a minimum, one hundred francs. The girl whose father does not receive the higher price suffers a great disgrace. In addition to the gifts of betrothal that are customary on the festivals, the bridegroom contributes wheat, olive oil, and the like to help the bride's father with the expenses of the wedding feast. If the father of the bride is generous and good-hearted he will provide a dowry for his daughter equivalent to the bride price and sometimes he will add extra money from his own pocket.

He who has only daughters profits from the bride price; nonetheless, the father of girls is mainly concerned that they not fall to a man of evil deeds.

The items of the dowry are appraised by the assessors[3] in the presence of the bridegroom at twice or three times their value and price, and are so written into the marriage contract[4] (see Tractate *Ketubbot,* 66).

As soon as the wedding festivities begin, the bride must demonstrate her bashfulness. She runs from her parents' home to the home of one of her relatives,[5] wrapped in a veil of modesty. Her face remains covered, and she is not to be seen with any man until the time of the wedding ceremony.

The groom must also depart from the house of his father.* He is accompanied by a youth, one of his friends, who is called the *shushbin.*[6] It is his task to watch the groom through the days of the wedding festival.

Before the wedding festival, the groom sends a species of an herb called henna to the bride's house (see Section 8, Note 11), so that the bride and her female relatives can paint her hands and feet red.[7]

The wedding celebration precedes the festival of Sukkot.[8] On the eve of the eighth of Tishrei, the bride is brought from her house of exile to her father's house. On the eve of the ninth of Tishrei, the bridegroom brings a basket of women's cosmetics wrapped in a silk sheet, together with the *bsīsa,* to the bride's father's house. (See Section 67, Note 48.)[9]

After the Day of Atonement, they take a hand mill and a plow, spread kerchiefs over them, and seat the bride on the kerchiefs (as a sign of her mastery of plowing and milling).[10] After that, they paint her hands

---

*A young man from Yefren named R[abbi] Ḥaim 'Ovadiah grew up in my home in Tripoli so that he could study the Torah. At his wedding festival, in his home town, he did not flee from the home of his parents, as is the custom there. The crowd complained about him, saying, "How dare he behave so shamefully and display such arrogance by not fleeing from his parents' home?" But he ignored the words of the crowd and paid them no mind. He just said, "Why should I flee; am I a thief?"

and feet. They also expose her hair, letting it flow down before the crowd,[11] while her face is covered with the kerchief. They sprinkle ground myrtle bud powder on her, and other perfumes sent by her groom.

The evening on which the bride is led from her father's house to her husband's house is called *lilet a-raḥla* (the night of the journey). Prior to her departure from her father's house, the bride must swallow seven twisted cotten wicks dipped in olive oil.[12] The bride walks slowly the entire way, her face covered by a veil, while two women support her, one on her right hand and one on her left. The rest of the women clap hands and sing love songs composed for the bride. Wax candles and a torch are carried before her. The men chant hymns very loudly.[13] When she arrives at the groom's room, she takes a chicken egg out of her bosom and throws it against the wall of the house so that it soils the wall. This is a reminder of the destruction of the Temple.[14]

The seven blessings[15] are recited on the night preceding the eve of the festival of Sukkot. The Rabbi reads the marriage contract aloud to those assembled in order to make public the sums written therein. This is done because sometimes the witnesses do not sign the marriage contract.[16] The public reading by the Rabbi is sufficient. For the most part, there is no marriage contract that is not the subject of a disagreement between the relatives of the bride and groom. Sometimes the seven blessings are not read until midnight.

During the day of the eve of the festival of Sukkot, the bridegroom may not leave the portals of his house, for this is his wedding day, the day which gladdens his heart. Instead, he remains dressed in beautiful clothes and makes glad the woman whom he has chosen, as he is given to her entirely for one day.

On the morning of the festival of Sukkot, his companions gather to parade him to the synagogue. He is wrapped in a fringed prayer shawl, and walks with very small steps, accompanied by hymns. If he takes a large step, one of his companions whispers in his ear, "Keep your steps slow, have you another day of joy like this?"

The groom rises and blesses the Torah scroll, to the sound of hymns, and then the prayer leader passes a small glass of brandy to all those present in the synagogue. This takes place after the groom finishes reading the portion of the Torah beginning, "And Abraham was old . . . ,"[17] in a special Torah scroll prepared for that reading. He pledges money to the Land of Israel funds, and then the Scripture beginning, "I will rejoice in the Lord . . . ,"[18] is read.

Every bridegroom is obligated to serve as a prayer leader at least once during the festival, reading the Additional Prayer[19] of the festival. If he is not familiar with it, another person may prompt him by whispering. All the grooms in one synagogue pull straws to see who will read on the first day, who on the second, and so forth.

Also, when the groom returns from the synagogue, dressed as he was when he came, his friends and comrades come to his house, eating and drinking and making merry at his table. For one month he does not enter a room where his parents are found together with his bride, for he is embarrassed to face them.

NOTES

1. The local term is *mimzūza*.

2. I have translated *mohar* as bride price, but the term is not entirely appropriate. The reference is not to a payment that effects the marriage itself, but to a betrothal agreement. The local term is *shart* (stipulation), a payment indicating the intention of the families to give their children in marriage, and comparable to the *tena'im* agreement elsewhere. See *Encyclopaedia Judaica*, vol. 4, p. 754.

3. This is done on the day of the wedding, or on the preceding day, by the notables of the community.

4. The *ketubbah*, which specifies the obligations of the husband, including the amount the woman is to receive in the event of his death, or of their divorce.

5. This avoidance custom is apparently quite old in Tripolitania, and evidence of it is found in a sixteenth-century document (Frieman 1945:111). Analyses of avoidance practices in Middle Eastern weddings are found in Peters (1965), Barth (1971), and Mason (1975:660). These various authors deal with Cyrenaican material. See Hirschberg's (1974:171) remarks on possible Berber influence.

6. The term in the local dialect is *shuash*.

7. Henna is the shrub *Lawsonia inermis*. While henna is used in celebrations throughout the Middle East, it may have special significance to Jewish groups, who are forbidden by a biblical injunction from using tatoos as a method of beautification. Hakohen provides the following information on henna (Section 8, Note 11, ms. p. 18a): "Henna: an herb of the garden-seed variety [*sic*]. The leaves are similar in form to myrtle leaves. The women grind these greens in order to beautify their hands and feet with color. Formerly, Tripoli imported henna by sea from the city of Gabes in Tunisia. Recently, however, the farmers have learned how to plant it. They have been pleased with their efforts, for they have earned a great deal of money from it."

8. The celebration of all the weddings at the time of Sukkot (the Festival of Booths in the autumn) may be rooted in the local economy. Since a large portion of the Jews of Yefren were itinerant peddlers, it was only at the holiday season that everyone could be present to partake in the celebrations. In addition, it may be that at this season of the year the Jewish artisans were well supplied with gifts in kind, paid after the harvest, by their steady Moslem clients. It is also possible that the custom has some connection to the following talmudic passage (Tractate *Berakhot* 59b): "At what period of time does one recite the benediction on rain? After the groom goes forth to meet the bride."

9. Hakohen's Note explaining *bsīsa* is translated in n. 38 to Section 97.

10. This act probably symbolizes conjugal relations, in addition to stressing domestic duties. See Bourdieu (1977:45, 208, n. 78) and Richards (1956:164).

11. After marriage, a woman should not expose her hair to men outside her family.

12. Cotton wicks are also used in memorial lamps and may be symbolically associated with the perpetuity of individual life and family ties (Goldberg 1973b), which are highlighted when a woman moves from one family to another.

13. The men lead the procession.

14. This is almost certainly a secondary interpretation, since the sexual symbolism is transparent. Hakohen describes how a similar custom is practiced among the Jews of Tripoli (Section 89, ms. p. 195a), and raises the question of the meaning of the symbol: "When she [the bride] reaches the groom's house, the people refrain from entering until the groom ascends the roof, and, with all his might, throws a jug full of water crashing to the ground—in memory of the destruction of the Holy Temple. The women cry out [*zgharit*] with joy, but it would be proper to sing a lament, because the crash recalls the mourning over the Holy Temple." The bride must step through the broken pieces of the jug to enter the house. Then she throws an egg against the wall.

15. The standard blessings recited at a marriage ceremony (Hertz 1948:1006).

16. This appears to neglect the law, but it may in fact stem from the desire to observe the law. In Rabbinic law, a kinsman is not a legally valid witness and would nullify the marriage contract if he were to sign it. As many people in Yefren (and the other small communities) were interrelated, there is a chance that almost everyone is related to either the bride or the groom. By not signing the contract, this possible complication is avoided.

17. Genesis XXIV. This describes Abraham's search for a wife for his son.

18. Isaiah (LXI:10).

19. A fourth prayer service in addition to the three services normal on weekdays (Idelsohn 1960:xvi).

Women's Household Routine

(SECTION 100)

When a man spends a great deal of money to obtain a wife for himself he does not waste it, because the women of the region stand behind the prince of their youth.[1]

They are very industrious, both in the house and at work in the fields. They do all those tasks, mentioned in the Tractate *Ketubbot* [Babylonian Talmud], page 59, which a wife does for her husband, such as grinding, baking, and so forth.[2] They do them all except for making the bed (because they have no beds).

They grind flour in a mill made of two wide, round stones, the upper and lower millstones. They grind the barley with the millstones during the early morning[3] watch.* They grind enough to feed the entire household for that day. While working, they sing special grinding songs. The woman who does not get up in the early morning to grind can never erase her shame. She is called lazy because people say, "How is it possible that she will not rise when it is still night to prepare food for her household?"

The new bride, however, is exempted from grinding for a month after the wedding because in the dowry brought from her father's house there is enough flour to provide meals for that time. She is free to delight herself with her lover until dawn.

Recently some camel-driven mills were established in Yefren; however most of the women continue the old custom of grinding by hand. The women bake bread, thick round cakes, and wafers on the walls of an oven that opens from the top. They light the oven with straw, rakings, peat, and wood.

They wash their clothes infrequently because they are not too concerned about cleanliness. Instead of soap, they generally launder with a substance made of natron,[4] which they hew out of a well-known cave. In the year 1899, as they were leaving the cave, part of the mountain collapsed on them. Some of the women were only slightly injured, but some perished.

The women of the region cook diligently in earthenware pots, copper pots, and kettles. They cook on flames, while columns of smoke rise straight up from the kindled wood and broom roots.

The woman of Yefren nurses her child with excessive compassion. She carries him on her shoulders or puts him in a cage-like cradle, which is suspended by ropes so that it swings back and forth and rocks the baby to sleep.

The women work in wool. They spin sheep's wool and weave sheets and embroidered carpets. The work is clean, and done in a traditional manner, both in the equipment used and in the style of the weaving. In years that bring a large profit, a woman takes an extra burden upon herself. "She perceives that her merchandise is good: her lamp goes not out by night. She puts her hand to the distaff, and the palms of her hands hold the spindle."[5]

The women are exempt from the task of bed-making, one of the seven tasks a woman is obliged to do for her husband that are listed in

---

*We thus can understand the intention of the verse (Proverbs XXXI, verse 15), "She rises also while it is yet night, and sets forth provisions for her household, and the portion for her maidens." The first time I went up to the mountains, I was astounded; early in the morning, I heard music that seemed to come from the ends of the earth, the thundering noise of wheels and songs that were strange to my ear. I asked, "What is this awful noise throughout the town?" and was told that this is the time set aside for grinding the grain.

the Tractate *Ketubbot*. They are exempt from this because they do not have beds, pillows, or blankets to lie on. Instead, they cushion the ground beneath them by spreading mats of straw and sacks on the floor, or by using carpets or skins. They lay their heads down on a slab of rock which protrudes from the floor of the house. Sometimes they roll over and their head ends up in a depression, with the body higher than the head. Despite this, they get up strong and healthy because this is what they have become accustomed to. They go to bed when it gets dark, and their sleep is sweet.

Instead of bed-making the women draw water and chop wood. They draw the water from the well named Ba'isi, which is in the wadi.

On Friday mornings[6] the women go out, organized in families, scattering afar in the forest and the fields. They go barefoot over thorns and briers, the distance of a two-hour walk, to gather enough straw and wood to bake and cook throughout the following week. They return at noon, each carrying a bundle of wood on her head weighing about fifty kilograms.

It was to no avail that the Rabbinic authorities in Tripoli issued a decree threatening to excommunicate all the women who went out to chop wood.[7] The women paid no heed to the decree, for any woman who did so would have been considered lazy, and no one wished to bear that shame. They did not pay heed to the decree, saying that it was unjust: "Our forebears who did the same were like angels,[8] and no one protested against them."

In addition to all the painstaking chores that the women do, they also lend a hand in plowing and reaping and related work in the nearby fields. They help beat the olive trees and work in the olive press. Not only that, they all raise egg-laying chickens, and all the while their children flitter about.

NOTES

1. This statement should be contrasted with a well-known maxim in the Talmud that "A man should sell everything that he owns and marry the daughter of a scholar" (Babylonian Talmud, Tractate *Pesaḥim* 49a). The attitude reflected in this chapter may be that of a city dweller admiring the industry, devotion, and "unspoiled" character of village women.

2. These tasks are grinding, baking, laundering, cooking, nursing, making the bed, and weaving. In this section, Hakohen follows the order listed in the Mishnah, except that he reverses the last two items.

3. The early morning grinding is also mentioned by Benjamin (1859:291).

4. Sesquicarbonate of soda.

5. Here Hakohen simply quotes two verses from the chapter in Proverbs he cited above (XXXI:18–19).

6. The eve of the Sabbath.

7. Presumably because of the immodest exposure to men involved in this activity.

8. A Talmudic saying (*Shabbat* 112b) suggests that the people of former generations were like the "sons of angels." In comparison, the present generation are simply "men."

Death

(SECTION 101)

When a person dies, the women begin to cry and wail so that the people will gather to pay their last respects. All the Jews stop work. They do not light a fire until after the deceased has been buried.

The coffin of the deceased is taken out. The women surround the coffin holding sticks in their hands with which to beat on it and sound the call far and wide. This beating is called *tabel* (drumming).[1]

One of the women sings a lament, and her companions respond as a chorus. They wear kerchiefs on their heads and dance, gashing their skin, as is their custom.[2] The female relatives of the deceased pair off two by two, embracing one another, each one with her head on the neck of her companion. They wail in anguish and recall the good qualities of the deceased. For example, if he was a scholar they say: "Woe, the reader of the Torah i-i-i-i" or "beloved of all the people i-i-i-i."

They do not have a burial society.[3] The mourning relatives of the deceased, and no one else, wash the body, dress it in shrouds, and carry the wooden coffin[4] on their shoulders to the cemetery. Strangers are forbidden to come near and help. No Jew is permitted to bring them shrouds, or soap, or any other item, either as a purchase or as a gift. The members of the community may not conduct business with a mourner during all the days of mourning. They cannot derive benefit from his possessions, nor may he benefit from the possessions of others. One is not permitted to talk to a mourner except when absolutely necessary and then only quickly and briefly.

The deceased is buried in the newly dug ground. Those who are fastidious about religious observance dig their own sepulcher and leave a verbal testament, saying, "In the sepulcher which I have dug, there you shall bury me [Genesis L:5]."

After the deceased is buried, the mourners and the people around them gather for the comforting of the mourners in an open place under the sky that was purchased long ago with synagogue funds.

When the mourners return home, they bring with them grass from ownerless fields for the meal of recovery,[5] for other people will not give them a thing.

The whole neighborhood of the deceased is cleansed of water and leaven.[6] The mourners eat only *maṣah* wafers during the mourning period. These wafers are called *ftira*.[7]

Should a stranger die there, he is left lying until a brave-hearted man volunteers to do what is necessary on his behalf. If a stranger receives word of a death in his family, all the Jews keep their distance from him during the mourning period.* They do not speak to him, neither of good nor of evil. They do not even give him a kettle with which to cook, either as a purchase or as a gift. He can only find refuge among the Berbers till his period of mourning is over.

*In 1885, I was there with a Tripolitan Jew named Khamus Kuandi. He received word of a death in his family, and he removed himself from the community, going to sit in a Berber's home for the period of mourning. The gentleman in whose home we were guests was Eliyahu ʿAtiya, a local notable. He boldly set aside the custom and brought Kuandi back to his own house, against the wishes of the people. I, the author, had in my belongings a revolver that I carried for protection against highwaymen. Kuandi took the revolver in his hand in complete innocence, and, as if by the work of the devil, he hit Mr. Nissim ʿAtiya, the brother of our host, in the shoulder with a lead bullet. The whole town rose up, saying, "Mr. Eliyahu ʿAtiya was punished by the Creator because he desecrated the honor of our forebears. He burst the bounds of custom and made light of mourning." Nevertheless, they hushed up the incident so that Kuandi would not fall into the hands of the government. Nissim was saved from death because the Berber doctor cut out the bullet from his flesh. Even so, the people were agitated, fearing that evil would befall them because the custom had been ignored.

I happened to walk in the wadi, and a woman was drawing from the well. I said to her, "Please, would you give me a little drink of water from your pitcher?" The girl screamed and drew back, saying, "Who gave the evil man permission to speak thus?"

I began to tremble and stepped closer in order to ask her what obscenity I had uttered. At that, she retreated even further and screamed in a loud voice, "Come save me from this wickedness." I thought to myself, "Perhaps the people will believe her, that I spoke obscenities; after all, I am a stranger in the land." So I stepped back and, speaking soberly and softly, begged forgiveness, explaining, "I am a Jew, a stranger in the land. Please tell me how I have sinned and what was the obscenity I uttered."

She gazed down on the earth, as if she were only speaking to the ground, which has no laws of mourning, and she said, "Who gave the mourner permission to speak to me?"

I suddenly became bold and said, "I am not Kuandi, the mourner." She then spoke directly to me, saying, "Are you Mordechai Hakohen, the merchant? Excuse me, I offended you; I mistook you for Kuandi, the mourner. Please, drink now, sir."

I discussed the reason for this foolish custom with the leaders of the Jews. They said to me, "Behold the verse in the Scripture, 'I gave none of it for the dead.' "[8] Then I explained to them the meaning of the verse, and I proved it, saying that the RaMBaN was correct in his letter when he likened them to the Karaites.[9]

They customarily refrain from shaving for a full year after the death of a father or mother. But if the beard becomes too heavy, they trim it with scissors.

They do not place tombstones over the graves because the Berbers break them.

They hold memorial gatherings at the end of one month, at the end of six months, and at the end of a year. At the memorial gathering, they prepare a meal for all the community. Then they pray the afternoon and evening prayers, listen to a Torah lesson, and read portions from the Mishnah.[10]

From the time of Ghoma's death, the land has been peaceful throughout the period of Turkish rule.[11]

NOTES

1. Hakohen's Note 39 in Section 40, ms. p. 74b, describes this practice: "It is customary for the Ishmaelites to make a drum, a loud instrument called *ṭabel*. This is how the *ṭabel* is made: a flat skin is fastened over a large wooden bowl. When one beats upon it, the sound can be heard over long distances. They beat this drum during wedding celebrations to accompany their singing, and also while wailing for the dead, as was customary among the Jews in ancient times. The sounds of the drum make up distinct conventional signs and signals. In the case of rebellion and war, there are two quick beats and one delayed beat. If they want the people to gather, they beat at infrequent intervals, and so forth.

"Perhaps we can understand the etymology of the terms that our forebears gave to the sounds of the *shofar*. These are called *teqi'ah* [a stem meaning "to insert strongly," *e.g.* a stake in the ground], *teru'ah* [a stem meaning "a loud noise"], and *shevarim* [a stem meaning "to break"]. One can see, upon examination, that they are the names of beats. In Arabic too the word "beat" is used in reference to the ram's horn and the trumpet, and all sorts of instruments are called *drab* (beats). The terms *teqi'ah, teru'ah,* and *shevarim* at first referred to drum beats. Afterwards, when wind instruments were invented, the terms were borrowed and applied to the sounds used to assemble the congregation, for the march of the camp [Numbers X:2], and so forth."

2. This directly contravenes biblical law (*cf.* Leviticus XIX:28).

3. In most communities, funeral preparations are the responsibility of a special group or set of individuals, as was the case in Tripoli.

4. The coffin is used to carry the body to the cemetery, not as a burial casket. The body is buried in shrouds.

5. This is called *se'udat havra'ah*. The standard Jewish practice is for mourners to be provided with a meal after returning home from the funeral, thus officially beginning the week-long mourning period. Here, because of the taboo placed on the mourners, they must take grass from ownerless fields.

6. It is a widespread practice to throw water out of the house of a deceased person, but the custom of getting rid of leaven is unusual. Perhaps it developed as a "logical" correlate of eating the *maṣah* (unleavened bread).

7. This is the local Arabic term for these large "wafers." It is homophonic

with the Hebrew *feṭira(h)*, meaning "passing away" (dying). Perhaps this custom derives from the linguistic usage.

8. Deuteronomy XXVI:14. The verse means that the tithe which the Israelite offers should not have been used for ritual purposes involved with the dead.

9. The reference is to Maimonides' letter that was cited in Section 98. In both the avoidance of contact with menstruating women and the avoidance of mourners, the Jews of Yefren observe taboos not required by standard Jewish practice. The statement that they are like Karaites suggests that these practices are due to an overly literal interpretation of the Torah, while Maimonides' letter also suggests that they may have adopted these practices from their non-Jewish surroundings. Given the relative isolation of the Yefren community from Rabbinic centers, these customs develop and persist in the absence of a religious authority which might modify them.

10. The word Mishnah contains the same consonants as the Hebrew word for soul, NShMH. The practice was based on this equation, and became very popular through the influence of Lurianic mysticism (Scholem 1946:285).

11. This sentence appears to have been inserted after the main part of the text was written. Hakohen thus concludes the description of the Jews of Yefren and moves on to a less detailed survey of the other rural communities. Ghoma, the Berber leader, is discussed in various sources (Slouschz 1908a; Féraud 1927; Rossi 1968; the Editor's Foreword to Chapter One).

CHAPTER FIVE

The Other Small Communities

Editor's Foreword

After providing an extensive description of the Jews of Yefren, Hakohen goes on to give briefer accounts of the other Jewish communities in the hinterland. Some of his information is best analyzed in terms of continuing demographic trends (Goldberg 1971). When we compare his population estimates with other figures, they appear to be on the high side. A number of the communities he visited are quite old (Yefren, Ghuryan, Mesallata, Zawia, 'Amrus, Tajura, Zliten, Misurata); Jewish residence there has been continuous for at least several centuries. Other towns (such as Zuara, Zanzur, Khoms, and Sirte) have been founded only recently. The new coastal communities presumably were settled as a result of increased security in the countryside after the Turks established their rule. Later, after the Italian takeover, other new communities were formed in the interior, such as Terhuna, Beni'ulid, Nalut, and Mizda. These new towns probably were familiar to peddlers such as those met by Hakohen and Slouschz south of Jado (see Section 90). Later, under favorable conditions, these men established more permanent residence there together with their families.

The increase in the number of small communities should not, however, obscure the basic trend in the population as a whole. By examining the figures over the last century (Goldberg 1971), we see that the Jewish population of the city of Tripoli grew at a much more rapid rate than the Jewish population of the towns. There was no large migration from other countries and there is no direct evidence of a swift drop in infant mortality in the city as compared to the countryside. It seems, then, that throughout this period there was a continual, if undramatic, flow of Jews from the rural towns into the city (Goldberg *et al.* 1979). This parallels the general flow of the Moslem population (Harrison 1967). It also sug-

TRIPOLITANIA

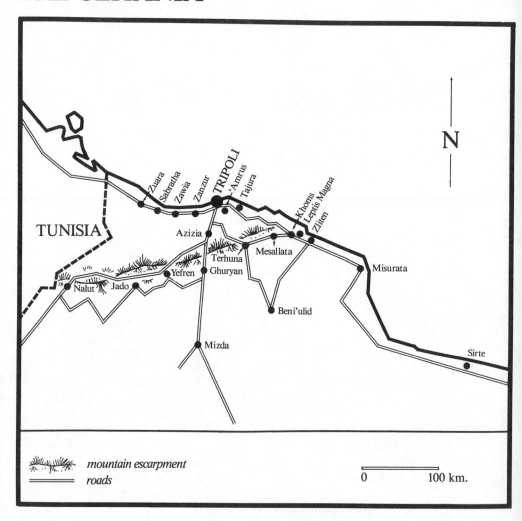

TUNISIA

Zuara
Sabratha
Zawia
Zanzur
TRIPOLI
Amrus
Tajura

Khoms
Leptis Magna
Zliten

Azizia

Mesallata

Terhuna
Ghuryan

Misurata

Yefren

Nalut
Jado

Beni'ulid

Mizda

Sirte

N

mountain escarpment
roads

0   100 km.

gests that we should not look for sharp differences in the customs of the Tripolitan Jews as compared to their rural counterparts (Goldberg 1974a).

Hakohen's portrait of the different villages is somewhat monotonous. The Jews specialized in trades and crafts. Their status as Jews entailed certain liabilities. Their communal organization revolved around, or was given form by, life in the synagogue, whose history and welfare were an indication of the well-being of the Jewish population. Hakohen's emphasis on synagogues and cemeteries is not an *idée fixe;* instead it reflects the view of the villagers themselves. After they had moved to Israel, the Jews of Ghuryan sometimes asked me if I was able to visit their original home in Libya. When I said that I might, one man replied, "If you go there, let us know about the synagogue and the cemetery; that's all we care about" (Goldberg 1972a:33).

As we have seen, communal institutions rooted in religious laws were common throughout the region. Thus we find few differences between the "remote" mountain communities and the coastal oasis towns (Goldberg 1974a). The same kinds of institutions, though on a larger scale, were also found in the city of Tripoli. In fact, Hakohen's presentation of the material implies a kind of urban-rural continuum, without the sociological implications that Redfield (1948) gave to that term. The customs of the city of Tripoli are discussed at length in Part II of the *Highid Mordekhai* (Moreno 1924, n.d.). Part III, which we have translated in this volume, begins with a detailed account of the Nefusa Jews, who are the most remote of the village communities. For the most part, details about customs are omitted in describing the other towns; Hakohen merely indicates whether their customs are similar to those of the Nefusa Jews or to those of the Tripolitans.

We also do not find any basic shifts in the focus of religious authority or worship. In Morocco, the tombs of revered Rabbis are often the sites of pilgrimages (*cf.* Voinot 1948), but saints like these are hardly mentioned by Hakohen. In contrast, several synagogues which embody the standard tradition are centers of popular veneration. Similarly, in the town of Derna in Cyrenaica there is a venerated Torah scroll which is viewed as the physical manifestation of established Jewish religion (see Noy 1967), possessing special powers that in other areas are attributed to saintly Rabbis. Thus, although there are few men of learning in the villages—or, perhaps more correctly, *because* there are few—there is no claim to an alternative religious tradition, and the Rabbis of Tripoli are recognized as the standard-bearers of the law.

There is, however, one interesting story (Section 87, Note 67, ms. p. 187b) concerning a saint's tomb, and it concerns the city of Tripoli itself. Near *suq a-tlat* is the tomb of a marabout named ibn-Limam. A Jewish legend records that Rabbi Shim'on Lavi, who is considered to have restored Judaism in Tripoli in the sixteenth century (see Section 97, n. 7, and Hirschberg 1969:182), requested permission of Suliman Dey Pasha to be buried not in the Jewish cemetery but near ibn-Limam's tomb. The precise location of Rabbi Shim'on's grave is unknown. Tradition has it that before the Rabbi's burial there, Jews would avoid passing near ibn-Limam's tomb at midday on Fridays. They believed that a spirit of madness would come forth from the tomb, seize a Jew, and force him to utter the profession of faith in Mohammed, prophet of God.[1] However, from the time of Rabbi Lavi's burial, the spirit lost its power. This belief in the evil spirit seems to suggest that Jews should keep away from the tomb when Moslems gather for prayer at the nearby Zawiat a-Dari'a mosque. It also implies that without the spiritual intervention of Lavi, the Jews of Tripoli were in danger of being assimilated by the Moslem majority. This belief thus states, in a different form, the view that before the Rabbi's arrival in Tripoli religious ignorance was widespread, and that for all practical purposes he had to convert them. Presumably Tripoli was the center from which Lavi's influence, as well as later Rabbinic influences, reached the outlying villages.[2]

The Jewish community in Benghazi, described at length in Section 110, also derives primarily from Tripolitania. Hakohen's argument that the settlement of the Jewish community in Benghazi was continuous from antiquity to his day is not convincing. Instead, the town seems to have been settled in modern times in the fifteenth and sixteenth centuries by Moslem and Jewish merchants from Tripolitanian towns, particularly Misurata (Evans-Pritchard 1949:41; Bulguma 1968:44–45). The dialect and customs of the Jews are essentially Tripolitanian, even though there may have been specific influences from Alexandria and other communities to the east.

Hakohen calls Benghazi a "village," like the other Tripolitanian towns, and the small nineteenth-century population there appears to have contained a large proportion of Jews. The Jewish community was under the jurisdiction of the Rabbinic court in Tripoli, but with the growth in the community's size it began to develop its own institutions. As noted in the Editor's Introduction, Hakohen served on the Rabbinical court in Benghazi after 1920.

NOTES

1. A Jew can agree to the first half of the Moslem profession of faith, "There is no God but Allah," but he cannot accept the second half, "Mohammed is the apostle of God."
2. See Goldberg (1974c).

Ghuryan

(SECTION 102)

In the mountain range[1] there is a small settlement called Ghuryan[2] (caves), about a twenty-two-hour walk southwest of Tripoli. There they dwell in houses built in the caves.[3] Each courtyard consists of an area about ten meters square that has been dug out. The depth is also approximately ten meters. One descends to the courtyard by way of an opening on the ground level that has a bolted door. One goes through the door and down a dark underground incline, about fifteen meters long, until one reaches the entrance of the courtyard. This wide entrance receives light through the open courtyard.

The rooms, on the sides of the court, consist of caverns dug into the bosom of the earth. They have no windows, but they receive light from the sun, which shines down into the courtyard; in this way they are similar to other walled houses built around a courtyard in which only the surrounding rooms have ceilings. A person walking across the fields is actually treading on the roofs of these cave rooms. If he has to talk to the owner of one of the houses, he does not have to go to the trouble of going down into the dark, through the door that leads to the inclined entrance. Instead, he looks down from the roof of the rooms, and the owner comes out of his room to talk to him. These rooms are protected from thieves because the doors are thick and strong, made with blocks of olive wood.

They drink rain water from cisterns dug out in the fields. In dry years, when the water in the cisterns does not suffice, they supplement their needs from the springs which flow from the clefts of the rocks. There are some streams of water that flow all year round. Ghuryan and Yefren are a twelve-hour walk apart. In Qiqla, there is a place called Assuadna which is a four-hour walk from Yefren and an eight-hour walk from Ghuryan. There, a stream flows in a ravine called Wad Assuadna. Between Assuadna and Ghuryan is a stream called Wadi Misqa. There is also a stream called Wadi Ghentan. Also, in a place called Rabta, there are two streams, one called Wadi Rabta a-Sharqiya (the Eastern Wadi Rabta) and the second called Wadi Rabta al-Gharbiya (the Western). Long ago, the early Romans paved an aqueduct so that the waters of Rabta could descend from the mountain to the wide plains called Gaṭṭis. However, when the Vandals gained the upper hand and took the district by force from the Romans (as I have described in Section 12), the aqueducts were abandoned and the soil of Gaṭṭis remained parched. Even now, the remains of the aqueduct built by the Romans can still be recognized.

The district of Ghuryan itself has many springs. At the foot of the mountain in the Plain of Gaṭṭis is a perennial stream called Wadi al-'Ugla. At the foot of the Ghuryan Mountains is a stream called Wadi Bujilan. Above, in the mountains, is one called Wad Dannui, one called Wad Ghan, one called Wad a-Nekhal (the wadi of dates), one called Wad al-Kemishat, one called Wad a-Ṣlahat, one called Wad Bu-'Ayyad, and one called Wad Teghessat, which is the closest to the government castle built by the Turks.

Her[4] soil is fertile; shrubs and all kinds of grassses grow plentifully. There are olive trees, dates, palms, and grapevines in abundance. However, there are very few garden crops because of the indolence of the inhabitants. There are many fields sufficiently watered by rain as well as ones irrigated by perennial streams. The choicest saffron grows there in abundance.[5] One kilogram is sold for approximately sixty francs. The soil is good for growing many varieties of fruit trees, but the inhabitants do not work the soil well; they retain only remnants of the skills they inherited from their forefathers. (Let us hope that as the district is captured by the Italians they will reveal their ability to work and the land will give forth its fruit.)

The Jews settled in the district of Ghuryan in the second century of the Christian era, as mentioned in Section 11.[6] (It is quite possible that Jews lived there even before that time, but we have no definite proof of it.)

At about the time of the capture of Tripoli by the Darghut Pasha, as mentioned in Section 20, wars broke out in Algeria. In the year 1555, a Jew named Ḥajjaj fled from the city of Oran in Algeria and settled in the land of Ghuryan. He was an expert ironworker, knew how to repair weapons, and was an expert marksman. He was also proficient in medicine. He was an orator who captured the hearts of his listeners with the smoothness of his speech. The people received him gladly and gave him honor. They then chose him as their chief. He instilled in them the courage to throw off the yoke of the rule of Tripoli.* They declared a revolt with him as their leader.[7]

---

*In a Moslem book called *Ta'rīkh Ṭrablus al-Gharb (The History of Western Tripoli)*, side 218, it is written, "In the year 982 (their date, which is equivalent to the Hebrew 5334, or the Christian 1574) a man named al-Ḥajjaj arose in the town of Ghuryan. The poor masses followed him. . . ." Perhaps he is the same Jew, Ḥajjaj, whom I found in the manuscripts of Abraham Khalfon. Even though the Moslem book makes no mention of his nationality, there are many entries with the Jewish name Ḥajjaj in the ancient property registers. But in this book the name is written al-Ḥajjaj. The *al* at the beginning of a word is a definite article, and personal names do not take the definite article at the beginning of the word. On the other hand, there is a tribe living in the Fezzan region called al-Ḥajjaj. Only the Almighty knows with certainty. It is also possible that Ghuryan is really the Burion that is mentioned in Part I, Note 20.

In those days, there were many, many Jews there. One town was named Kammun after a Jewish lineage head whose surname was Kammun. Another town was called Abu 'Ayyad, also after the surname of a Jew. Another town named Jehisha is completely inhabited by a tribe of Jews called Hassan.[8] To this day, one can find remains and traces of the synagogue and the Jewish cemetery there. In a town called al-Gmamish one also can find a Jewish cemetery. Today[9] there are no Jews living in the Ghuryan area, except for about eight hundred Israelites divided into two settlements. One is called Tighrinna, and all of her inhabitants are Jews. This village is about a twenty-two-hour walk from Tripoli. The other village, called Ben'abbas,[10] is at the beginning of the Ghuryan region, a distance of sixteen hours from Tripoli.

NOTES

1. *I.e.* the whole range south of Tripoli.
2. Also written Ghurian, Gharian, and so forth.
3. See Despois' (1935) description of the "grand court" type of dwelling, and the references in Goldberg (1972a:35).
4. Presumably Wadi Teghessat; see Khuja (1960) on the town of Teghessat.
5. The saffron of the Ghuryan was mentioned by Leo Africanus in the sixteenth century (tr. 1847:743). In Section 43, Hakohen describes how the Jews of the Ghuryan were fined by the Turkish governor and made to pay in saffron.
6. The evidence cited by Hakohen in Section 11 is very weak, but we do know of Jewish settlements outside of Tripoli in Roman times (Hirschberg 1974:27, 40).
7. The story of this rebellion is discussed by Hirschberg (1965b).
8. One should not attach much sociological importance to Hakohen's use of the term "tribe" here (Goldberg 1967), or of the term "lineage."
9. The twentieth-century Jews of the region are depicted in Goldberg (1972a).
10. The community of Ben'abbas is the subject of a study by al-Ahmar (1976). There is a historical emphasis in this work, but no mention is made of the former Jewish community.

Customs of the Jews of Ghuryan

(SECTION 103)

The Jews are very diligent workers both at home and in the field, for they know how to plow and reap. However, they refrain from working the soil because of the strong religious hatred of the inhabitants, who steal the fruit of their crops and their labors, leaving them only a pittance to reap.

They are very haughty and pursue honors. They are always fighting over positions of leadership.[1] In the early days, most of them were wealthy, but now they are so poor that they must borrow from the Moslems and pay interest.

There are those among them who take two wives, even those who have children from their first wife.[2] If a man is not pleased with his wife, he takes her to the Rabbinic court in Tripoli, writes her a bill of divorce, and delivers it to her.

The Jews of Ghuryan are not learned in the Torah. On the Sabbath they study the Bible and Midrashim. They also get up in early hours of the morning to study the Book of the Zohar.[3] They don't understand what they read, but they still earn the reward of studying.

They are drinkers and also have an enormous appetite for large pieces of meat. Each person has a Mohammedan friend who stands by his side to help him against a fellow Jew who may oppose him. If a youth desires a certain maiden, but her father refuses to give her to him, then the youth's Mohammedan friend intervenes in the affair so that the youth gets the maiden against her father's wishes.[4]

They have the same customs for weddings, circumcisions, avoidance of the menstruant, commerce, and crafts as their brethren in Yefren. There is no difference between them, except that the Jewish form of slaughter is rejected by the Moslems. Should an animal be found ritually unfit, it is sold very cheaply.[5] Most of them know how to cut out the thigh muscle from the hindquarter, because the Mohammedans will not buy that part unless it is very cheap.

Besides their monopoly of crafts and commerce, most of the Jews are knowledgeable in medicine. They cure the sick with animals,* in-

---

*A Jew named Sa'id Shinin was traveling with a caravan one night when all of a sudden he let out a terrible scream and then stood dumb. His friends gathered around to find out what had happened, and they discovered that a serpent had torn his shoe and bitten his heel. A few friends began to bind his leg so that the poison would not spread to the rest of his body. Others sped like lightning to the nearby Bedouin tents. They brought back the interior of a certain reptile called *wīl* (lizard). They warmed this substance over a fire, then cut open the area of the bite with a razor and poured a little on it (because the *wīl* is constantly fighting the snake). Lo and behold, in a short time, the bitten man was saved. He stood whole and healthy; it seemed like a work of magic.

I, the author, was afflicted with some rotting molars. The decay began to spread to all of the molars, and I had a pain in one of them on the left side. The sheikh of the Jews in the town of Ghuryan was Rabbi Khalifa Ḥajjaj. He was learned in the Midrash and the Aggadah[6] as well as being a doctor. He cauterized the joint of my right thumb in order to treat the rot. From the minute he cauterized my thumb, the disease ceased. I asked him why, if the pain and rot were on the left side, he had cauterized the right side. He answered that the veins and arteries go from right to left and left to right.[7]

The same sheikh of the Jews is a wonderfully skilled gunsmith, and a marks-

sects, and reptiles; with herbs and other drugs; and with bloodletting and cautery. They have learned these methods both from their predecessors and from experience. There are some kinds of illnesses which European doctors have not been able to cure; despite this, the Arab doctors treat them easily, in a way that seems beyond comprehension. Perhaps they have some special supernatural power, or have discovered an unknown natural force.

The sheikh of the Jews is the intermediary between the Jews and the government. He collects the head tax and gives it to the treasury. The government bestows its authority upon him, including the power to imprison and to set free.[9]

Most of the men wear gold or silver earrings. As for the rest of their costume, it is no different from that of their brethren in Yefren, except that the people of Ghuryan wrap an old kerchief about their heads.

Jewish burial differs greatly from the Mohammedan practice. They dig a hole in the ground about three or four cubits deep, and at the bottom, on the side, they dig out a cavity, the length of the deceased.

man too. He could hit a bull's eye with a pistol at a great distance. All these skills he inherited from his forefathers. In the year 1885, the Turkish government sent a special doctor, a professor, and his assistants from Constantinople to study Arab medicine and medical practices. These Turkish doctors were very pleased with the work of the Jewish sheikh, Dr. Khalifa Ḥajjaj, in the town of Ghuryan. They saw the skill of his hands when he cut a stomach into sections and when he opened the brain membrane of an injured head. After the operation, he covered the membrane with the skin of a gourd. A few days later, a web of skin would form on the head and slowly pull together to form a new membrane. His operations on the rest of the limbs of the body were also very successful. In their presence, he operated on a donkey's stomach and removed a stone that was blocking the urinary tract. In their presence, he also cured a lung disease and other sicknesses by means of cauterization. He did everything quickly and efficiently, and showed them all kinds of drugs and herbs. The Turkish professor praised Khalifa. In addition, he also took some instruments Khalifa had made, for he was skilled in iron work. He could fan a charcoal fire and make his tools. The Turkish doctors thanked him for all his labors and returned to Tripoli.

At about this time, a Tripolitan Jew named Judah Lighzayil was injured by soldiers in the fields. They stole his money and shot him in the loins with a lead bullet. The governor, Ahmed Razem Pasha, brought the criminals to justice and ordered the surgeons to try with all their might to extract the bullet from his loins and save him from death. They seemed to toil for naught because the injured man was in a terrible condition. His relatives sent to the Ghuryan for the sheikh, Khalifa. He cleverly removed the lead ball by twisting, without causing any further injury. Because of that, Ahmed Razem Pasha honored Khalifa and gave him a diploma of certification attesting to his expertise in surgery.

In the year 1900, the head of the criminal courts was overcome by the pain of diseased and swollen legs. He sent a telegram to the Qaimaqam of Ghuryan requesting that he please send Dr. Khalifa Ḥajjaj as quickly as possible. Dr. Khalifa came to Tripoli and examined the illness. He prepared some drugs and

They place the deceased in this cavity, seal it with a wooden board, and afterward seal up the whole grave.

Prior to the burial, they arrange a sermon in honor of the deceased and distribute *bsīsa*,[10] made of parched grain kneaded with olive oil, to the children. They follow the practice of the Jews of Yefren in all of the other customs pertaining to death and mourning.

They have three synagogues. There is an ancient one in the village of Ben'abbas.[11] In this generation, they tore it down with the intention of raising a new building. However, Mohammedan troublemakers protested, saying, "It is forbidden to build a synagogue near a Moslem place of worship, and the Jews must move from there." It so happened that in a hole in the wall they found an ancient deed written on parchment stating the date of the founding of the synagogue. The Jews won the right to build without interference because the synagogue had been founded before the Mohammedans came to the region. The Mohammedans' house of prayer was therefore on the synagogue's premises.

covered the man's legs with a lead-plated sheet of tin to suck out the disease. The disease was healed as if by a miracle.

A certain Moslem notable named 'Ali Biram had a severe illness in which all his body was swollen. The doctors had almost given up hope for him. The same Khalifa bled him with a surgeon's knife. Foul and stinking fluid flowed from his body. In a short time, he regained his health. He saw that he had improved. He became angry and reviled the other doctors and praised Dr. Khalifa, saying, "He has never set foot in a medical school and despite that he is wiser than all the other doctors." Dr. Khalifa gave him these instructions: "Even if you feel as healthy as you were before, be very careful and do not eat anything which is not clean, nor any heavy food." However, 'Ali Biram, paying no attention to his words, said, "Now I am stronger than the doctor." He ate as many heavy foods as he pleased, couscous and ram's meat. He fell ill again and died. When this occurred, the doctors wrote and signed a document stating that Khalifa had murdered 'Ali Biram because the knife he had used in the bleeding had been rusty. The matter dragged on till 1902, when the government prosecutor charged Khalifa with the murder of 'Ali Biram. Khalifa was imprisoned and called to give an account of himself as a result of the doctors' decision. I, the author, hired a defense attorney for him for two hundred francs. The attorney argued in criminal court, saying that Khalifa had a diploma stating that he was an accomplished doctor and that the other doctors' claims were contradictory. They said Khalifa of Ghuryan had murdered 'Ali Biram because he had bled him with a rusty knife. However, they should only have claimed that Khalifa contributed to the death; one cannot say he murdered unless he came with the intention of killing. The criminal court sentenced Khalifa to a month's imprisonment because he did not check to make sure the surgeon's knife was not rusty.

However, the court of appeals cleared him of all charges on the basis that since the doctors' testimony was partially invalid it should be considered totally invalid. Moreover, Khalifa had a written medical certification.[8] (Khalifa passed away in 1913.)

There are two synagogues in the Jewish hamlet of Tighrinna. One is an ancient underground cavern without ornamentation and without windows. Close by the cave is a second, new synagogue built in 1885. When they laid the cornerstone, troublemakers challenged the act, saying, "It is not a good omen to allow the Jews to build a new synagogue." Khalifa Ḥajjaj, sheikh of the Jews, went out and gathered testimonies from the elders stating that this plot of land had already been sanctified. The Brilliant Sage, Rabbi Eliyahu Ḥazzan,[12] received a permit from the authorities in Istanbul to build without any interference.

NOTES

1. Judging by the situation among the Jews of the Ghuryan who resettled in Israel, they compete over prestige more than they do over actual positions of leadership (Goldberg 1972a).

2. From the cases I have studied, it seems that only a few prominent members of the community entered polygamous marriages (Goldberg 1972a:24–25). In Section 5, Hakohen states: "Some Jews, as well, have two wives, but for the most part the only person who takes a second wife is one who has had no children from the first and has not fulfilled the *miṣwah* 'Be fruitful and multiply!' " He also states (Section 38) that at the beginning of the nineteenth century, European Jews sometimes would come to Tripoli in order to marry a second wife.

3. The most well-known book of the Kabbalah, the mystical tradition.

4. Both in this instance and in the case of Yefren (see Section 99) it appears that there is significant leeway for young men (and women?) to make their wishes felt in the choice of a spouse (*cf.* Joseph 1974).

5. Because it cannot be sold to the Moslems (see Section 92).

6. Homiletic and folkloristic sections of the Rabbinic tradition.

7. Hakohen is surprised at the left-right reversal, but he takes for granted the effectiveness of cauterization (*cf.* Griffin 1924:176–177 and Tully 1957:119, n.1).

8. There are many stories of Jewish doctors in Middle Eastern lands who were subject to false accusations by Moslems envious of their successes. One well-known set of legends is based on an incident in the life of Maimonides (Baron 1958, Vol. VIII:250).

9. The role of the sheikh of the community is analyzed in greater detail in Goldberg (1972a).

10. This custom is somewhat unusual because *bsīsa* is usually associated with festive occasions.

11. Elsewhere, Hakohen (tr. 1969:69) reports seeing a plaque on a broken Torah case in that synagogue dating from the year 1559.

12. On Rabbi Ḥazzan, see the Editor's Introduction, VIII.

Zawia, Zuara, and Zanzur

(SECTION 104)

About a nine-hour walk west of Tripoli, not far from the coast, is the town of Zawia al-Gharbiya. The land there is very fertile, irrigated by water pumps from wells. The land is blessed with date palms, olive trees, all sorts of fruit trees, and garden crops of great commercial value.

In ancient times, many Jews lived in the environs of Zawia, namely in Zuagha, which was formerly called Tripoli.[1] Later, it was called Sabratha, and now it is called Zuagha after the leader of a Berber tribe. The Jews once dwelt in Zuara[2] too. They dwelt in Dahman and Sorman, but many years have passed since they were exiled from these places. At this time there are no Jews there; however, I saw the surname a-Sormani in an old ledger. In this generation, Jews have once again settled in Zuara. About forty Jews have come to engage in commerce. In the town of Zawia proper, there are only about six hundred people because the Jews there are not blessed with fertility.

Among the Jews, there are many who are extremely wealthy, according to local standards. Poor people are to be found among them also, but there is no Jew who goes begging from house to house because it is considered shameful for a Jew to receive charity. Most of the commerce is in Jewish hands, but some is controlled by Mohammedans who have recently begun to engage in trade.

The Jews are not learned in the Torah; they are haughty and pursue honor. Their customs are a mixture of those of Tripoli and those of the village Jews. Their food consists of putrid bread; neither is their dress fancy. However, the well-to-do have special, imposing outfits to wear when they go to Tripoli.

The local Mohammedans are the lords of the land. They cheat and murder as if the Turkish government were only a mirage. In 1906, a Mohammedan murdered the sheikh of the Jews, Furjallah Shlig, in the marketplace in front of many witnesses. Furjallah was the wealthiest man in the region. Despite this, the murderer, when brought to trial in the court of Tripoli, was declared not guilty, because of scheming false testimony. Witnesses appeared who contradicted the testimony of those who had seen the murder. These said, "The Mohammedan was with us at that time at such and such a place" (which was far away from the scene of the crime).

Many Mohammedans are dependent on the Jews who lend them money. Yet despite this, the Jews live among them only through cunning and by humbling themselves before the honor-seeking Mohammedans. Even so, many Jews have been murdered, and their blood cries out for justice.

The Jews have a ritual bath where rain water collects. In 1906, they began to dig a ritual bath behind the synagogue, fed by running water.[3] The governor of the town prevented them from completing the project, saying, "It is not fitting and proper that the Jews should introduce new things in the region."

The Synagogue. In the early days they had a synagogue some distance from the Jewish neighborhood. In 1780, it collapsed and the Jews wished to rebuild the ruins. A resident who hated Jews incited his Mohammedan brethren to disrupt the building of the structure. He was very rich and therefore his words were heeded.

The Jews then sent a letter of complaint to 'Ali Pasha Qaramanli, the Pasha of Tripoli, and he sent word of their disagreement to the Qadi and the Mufti, the heads of the Mohammedan religion. The Jews of Tripoli came to the aid of their brethren. They freely gave money from their pockets for bribes, and thus acquired a permit to build from the religious leaders, as had originally been planned. The resident who had opposed the building grovelled before 'Ali Pasha until the latter rescinded the permit. He would not allow the building of the synagogue unless the resident agreed to it. The Jews humbled themselves before the resident and gave him large amounts of money, but to no avail (this is described in Section 32).

The Jews of Zawia then chose the home of one Joseph Ṣror to serve as a synagogue with a Torah scroll. In 1797, they built Ṣror's house into a permanent house of worship. The Mohammedans maligned the Jews, denouncing them before Yusef Pasha Qaramanli, the Pasha of Tripoli, saying, "They have built a new synagogue without obtaining a permit." Yusef Pasha fined the Jews two thousand francs as punishment.

The Jews gave two thousand francs to the deputies to intercede for them and to appease Yusef Pasha's anger. However, the other deputies, who did not share in the bribe, continued to add fuel to the fire of his anger until he dropped a hint to thugs, who proceeded to destroy the synagogue and tear the Torah scroll into shreds. To Yusef Pasha the Jews cried out against the wrong, but in vain. They showed him the permit signed by the Qadi and the Mufti during the reign of his father, 'Ali Pasha. All their words were as straws in the wind.

On the new moon of Tammuz, 1798, all the Jews of the town of Zawia came to Tripoli and said to the Pasha, "We have come to live here because we, your servants, have no synagogue." Then the Pasha granted their request and handed them a permit to build a synagogue. On the twenty-eighth of the month, a Qadi came to the Pasha with a complaint, saying, "I fear you have sinned in exalting the enemies of the Mohammedan religion by building a synagogue, which diminishes the power of the government."

The Pasha was filled with anger and rage at the words of the Qadi. He sent an official to the town of Zawia to bring all the Jews to Tripoli, and he issued a proclamation that the Jews were not obligated to pay their debts to their creditors and that whoever accused them maliciously or spoke one deceitful word of them would be put to death.

The Jews came to Tripoli with all their belongings. The resident who had worked against them lost all his wealth, and his words were no longer heeded. The town deteriorated because the Jews were responsible for the commerce and industry, and the townspeople were unable to manage in their absence.

On the New Moon of Sivan, 1799,[4] Yusef Pasha received letters signed by all the notables of the town, saying, "Pardon us, lord. Please send the Jews back to live with us as of yore. Behold, the breadth of the land is before them. Let them trade therein and dwell in security." The Pasha granted their request, receiving from the notables a letter that guaranteed protection of the Jews. He gave the Jews a written permit to build the synagogue, and no one protested. They built a synagogue at Joseph Ṣror's house, and the place of the old synagogue was set aside for a cemetery. They lived in safety. (The preceding has been copied from the writings of Rabbi Abraham Khalfon,[5] from the aforementioned book.)

After a while, another spark of jealousy was kindled in the heart of three Mohammedans whose names were as follows: Mustafa ibn Muḥammad, Farḥat ibn Maami, and Hasin Zribuʻa. They hid some gunpowder under the floor of the synagogue in order to blow it up. However, they were unsuccessful, as their hiding place was discovered. In addition, they were afflicted with blindness, as is mentioned in Section 36.[6]

The synagogue faces north in the Jewish quarter. In the year 1895, they tore it down and built it anew. They also built another synagogue nearby facing east because the population had grown somewhat. It is customary there, when commemorating a death, to send bread and a piece of meat to every Jewish family, according to the number of people in the family.

About twelve miles[7] west of Tripoli, near the coast, is the town of Zanzur. It stands out in the district because of its fertile soil and its air, but it is like a thorny rose, for its inhabitants are mostly bandits and thieves.

Long ago, many Jews lived there, but they all scattered, and the only trace of them is an old surname in Tripoli, a-Zanzuri, derived from the name of the town.

About 1840, some Jews came back to settle there. At present, there are about forty Jews. Most of them are poor, living as peddlers. Some are cobblers, and others are blacksmiths.

In one of the houses a room with a Torah scroll is set aside for communal prayer. The teacher of the small children lives in another of the rooms. Half of the house is owned outright by the Jews, and the other half is rented. (In 1912, during the turmoil before the Italians captured the town, some Mohammedans, seized by religious hatred, desecrated the synagogue and burned the Torah scroll.)

The Jews have no special ritual bath, so the women use the sea for ritual ablution. The dead are buried in the cemetery in Tripoli. They do not have their own ritual circumcisor; when necessary, one comes from Tripoli. They do not have a ritual slaughterer; instead they buy kosher meat from Tripoli, which is near the town. When necessary, they call a Rabbi to perform the wedding ceremony, but the marriage contract is written in Tripoli.

NOTES

1. Tripoli, "the three cities," was the Roman name for the three towns of Sabratha (near Zuara), Oea (Tripoli), and Leptis Magna (near present-day Khoms; see Section 107).

2. Hakohen first gives the spelling Zuagha and then switches to Zuara. The latter is more common in European languages.

3. One of the requirements of a ritual bath is that it come directly from a natural source of water.

4. The text says 1759, but the Hebrew date, 5559 (1799), is correct.

5. On Rabbi Khalfon, see the Editor's Introduction.

6. Another incident, in 1879, in which the Zawia synagogue was desecrated is documented by Littman (1975:69).

7. Hakohen uses the Hebrew word *mil,* which he perhaps understood as equivalent to the Arabic *mil.* The former term appears in the Talmud and has been estimated to be about 1,470 meters. The Arabic *mil,* consisting of 4,000 cubits, differs from region to region and is upward of 2,000 meters in length. Hakohen's usage is not at all precise here. Zanzur and Tajura (Section 105) are both described as being "about twelve miles" from Tripoli; the first is about 16 kilometers from the capital and the second somewhat further. Both Mesallata (Section 106) and Khoms (Section 107) are described as being about "fifty miles" from Tripoli, and the respective distances are 135 and 120 kilometers. It may not have been possible for Hakohen to get more precise information at the time. The following anecdote is quoted by Harrison (1967:397) in a footnote: "So ignorant were the Turks of their own African dominion that at the outbreak of the war [1911], when the Sultan asked for a map, there was not one to be found."

'Amrus and Tajura

(SECTION 105)

A short distance east of Tripoli, towards the coast, is the town of al-'Amrus. About two thousand Jews dwell there.[1] Many of them are enormously wealthy, according to the standards of the town. They are miserly and are satisfied with only the bare necessities, with putrid barley bread. Similarly, their dress is not very elegant. As for trades, they are peddlers, cobblers, metalworkers, and manufacturers of wool combs. They are very industrious and cunning when it comes to acquiring money. In addition to their regular occupations, the majority lend money at interest to the Mohammedans. (In 1911, when Tripoli was captured by the Italians and many of the Mohammedans hurriedly fled to the desert, there were few porters left in the city. However, a few Jews from this town came to Tripoli,[2] rolled up their sleeves, and became muleteers and wagon drivers, and realized a good income from their enterprise.)

They are not learned. The ritual slaughterer is rewarded for his labor as is customary in the rest of the villages. He receives a piece from the neck, where the animal is slaughtered, a part of the liver, and a part of the small intestines, where the slaughterer's hand touches.[3] They have a communal fund supported by the tax on kosher meat and the sale of *'aliyot* to the Torah scroll. The money is distributed on the eve of every Sabbath to the teacher of the young children and to the poor.

They are very quarrelsome. Even though they are miserly, they will waste enormous amounts of money to win a judgment against their opponent. In 1913, the Italian . . .[4] decreed that marriage ceremonies must be performed by a functionary representing the Chief Rabbi in Tripoli.

One of the synagogues in 'Amrus, on the outskirts of the town near the Jewish quarter, opens toward the south. No one knows exactly when it was founded, but according to tradition it was begun in an earlier generation by a Jew named 'Amira. This very same synagogue is also considered holy in the eyes of the Mohammedans. The Jews of Tripoli vow to visit the synagogue, and make votive offerings of money and candles.

Near that synagogue is another one, opening toward the west. This one was founded in 1850. The money for the land and the building came from the communal fund. In 1904, still another was built near it with money from the fund. It has a ritual bath fed by fresh running water.

For burial, they carry the deceased in a wooden coffin on their shoulders to the cemetery in Tripoli. (In 1910, there was cholera in Tripoli and also in this town. The Turkish government forced the local Jews to bury those who died from the plague in the village.)[5]

About twelve miles east of Tripoli, in the direction of the coast, is the town of Tajura. Jews have been there since ancient times. Even in 1510, when Tripoli was captured by the Spaniards and the Jews of Tripoli were exiled, Tajura was not overpowered; it remained in the hands of the Mohammedans (see Section 20), and the Jewish inhabitants were not driven out.

At the present, there are only about a hundred and forty Jews there. Most of them are poor, burdened by the weight of exile and the religious hatred of the local robbers and thugs.[6]

The Jews are not learned, but they hold onto their faith as it was handed down from their fathers. Their customs are similar to those of their brethren who live in the town of 'Amrus, but they have their own cemetery.

They have had a synagogue from olden times. It is very holy and even the Jews of Tripoli make vows and contribute to it. Not long ago, they tore it down and rebuilt it.

(In 1911, during the interregnum, most of the inhabitants of the region fled in order to prepare themselves for a holy war against the Italians. The remaining Jews suffered revenge at the hands of the Mohammedans. Their property was confiscated and many were murdered, but this did not satisfy the desire of the Mohammedans. They vented their anger in the synagogue by tearing and burning the Torah scrolls.)[7]

When the Italians captured the area and peace was restored to the land, the Jews returned to the town, but they had no Torah scroll.

NOTES

1. 'Amrus was the largest of the Jewish settlements outside of Tripoli. Although it was only six kilometers from the town, it was a separate community.

2. See McClure (1913:86, 137) on the Jews of 'Amrus in Tripoli and their return to 'Amrus.

3. The ritual slaughterer inspects an animal to determine if it is healthy by feeling the inner organs, particularly the lungs.

4. A single word is unclear. In Section 71, Note 55, Hakohen gives the following information: "All the *ketubbot* are kept by the official scribe of *ketubbot*, Rabbi Shaul Adadi [see the Author's Introduction], and are also listed in the register and signed by the witnesses. (When the country was conquered by the Italians in 1911–12, it was decreed that the register should also list the ages of the bride and groom, their street and neighborhood, and so forth.)"

5. Hakohen mentions this earlier (Section 65, ms. p. 119a–b), and also tells of an outbreak in 1912 (*cf.* McClure 1913:96, 254*ff.*).

6. Incidents in 'Amrus and Tajura are mentioned in Littman (1975).

7. See Section 112.

Mesallata

(SECTION 106)

Fifty miles to the south of Tripoli is the town of Mesallata,[1] situated among the high mountains. There they use rain water for drinking. Each house has a cistern for the gathering of rain water. Each house has a cavern which is a toilet. They do not relieve themselves in the fields, as is the custom in Yefren and Ghuryan; instead, they relieve themselves in the cavern in a toilet.

The whole region is blessed with many olive trees, date trees, almond trees, and many other fruit trees. They also have some flowing streams, but not many.

There are about seven hundred Jews living there under the heavy yoke of the Mohammedans, the lords of the land. Several people have died in wanton crimes. Even though the officials are under Turkish rule, which bestows equal rights and freedom, it is as if the government notables, who are Arabs, are trained from childhood to disregard these rights and to seek the humiliation of the Jews, who do not believe in the Mohammedan religion.

The Jews have a tradition that their origin can be traced to the Island of Jerba, at the time of the Hilalian[2] conquest, and that they preceded the Mohammedans in settling the area. Later, a large population came to join them. Still later, some of them returned to their country, Jerba.

To this day, many places are called by names that the Jews were accustomed to use in the early days. There are places where the names cry out plainly that they are Jewish and one does not even have to guess their origins. For example, a wadi near the town of al-Khoms is called Wad al-Yahud (the wadi of the Jews). The remains of some old palaces are called *qṣar al-yahud* (the castle of the Jews). These palaces are near a tract of land belonging to a Mohammedan named Ben-Hanid. According to local tradition, his ancestors converted to the Mohammedan religion, but their origin was Jewish.

The Jews there do not give themselves family names based on crafts or place names or patronyms; each one is called by his father's name alone.[3] For example, Isaac Abraham, Moshe Amran, Joseph Menaḥem, Joseph Ghrad, and so on. There is one tribe,[4] however, called Magro, which is an Italian word. There is also a tribe called Zradba. According to their tradition, the original settlers came from Silin, which is between the town of Mesallata and the town of Khoms, but at present there is no Jew living there.

Among the Jews, both men and women engage in trade, and these circumstances have led some women to licentiousness.[5]

The Jewish quarter is close to the army base and the traders' market. Recently they have begun to extend into the Mohammedan quarter.

In early times, they used to grind grain by hand and bake bread on the walls of an oven that opened on top, like the rest of the villagers. Not long ago, they built camel-driven mills and ovens with an opening on the side. Nevertheless, most of the women cling to the old custom of grinding in hand mills and baking on the oven walls. However, the wheat for Passover is ground in the camel-powered mills. The *maṣah* wafers for the festival of Passover are baked daily on the walls of an oven that opens on top.

They observe the same customs as the Jews of Yefren and Ghuryan. There is no variation, except on the festival of Shavuot. Besides a water fight, in which they pour lots of water on one another, they also have the custom of reading the marriage writ of Shavuot, *Be-Simana Ṭava,*[6] in the synagogue on the second day of Shavuot. The honor of reading this hymn is auctioned publicly, as are the rest of the calls to read the Torah. After the purchaser has finished reading the hymn, they pour a container full of water over his head in the synagogue. This is considered a *miṣwah* and a sign of blessing.[7]

The former synagogue in the Jewish quarter was founded and built in 1815. It was then that they received a permit to build a synagogue. In 1862, they tore it down and two Tripolitans, Mr. Shalom 'Arbib and Mr. Shaul Ḥabib, built an impressive structure. However, we could not find the site of the former synagogue. It is a tradition among the elders that when the Mohammedans succeeded in capturing the area many Jews were exiled. The remaining Jews were oppressed and for many years, until 1815, they prayed in the home of Judah Makhluf.

About a two-hour walk from the synagogue, in a northeasterly direction, is a place called Khalfon, named after a Jew. There is a ruin called *ṣlat simḥa* (the synagogue of Simḥa). The only ruins left are ancient posts and the remains of the foundations. It is a tradition of the elders that a Jewish tribe called Khalfon, named after the head of a family Khalfon, once lived there.

Some remains of castles and a stopped-up well of running water are called by Jewish names. According to tradition, there were many, many Jews there. It stands to reason that this is so: the fact that they called the synagogue by the name Simḥa would indicate that there were other synagogues known by different names. If there had been only one synagogue they would have referred to it simply as "the synagogue."

The cemetery was in part taken over by the Mohammedans and incorporated into their cultivated fields. The Jews there only occasionally place engraved monuments on the graves.

The Jews are not very learned. On the Ninth of Av, 1906, I arrived with my friend, the researcher Nahum Slouschz. We saw many young men, riding donkeys, coming from afar to greet us. It is their custom to greet the Messiah, who will be poor and ride on a donkey.[8] They mistook Mr. Slouschz for the Messiah riding on a donkey. Astonished at the way he looked, they said, "Lo, he has come dressed in European garb, but he is rich and rides a donkey."

NOTES

1. The community of Mesallata is the subject of an historical-ethnographic novel (Ohel 1962).

2. See the Editor's Introduction.

3. On the question of names, see Goldberg (1967, 1972b).

4. One should not attach too much importance to Hakohen's use of the term "tribe."

5. Given the large number of men who engaged in itinerant trading in the small towns, it would be valuable to have a more complete picture of family life in these communities.

6. Shavuot commemorates the "giving of the Torah," that is, the revelation at Sinai. Mystical tradition envisioned this event as a marriage between God (the bridegroom) and Israel (the bride); this is expressed in the custom of reading a liturgical marriage writ on that festival (see Scholem 1965:138–139). For the specific text, see Tefilat Yesharim (1958:408–411).

7. See the Editor's Foreword to Chapter One on spiritual closeness to the land.

8. The belief in the Messiah coming as a poor man riding on a donkey is based on Zechariah IX:9.

Khoms

(SECTION 107)

The town of al-Khoms is about a six-hour walk in a northeasterly direction from the town of Mesallata. It is on the coast about fifty miles from Tripoli. The Arabs call it Liqqata. It is near the ancient ruins of the city of Lebda.[1] In ancient times, there were many Jews there because Septimius,[2] Emperor of Rome, exiled many Jews from Tripoli to the town of Lebda (see Section 11). However, we have no particulars as to what befell them or how their settlement there ended. According to tradition, the place where the Turkish government building is now located was once the Jewish cemetery.

In 1871, the town became well known because the Jews returned to live there. The *halfa* (esparto)[3] trade was revived, and *halfa* grass is to be found in abundance there (see Section 8, Note 10).

The Jews control commerce, and shape it as they see fit.[4] Trade is almost at a standstill on the Sabbath and Jewish holidays. The market, stores, and houses have been rebuilt. The price of land has risen because the town has been revived. Jews and non-Jews live in the same neighborhood.

All of the inhabitants use one ancient well called al-Ḥasi, whose waters are light and good. Most, if not all, of the 410 Jews who live in

Khoms are refugees from Tripoli who were not able to support themselves there, but have prospered here. There are even those who have earned a fortune and are considered wealthy.

They follow the custom of Tripoli except in the order of the confessional prayer on Monday and Thursday mornings,[5] for which they choose to follow the custom of Jerusalem. The students of the Talmud and Torah receive their lessons sitting on straw mats spread out in random fashion on the ground. Their legs are crossed under their thighs and their heads are bent.[6]

The Italian government cast her protective eye upon them and founded a school for boys. The reading and writing of Italian are taught, as well as arithmetic and Hebrew. There is a school for girls in which reading and writing in Italian, as well as mathematics and sewing, are taught. The Turkish government also established schools there, and in the rest of the towns, to teach arithmetic and reading and writing in Turkish.

The charity fund is supported by the money paid for the privilege of being called to the Torah and by the *gabila*[7] money, the tax levied on kosher slaughtering. The money in the fund is distributed weekly to the prayer leader of the community, the teacher of small children, and the ritual slaughterer, as well as to the poor.

The Synagogue. In early days they would pray in the attic of an inn owned by a Mohammedan. He charged them a hundred and fifty francs rent per annum. However, he wanted to increase the rent.

A wealthy and influential Tripolitan named Mas'ud Nahum bought a parcel of land in the town and built houses and storehouses there. Along with these, he acquired land to build a synagogue fifteen meters long by fourteen meters wide. He constructed a fence around the plot and prepared all the materials needed for the building. However, some Mohammedans interrupted the building of the new synagogue. The Qadi, the head of the Mohammedan clergy, agreed to issue an order to stop the construction.

In 1904, Mas'ud acquired a written permit from Constantinople to build the synagogue, and no one could override him. However, he passed away before he was able to finish his project. Before he died, he wrote in his will that the synagogue should be completed with funds from his estate. He also willed money for the Serusi School in Tripoli[8] (see Section 83). In 1905, the wealthy Mr. Rafael Nahum (brother of Mas'ud, may his soul rest in peace) willingly fulfilled the stipulation.

The synagogue is built like a fortress on marble columns. The floor is also made of marble. There is a special room for the study of the Book of the Zohar during the early morning. In the synagogue, to the left as you enter, is a room with cubbyholes in the wall for the storing of prayer shawls and phylactery pouches. Those who happen to arrive late in the morning and find that their friends have already reached the middle of the prayer service begin their prayers in this little side room so that their voices don't mix with those already praying. When the first group has finished their prayers, the second group moves into the main room to finish theirs. (The first synagogue, which had been in rented quarters, remained empty, and did not house any more tenants. All who occupied it, either Jews or non-Jews, left it in a hurry.)

To the right of the court, as you enter, is an attic used as an inn for guests. Above is the women's section, from which they can see the Torah scroll.[9] On a board on the wall of the synagogue is the list of those who have volunteered to receive the *shaliah kollel* from the Land of Israel in their homes. Also listed, in the order of their turns, are the names of those who have extended invitations to guests to dine in their homes.

About a thirty-minute walk eastward from the town, on the seacoast, is the city of Lebda. Though the city is destroyed, it is obvious from the ruins that it was once very important. The remains of lovely mansions, blocks of marble, hewn stones, and columns of marble are found there. Everyone who passes by is amazed at the building talent of the former generations, which is like the building of giants. There are many pieces of statues, made of marble and other kinds of stones, scattered all over, some above ground and some buried in the sand. Some have Latin inscriptions on them. The local stonecutters always break the inscribed stones and sell them to the builders (alas for their loss). A great portion of the city has been claimed by the sea.

Nearby is a river. The exact founding date of the city is unknown. (According to the writings of R. Abraham Khalfon, which I have consulted, Lebda was already well established in the reign of Septimius Severus of Rome, because the self-same Septimius decreed that the Jews of Tripoli be exiled to Lebda (see Section 11). Even during the period of the Second Temple, during the reign of the Ptolemies in Cyrene, many Jews from Mesopotamia came to settle in the vicinity of Lebda and Tripoli. These were in addition to those who joined the masses of Jews drawn from Alexandria in Egypt to Cyrene. I recall that in my youth I saw a manuscript by R. Abraham Khalfon stating that "twenty-four[10] . . . Jews came." However, I wasn't able to fully understand the words because the writing was erased and covered with mold.)

Near the cape called Ras al-Bental, along the shore between the towns of Tajura and Khoms, are the remnants of settlements and cemeteries. Here, too, one can find hewn stones inscribed in Greek and in strange letters I could not decipher. (It might be Phoenician writing, but I have not seen the letters since my youth.) In 1906, on an island in the sea called al-Me'agel, my friend, the researcher Dr. Slouschz, and I saw many graves and human skeletons and bones scattered about. I saw a stone inscribed with two Latin letters.

For the following two reasons, it would seem that all these places had no Jewish inhabitants. The first is that my careful scrutiny did not reveal any Hebrew inscriptions. The second is that it is customary for Jews to bury their dead deep in the ground. But not having seen something does not constitute proof. In time, some evidence may appear that will refute my hypothesis. As for the inscriptions, are there not many sayings scattered throughout the Talmud attesting to the fact that the Jews also wrote Greek?

NOTES

1. The ancient Leptis Magna.

2. Hirschberg (1974:53) gives the following information: The Roman Emperor Septimius Severus and his son Caracalla (real name, Marcus Aurelius Antoninus), who ruled in the second to third centuries, were known for their fair treatment of the Jews. Both Caracalla and his father allowed Jews to hold positions of honor. Septimius Severus was born in Leptis Magna, and Caracalla was brought up with Jews in Africa. When he was seven, Caracalla discovered that one of his friends had been severely beaten, simply for being a Jew. Caracalla, very upset, blamed his father and his friend's father. Caracalla may also have been the friend, often mentioned in the Aggadah, of Rabbi Yehudah Ha-Nasi, compiler of the Mishnah.

3. This grass was exported, mainly for the manufacture of paper. The grass exported was *stipa tenacissima,* often confused with the less strong *lygeum spartum.* The former is known locally as *halfa ghedima,* while the latter is *halfa mahbula.* Note 10 in Section 8, ms. p. 17b, reads as follows: "*Halfa* is a species of grass that grows in the mountains. It is called *helef* in the Mishnah [Tractate *Kelim* 17:17]. It consists of strands which can be split into smaller strands, as thin as hair. The merchants export it to Europe for making paper and other products. In former times, the monetary value of this grass was not recognized, and it was used for animal fodder. It was also used to make braided baskets and wicker baskets used in oil presses. In 1867, a certain Christian, who was a British subject, sent a sample of the grass to England, and was well rewarded for his effort. In 1870, the merchants discovered its commercial potential[?]. The trade in *halfa* has now grown a great deal, and the merchants have installed steam presses to pack the bundles in order to facilitate transportation on steam ships." (See Rossi 1968:35.) The gathering of *halfa* was first carried out in quite a destructive manner, by pulling it from the roots so that it did not replenish itself.

4. Moreno (1928:51) cites an Arabic proverb to the effect that "a market without Jews is like a document without witnesses."

5. The *widdui* (Idelsohn 1960:111). The difference concerns the order of the individual sections that compose the *widdui.*

6. The implication is that one might have expected a more "modern" form of instruction in a town whose Jewish population came mainly from Tripoli.

7. See Goldberg (1974b:146) on the term *gabila.*

8. One of the schools organized in the effort to modernize education (Kaha-lon 1972).

9. Women are not required by law to participate in the prayers and usually do not. Therefore, most of the village synagogues did not have a special place for women. Many women do attempt to be present on the Sabbath to view the Torah scroll when it is publicly displayed and read.

10. He remembers only the initial two digits of the number.

Zliten

(SECTION 108)

A nine-hour walk eastward from Khoms, not far from the coast, is the town of Zliten. Between the two towns are the remains of many ancient palaces.

The lands of Zliten are fertile with fruit trees and vegetables. The inhabitants irrigate the fields with water drawn from wells. In the old days, there were many Jews there, but in our time there are only about 640 souls.

There are no exceedingly wealthy men among them. Also, they are not very learned; only a handful read the books of the Midrash. Their quarter is near the government palace and the market. Most of the commerce is in the hands of the Jews, especially the *halfa* (esparto grass) trade.[1] The exile weighs heavily upon them. They cannot hold their heads high because of the religious hatred of the Mohammedans, the violent and haughty rulers of the land. Several people have been murdered.

From the first of the month of Av, they eat no meat, even on the Sabbath.[2] On the night after the Ninth of Av, it is customary for every-one to slaughter a chicken. In all other ways, they follow the custom of their brethren in Mesallata. It is a tradition among them that the deed for the cemetery was written in the name of a Jew named Sharir ben 'Affan.

One synagogue is called *ṣlat abu-Sha'if*. A very ancient synagogue, it is located at the edge of the town close to the Jewish quarter. It is accorded great honor. People come from far and wide to visit and pay tribute to it with vows and gifts and charitable offerings.[3] It is used for prayer only on those days when the Torah scroll is read.[4]

In 1868, religious hatred was aroused among the local Mohammed-ans, and one night they set fire to the four corners of the synagogue. All the Torah scrolls and the ornaments were consumed by the flames. The Jews risked their lives, but were unable to put out the fire. When it came to investigating the fire, the officials acted as if nothing had occurred. The Jews of Tripoli lodged a complaint before the government council and their plea was not answered. They then notified the Alliance Israélite Universelle in Paris, and they also sent word to Sir Abraham Camondo Effendi[5] in the capital city of Constantinople.

After a while, a letter from Constantinople with the royal seal was received by the Pasha of Tripoli. The letter levied a fine against the Mohammedan inhabitants of Zliten in order to rebuild the destroyed synagogue into a magnificent structure and to buy new Torah scrolls and anything else that might be needed.

In 1870, the Pasha of Tripoli and his assistants came to the town, and they were the first to lay the foundation stones of the building; a handsome edifice was built, by local standards. The Mohammedans kept silent because it was a royal decree and no one would dare question it.

Those who were suspected of the crime of arson were sentenced to long terms in irons; their wealth was confiscated and they received corporal punishment as well.

But the flame of religious hatred was not extinguished in the hearts of the criminals. On the night of the twenty-ninth of Tevet, 1903, the spirit of fanaticism entered the hearts of these criminals. In the dead of the night, they climbed on the roof of the synagogue, carrying in their hands tools of destruction, kerosene, and matches in order to pry an opening in the roof and burn the synagogue. They worked until the light of day, but without success for, by chance, the place where they were working contained the supporting beam of the roof. The criminals fled at daybreak in such a hurry that they left their tools and the kerosene that they had prepared for the kindling of the fire. The Jews reported the incident to the government officials. They also informed the Alliance in Paris by letter. As a result, the Turkish government ordered the governor of the town of Zliten to give special attention to the protection of the synagogue. Even though no unequivocal evidence was found that could convict them, in time the criminals received their just reward. In the year 1905, they went from bad to worse and became highway robbers. The government sent police to bring them before the tribunal to stand trial and account for all their misdeeds. One of the suspected bandits shot a policeman with his pistol. He and his companions then fled to a hay storehouse and, standing with guns ready, they warned everyone, saying, "Anyone who tries to enter the building takes his life in his own hands."

The governor of the town surrounded the storehouse with armed soldiers and issued an order to make an opening in the roof and pour in kerosene. These self-same suspected criminals died in the flames of the burning fire.

There is another synagogue in the Jewish quarter which was founded anew in 1892 by a woman named Ḥidria, the widow of Mr. Eliyahu Kaḥalon. She was the first to work for the construction of the building.

She also contributed six hundred francs toward the building. The community regularly prays in this synagogue, morning, afternoon, and night.

About a four-hour walk from Zliten is a mansion held by the Mohammedans called *knis al-Yahud* (the synagogue of the Jews), but the Jews call it simply *qaṣr* (palace) *a-Sha'if*. It would seem that he is the son of the abu-Sha'if mentioned above. The whole area belongs to one of the Mohammedan tribes who are called al-Brahama (Sons of Abraham).

At the eastern corner of Zliten is a plain about a six-hour walk wide, called a-Sha'ifa (the Shaifa). Perhaps it is named after a family head called abu-Sha'if. In this plain, there is a long and wide area called a-Dafnia (graveyard). This area is not fit for farming as it is covered with mounds of stone. In 1906, I was able to acquire one of the stone blocks found there. It had the following inscription in Assyrian letters:[6]

> This[7] is the grave of . . . from . . . Bir Rabbi Nissim . . . who was removed to her eternal resting place on . . . of the month of Kislev, 947. May the Eternal, in his compassion, cast her lot with Sarah, Rebecca, Rachel, and Leah in the Garden of Eden and fulfill the Scriptural verse: Thy dead shall be . . . my body shall rise again.[8] Amen.

This stone is now in Paris. The date 947 (1186) written on it is proof that even in the fifth millennium the Jews were accustomed to drop the thousands' place from the reckoning of the years from Creation, as handed down to us. Witness the fact that the date is not written ר"א תתקמ"ו or at the very least דתתקמ"ו (4947). If you will refer to the book *'Even Sapir,*[9] Part II, page 13, in the note you will see that according to his view, our forefathers did not leave out the thousands. This custom was introduced in the sixth millennium since the Creation. It is therefore impossible to say that what is inscribed in this stone, 947 since the Creation, means 947 of the current millennium.[10]

NOTES

1. The export of esparto grass was developed on a large scale in the last third of the nineteenth century.

2. The day on which the Temple was destroyed, commemorated by fasting and lamentation.

3. During the present century, the Busha'if synagogue was the focus of a regional pilgrimage that took place on the *hillula* (commemorative feast) of Rabbi Shim'on Bar Yohai, reputed author of the Zohar (Zuaretz *et al.* 1960:123–125). This synagogue is not far from the site of the tomb of Sidi 'Abd es-Salem, one of the main Moslem shrines in Tripolitania (Cesàro 1933 and Editor's Foreword to Chapter One).

4. The Sabbath, Mondays, and Thursdays.

5. A leader of the Jewish community in Istanbul. Camondo supported a school there which provided a European-style education (see Hirschberg 1969:199–200, 215–216). The request for his intervention in the Zliten affair is documented in a letter (see Note 90, "Jewish-Christian Conflict in Benghazi") from Shaul Lavi to Adolphe Cremieux, President of the Alliance (Littman 1975).

6. Standard Hebrew script.

7. There are slight differences between the accounts of Slouschz (*e.g.* 1927:53–58) and Hakohen concerning this inscription and those cited in Section 109.

8. Isaiah XXVI:19.

9. Ya'aqov Sapir was a Rabbinic emissary who visited Jewish communities in the Near East and wrote of his travels in the book *'Even Sapir* (1866).

10. According to the Hebrew calendar, the year 1906, for example, was the year 666 of the current (sixth) millennium.

Misurata and Sirte

(SECTION 109)

About a twelve-hour walk eastward beyond Zliten is the town of Misurata. The center of a large area, it is an important market. Merchants travel there from as far away as Fezzan, which is to the south of Tripolitania. The land is very fertile. Dates and olive trees are found in abundance, as in the rest of the region. The inhabitants also grow other varieties of fruit trees. They have many marvelous vegetable gardens, which they irrigate with water drawn from wells.

There are two ports at which boats tie up. One, not far from the government palace, provides protection for small single-masted vessels. The second port, for large ships, is located at a place called Qaṣr Aḥmad. It is about a two-hour walk from the government palace. Neither of these ports has wooden or stone docks to transfer passengers and goods from the fishing boats to shore.

The government palace is in the neighborhood of Matin. There are warehouses for the goods there, as well as an open-air marketplace. Trade is very heavy on Sundays because crowds of people come from all directions for the market day. On Thursdays, there is a regular market day in the quarter called Yidder, not far from Matin.

Jews have always lived there. They are not learned. They have no historical records, nor is there any tradition as to when they settled there. There are about nine hundred Jews divided between the two quarters, Yidder and Matin. Most of the Jews live in Matin.[1]

The Mohammedans also have begun to be traders and artisans, occupations which once were wholly the province of the Jews. Nevertheless, most of the trade is still in the hands of Jews because they are more knowledgeable in matters of commerce than the Mohammedans. There are some Jews who venture far out to engage in trade; they deal in spices as far away as Marzuk, the capital of Fezzan in the south. They come home only in the month of Nisan and in the month of Tishrei to celebrate the joy of the festival with the members of their family.

Even though they profit handsomely in trade, there are no outstandingly wealthy men among them. They have no contact with farming. Most of them are quarrelsome and pursue glory, saying, "I will achieve office and be honored." They also quarrel in the synagogue.[2]

They pay wages to the teacher of small children out of the communal fund, and also distribute part of it to a few poor people. He who acquires the certificate of a ritual slaughterer is called "Rabbi,"[3] and it is a great honor for him. The ritual slaughterer receives, as wages for his labor, those parts of the animal that are customarily given in all the villages.[4]

There is an ancient synagogue in the neighborhood of Yidder. In the neighborhood of Matin, in the Jewish quarter, there is also an ancient synagogue. In 1884, it was torn down and replaced by an imposing edifice, according to local standards, which was built by the synagogue overseer, Mr. Yiṣḥaq Ḥakmon, and by Mr. Khamus Jinah. Adjacent to the synagogue is a room to house guests that also contains a spring. This room, which one reaches by walking down some steps, serves as a ritual bath.

At the edge of the street of the Jews, in the neighborhood of Matin, is a synagogue called *ṣlat* (synagogue) *mevorakh,* which also was founded anew. Originally, it was in the dwelling of Mr. Mevorakh Jinah. In 1893, he brought a Torah scroll there, and a synagogue was established.

We know of no holy man, neither recent nor ancient. However, near the seacoast, about a forty-five-minute-walk from Matin, is a *qubba*[5] that contains a tomb considered holy by the Jews and the Mohammedans alike. They pay homage to the tomb, light candles there, and burn incense. Miracles are ascribed to it. The Mohammedans call it *sī merbaṭ.*[6]

No one knows when the cemetery was founded. The Mohammedans use a large portion of it for farming. The practice of inscribing the name of the deceased and the date of death on the site is not customary among the Jews; it is done only rarely. In 1898, the Jews experienced a reawakening and built a wall around the cemetery. They still maintain it to this day so that no stranger can encroach on the territory of those buried there. When they were digging the foundation for the wall, they found, nestled in the earth, some stones with Assyrian[7] writing on them. It is the custom that he who finds an Assyrian inscription must bury it, and whoever is first to do so is the most praiseworthy, so they quickly buried those stones in the earth, as was their wont and custom. However, they neglected to bury some of the stones, which thus survived and were placed in the synagogue's vault for tattered books.[8] In 1906, I went with my friend, the researcher Dr. Nahum Slouschz, to investigate Jewish life there. I was able to acquire these stones, and they are now in Paris. Here, dear reader, I have copied for you what is inscribed on them. I have indicated the missing parts by dots.

This is how they read:[9]

1. This is the tomb of the honored R. Shim'on Hazaqen,[10] the son of Rabbi Nissim Hazaqen. May the Merciful give him his part in the garden of Eden, Amen and amen. . . . for his house of eternity in the year 5009.

2. This is the tomb . . . Abraham, son of the honorable . . . delegate of the community,[11] he departed this world, having his years cut short, in the month of Shevaṭ in the year. . . . "Sweet is the sleep of the toiler, if little or if much he consumeth."[12] This alludes to those who labor in the Torah. May the Merciful give him his part . . . with those who are occupied with the Torah. The reckoning is according to the Creation and the wise will understand.

3. . . . of Rabbi. . . . May he find refuge in the spirit of God. . . . age in the year 52. . . . May the Merciful give him his part . . . sleep as R. . . . . . . Moses and Aaron and with [the seven categories][13] of the righteous in the Garden of Eden. May his death . . . as an atonement for all his sins. . . .

4. Departed to her h[ouse] of eternity, Ghezali the daughter of Rabbi Balḥiya, may her soul rest in Eden; the wife of our Teacher and Rabbi Sa'adia, son of the honorable Moses, may his soul rest in Eden. Whose years were cut short. . . .

5. This is the tomb of Ḥasana, daughter of Rabbi 'Ayad, may his soul rest in Eden; the wife of David, of peaceful memory. May the Merciful place her portion with Sarah and Rebecca. She departed for her house of eternity in the year 5502.[14]

These are copied from the tombstones that I managed to acquire. See Section 108 for the version of the stone that I acquired in Misurata, which was brought from Dafnia from a place called a-Zrig. The following are the inscriptions on the two stones found in Jebel Nefusa in the town of Fassato, which is mentioned in Section 90. These stones are in my possession:

1. Gathered into the Garden of Ede[n] . . . bequeathed unto all Israel. Rabbi . . . son of Mamah, may he find refuge in the spirit of God. In the month of . . . in the year 5. . . since the Creation of

the world. May the Lord give him his portion and lot in the Garden of Eden with the seven categories of the ri[ghteous]. Moses and Aaron . . . among the dwellers among the plants . . . the verse . . . your dead. . . .[15]

2. Gathered unto the Garden of Eden he bequeathed life to all Israel, Rabbi Temam, his rest is in Paradise, son of Joseph, his rest is in Paradise, *papa*. On the second day, the twenty-second day of the month of Shevaṭ in the year 4919[16] since the Creation of the world. May his resting place be under the tree of life and may his lot be with the seven categories of the righteous. Amen and amen.

In 1890, Doctor Abraham Navon[17] sent a copy of these two inscriptions to the Alliance Israélite Universelle in the city of Paris. Isidore Loeb, the author,[18] took it upon himself to send a letter to me asking about the meaning of the word *papa* that is engraved on one stone, because he has other stones from Jebel Nefusa with the same word inscribed on them. At that particular time, I did not have the opportunity to examine it carefully, and so my answer to him was, "Only God knows." However, at a later date I delved more deeply into the matter, and it seemed to me that the word *papa* is an acronym for "Here in Fassato,"[19] the region in which he died. My interpretation was mentioned by my friend, the scholar Nahum Slouschz, in the book describing his research in this region. However, he did not accept my idea, and it is clear that he has a different explanation. We repeat, "Only God knows."

The Jews of Misurata told me that many years ago they found a stone with the inscription Kohen on it. However, the stone was buried, and they do not know where. In addition, before they buried it, they did not know enough to pay attention to the date engraved on it. Curiously, among all the Jews of Tripolitania, there are no Levites,[20] except for those that settled here from the Island of Jerba or from other countries. As for myself, the writer,[21] my origin traces to Italy at the time of the upheaval created by Napoleon Bonaparte.

What is clear from all the inscriptions is that in Tripoli proper and its hinterland, from the fifth millennium to the sixth millennium and until this day, Jewish settlement has never ceased.

It is also quite clear from the inscriptions on the stones that the early Jewish settlers did not come from the Karaite sect.[22] Among the present-day inhabitants are those who know how to interpret the Torah; they believe in retribution for their deeds, preservation of the soul, and the resurrection of the dead.

The town of Sirte is in the southeast, close to the seacoast between the regions of Misurata and Benghazi (Cyrene). It is known far and wide as a busy trading center because it is close to the land of Fezzan and to central Africa. Caravans stream into the city from the south and the surrounding areas. Settlers from Cyrenaica were drawn there before they were attracted to Tripoli. There are many ancient palaces there and a great many stones scattered all over. There are engraved seals with Latin and other ancient inscriptions. From time to time, ancient caves are discovered.

In former days, there were Jewish settlers there. However, we know no details of whence they came and why. There are no remains of their settlement. Recently some Jews, about fifty souls, came from the town of Misurata to settle there. They arranged for a ritual slaughterer and for a prayer leader for the synagogue. They engaged in trade and were very successful. They were influential in building the region's reputation for trade.

NOTES

1. See Blake (1968) on Misurata. It appears that, in the past, Yidder was the main Jewish quarter. It may be that insecure conditions caused many families to move close to the government palace at Matin (*cf.* Littman 1975:69–71).

2. As I have discussed elsewhere, the "office and honor" referred to is primarily competition for prestige. The synagogue serves as one of the main arenas for this competition (Goldberg 1967, 1972a).

3. *Rav* is the term used here, meaning Rabbi. Hakohen probably means to distinguish it from the term *rebbi,* which is used by the Tripolitanian Jews to refer to minor religious specialists, such as a slaughterer, circumcisor, or teacher. Sometimes the term is used only in a particular situation, as, for example, when a man is serving as a prayer leader. The same individual would not be addressed that way on other occasions. (See Deshen 1970:10–11.)

4. The neck, the liver, and the small intestines.

5. A small square building with a domed roof. This may be the same place mentioned in Section 18, which Hakohen suggests as the burial place of Rabbi Trabuto. The latter was a Jew of Spanish origin who is known to have come to Misurata in the sixteenth century. It is not uncommon to find tombs in North Africa which are revered by both Jews and Moslems (*cf.* Voinot 1948).

6. From the term "marabout," although Hakohen believes that *merbaṭ* in this case may represent a linguistic evolution of the original name, *trabuto.*

7. Standard square Hebrew letters.

8. Any written text containing God's name may not be discarded, but must be buried or kept in a special room, usually called a *genizah.*

9. There are differences in the texts of the inscriptions as recorded here by Hakohen and published by Slouschz (1927:53–58). In order to reconcile these differences, one would have to consult the gravestones themselves. I have translated only the straightforward portions of the text. Photographs of the tombstones are found in Slouschz (1909).

10. The R. stands for Rabbi. The surname means "the elder." The year is 1247.

11. This is the translation of an abbreviation of *shaliah ṣibbur,* which refers to a prayer leader.

12. Sometimes Hebrew dates are given by citing a biblical word or phrase whose letters have the numerical value of the date intended. Slouschz (1927:56) gives the date as 1447. The verse is from Ecclesiastes IV:11.

13. See the expression in the first inscription from Fassato, below.

14. 1742.

15. Probably the same verse that appears on the tombstone found near Zliten (Section 108).

16. 1159. These two inscriptions are discussed by Slouschz (1927:191–201).

17. The director of the Alliance school that was established in Tripoli in 1890.

18. A Rabbi and scholar, Loeb was secretary of the Alliance Israélite Universelle (see the Editor's Introduction).

19. The Hebrew is *po(h) fassato.* The *p* and *f* are written with the same character in Hebrew, differing only in the diacritics.

20. Slouschz used the absence of Kohanim as support for his theory that the Rabbis had wrested leadership from the Kohanim in the area.

21. The author is also a Kohen.

22. See Hakohen's Notes in Sections 98 and 101 above.

Benghazi and Derna

(SECTION 110)

About 360 miles from Tripoli, eastward by sea (because the desert is a roundabout way), is the region called Benghazi (Cyrene), named after a family head called Ghazi and his son called Ben-Ghazi. Formerly the region was called Ben-haris[1] after a family head called Haris.

This land is where settlement first took place in the country of Libya, as mentioned in Section 9. The land covers a very wide area. There is twice as much commerce as in Tripoli because many traders are drawn there. In addition to those from Central Africa, there are ships from Crete and Egypt. The land is blessed with grain and stocks of cattle and sheep. No one has estimated the value of the grain, the livestock, the sheep's wool, hides, and so forth that make up the sea trade every year. The town imports an enormous amount of goods as well. In years of drought, it imports a great deal of corn.

It has a very large population. At every opportunity, they engage in robbery and violence; they are afraid of nothing. Religious hatred is their strongest passion[2] and is imprinted on their hearts. Nevertheless, the Turkish government honors the Jews and watches over them with vigilance to prevent outbreaks of religious hatred.

The volume of trade increases sharply when the grain is gathered from the threshing floors, that is, in the months of August and September. The Jews are the principal artisans and traders, but recently the Mohammedans and Christians have begun to try their hand at trade. The result, because the Jews are more expert in the ways of commerce, is that hatred toward them has increased. (They wear elegant clothes.)[3]

The merchants help each other and carry on business transactions based on trust. Anyone who wants to receive goods on credit may come and take them, and when he has enough means at his disposal he settles his account. All this is done without any cheating whatsoever. When one of the merchants comes upon hard times, so that he reaches the point of bankruptcy, the other merchants spare him from dishonoring his name, feeling obligated to come to his aid. They do this with verbal support and with their merchandise. They still lend money to him without promissory notes. However, in recent times, dishonesty has begun to spread, even among the merchants. The Turkish government enforces the law by meting out heavy punishment to the cheaters, even though there may not be clear-cut evidence to support the case. This is done in order to dissuade other wrongdoers from going astray and troubling the land.

There are those who have become wealthy, in terms of the standards of the region, from what they have accumulated through trade. They themselves are not learned in the Torah, but they honor the Torah and those who study it.[4] One finds there traveling solicitors who sail the seven seas and spend their days knocking on the doors of the rich. They adorn themselves in long garments, a Rabbinic cloak, and thereby acquire the title "Rabbi." They are received with reverence and joyous hearts. The multitude bestows gifts of money on them, each man according to his abilities, large or small. They are especially generous to a *shaliah kollel*[5] from the Land of Israel. In their eyes, he is considered a holy emissary, and they are blessed by his presence. They stray not from his commands, neither to the left nor to the right. They fulfill his every request with an eager heart all the while that he is a guest in their midst.

Despite the fact that the Jews are very successful, they humble themselves before the Mohammedans, who are the rulers of the land. They call them respectfully *sīdī*,[6] because the Mohammedans are vain and jealous of their honor, lest someone from the other religions treat them with contempt.

Those Jews who are citizens of foreign countries, even though they are protected and shielded by their consuls, who seek freedom for all their nationals, still humble themselves above and beyond what is called for. They foresee the distant future and fear the wrath of the oppressor, the religious hatred which lies hidden in dark recesses, taking vengeance when the opportunity arises.

Most of the merchants are very strict in their religious observance. They come to the morning, noon, and evening prayers daily. They are careful to observe the Sabbath as prescribed. They do not marry gentiles and they refrain from partaking of their wine and their food. They do not cook meat with milk. They do not eat the thigh muscle or the flesh of animals which have not been ritually slaughtered. On the Sabbath and holidays they are very careful to refrain from touching anything that is "forbidden,"[7] not only those things mentioned by the Rabbis but other things as well. If someone is ill, they go to visit him at home on the Sabbath before the Sabbath meal.

In 1836, Judge Rabbi Nathan Adadi[8] visited Benghazi. He noticed that the ritual slaughterer was not skilled in his craft. He insisted that Rabbi Joseph Romani come to Tripoli to learn to be a slaughterer and inspector,[9] and so he did.

(However, when the region was captured by the Italians some of the simple people began to scorn the customs which they had inherited from their forefathers, saying, "He who keeps the old customs removes himself from modern society.")

In the early days, there were not many settlers in Benghazi because there was not enough food to support the population. In the beginning of the seventeenth century, according to the Christian reckoning, there were but four Jewish families: Buaron from Misurata, Barḍa from the town of Tajura, and Ḥayun and Temam from Tripoli. Even though Benghazi's soil is not suitable for raising food crops, she is able to import an enormous amount by sea from Crete, Egypt, and so forth. Many caravans come to Benghazi by way of the great wide desert. They come from Central Africa, bringing ostrich feathers, ivory, gold dust, and so forth. The Jews grew in number there, and trade developed.

One of the Jewish merchants, who came from Constantinople and settled in Benghazi, was a close friend of important Turkish officials. He violated an ordinance[10] and gambled in front of witnesses. The Rabbi of the Congregation, the Ḥakham Raḥamim Farjun (may he rest in heaven), did not defer to him but posted a notice in the synagogue clearly stating that "So and So" had violated the rule. As a result, the congregation ostracized him. No one would speak to him. The gambler spoke to the officials of the government and asked them to support him. He wrote a letter of complaint to the governor stating that Rabbi Raḥamim Farjun, the leader of the Jewish congregation, had imposed a ban[11] on him which enjoined any Jew from speaking to him, and that this violated the law enacted by our Lord the Sultan, 'Abd al-Ḥamid.[12]

The governor invited the Rabbi to appear before him because he had violated a government regulation. The Rabbi responded, saying, "I did not impose the ban. When I accepted the post of Chief Rabbi I received a list of those areas for which I was to be responsible in fulfilling my duties of office. Included in the list was gambling. Gambling is a corruptive influence, one of the repugnant vices in which many people were sunk. As a result, an ordinance was passed, with the agreement of members of the former generation (who all signed it), that whoever plays dice will not be spoken to by any member of the congregation for a period of three months. When I received the testimony of eyewitnesses, it was my obligation to inform the congregation. I fulfilled my responsibility. The congregation, on their own, separated themselves from him. I did not instruct them to refrain from speaking to him." The governor, upon hearing this, upheld the Rabbi, saying, "You have permission to continue, and may you be successful."

The gambler was not content with the ruling. He hoped that if he told the consuls of the other governments that it was contrary to the principles of freedom they would intervene in the issue and see to it that the Rabbi was punished.

The French consul met with the Rabbi, and the Rabbi explained the matter to him. He also explained the reason for the ruling. It seems that gambling used to be rampant among the population, and they lost a great deal of money. It happened one night that a man played and lost all the money he had with him. His friends advised him to take his wife's kerchief,[13] without her knowledge. With it, he would be able to win back all he had lost. While his wife was sleeping in her bed, he took the kerchief, but he lost the kerchief too. His wife was forced to stay in her bedroom because she had no other kerchief to wear. From the day the decree was promulgated, the population mended their ways. Then the consul agreed that the Rabbi was in the right, and he said, "I, too, join forces with you."

After the region was captured by the Italians, some youths tried to undermine the decree. They counted on the government to assist them, but the government would not give them permission to ruin things.

The communal charity fund is supported by the money collected from the sale of '*aliyot*[14] to the Torah scroll, from the *gabila*[15] on kosher meat, and so forth. Each week, about 1,200 francs are distributed to the teachers of the small children and to the poor. When the congregation sees that the funds are running low they raise the *gabila* tax.

There are about 1,200 Jews there now (that is, in the year 1906, but I heard that in 1910, there were 2,850, and in the year ____[16] their number increased to ____). Most of them are refugees from Tripoli, unruly and given to chronic gambling, the source of all the corrupting vices. Unable to raise money in Tripoli, they moved to Benghazi. They were successful in their business and amassed wealth because the town is a sanctuary, prohibiting every sort of gambling: one cannot find a stakeholding document there.

In former days, dice playing was very widespread, and many Jews lost their wealth.[17] In 1840, a visiting scholar named Rabbi Moshe Ashkenazi passed through there. He was a judge and head of a Rabbinic college of the Holy Congregation of Vienna.[18] He saw their misfortune and the decay that grew as a result of the gambling. Possessed by zeal, he gathered to him the notables of the city, and with their agreement he promulgated a decree in writing, with full authority and signed by all. The ordinance prohibits all forms of gambling and stakeholding. He who breaks the law, even if he is one of the most influential members of the community, will be called impure and the punishments of *herem* and banishment[19] will fall upon him. He will remain isolated and rebuked. No Jew will speak to him. He will not be able to take part in any holy endeavor for three months.

This written agreement is still preserved in the hands of the Rabbi of the community. The Jews deviate not from that which is written, neither to the right nor to the left. There was one notable, a foreigner, who erred and broke the agreement. The Jews withdrew from him so that the *herem* would not contaminate them. The man could not stand it any longer, and fled from there as one flees from a serpent.[20]

In the marketplace is a synagogue called *a-sla likbira*.[21] It was built as a synagogue in 1870. Afterwards, the community acquired the ground around it. Upstairs is a room expressly set aside for the study of the Book of the Zohar[22] during the early morning. There is a balcony for the women's section. There are windows through which they can see the Torah scroll. The women spread their palms toward the script[23] of the Torah scroll in supplication for long life and sustenance for their families. They do this because they do not know how to pray.

In the yard of the synagogue, downstairs, is a room set aside for the latecomers, those who arrive when their friends are already midway in the prayer service. The courtyard of the synagogue was consecrated by the Honorable Moshe Temam in the beginning of the eighteenth century, according to the Christian calendar. Afterwards, the Congregation bought the remainder of the rights. They follow the same ritual of prayers as do their brothers, the Tripolitanians. However, in the prayer of confession said on Mondays and Thursdays[24] they follow the liturgy of the Land of Israel, as instituted by a *shaliah kollel* who came from there.

On the outskirts of town, not far from the seacoast, is a synagogue called *slat li-bramli* because the land was bought by Rabbi Jacob Libramli. He purchased a ruined building from a Mohammedan named al-Haj 'Abdullah Ga'ida in 56__[25] for a sum of 4,000 francs, cash. He was aided in this effort by the Hakham Rabbi Rahamim Farjun, the honorable David Dani, and Rabbi Yosef Teshuva. The building was completed in 1914. Its height is eleven meters, its length twenty meters, its width twelve meters. The total cost of the land and the building was

____ francs, excluding the cost of the planks, the ceiling beam, and the cement for the floor, which were contributed by the children of ____. There is a room in the synagogue yard for the *Shomrim Laboqer*[26] society. In an upper story, there is a section for the women who come on the High Holidays. The committee of the *qehillah*[27] meets there to deal with community matters, and the place is also used by the Rabbinic court.

Another synagogue was built recently, in 1906. In that year, however, before it had been completed, a fire broke out one night in the storehouses of the Benghazi marketplace. Most of these storehouses belonged to Jewish merchants. Thus, many of the wealthy Jews were impoverished because of the fire. What was saved from the flames was stolen during the conflagration by looters, as if whatever was left was ownerless property. The construction of the synagogue was suspended because the wealthy could not manage to contribute enough money to cover the costs.

There was a Talmud Torah[28] which had seriously deteriorated. In 1906, a few members of the community got together to revive it. They appointed Mr. Lalu (Eliyahu) Gewili to be the director and overseer. He undertook this holy task with love. He ignored his business in order to supervise the pupils. He watched over their ways and instructed them in the habits of cleanliness and success, seeing to it that they did not neglect their studies. He gathered all the wayward youths who loiter in the streets and marketplaces, so that the number of pupils attending the Talmud Torah school came to eighty. He went from door to door collecting funds from the rich for the teachers' salaries. He also introduced benches for the pupils to enable them to sit with heads held high and legs free, not like the old custom of sitting on straw mats with feet tucked under and head bowed.

There is a separate room specifically for the elder children.[29] This school was established in the new synagogue mentioned above. In those days, students made progress in cleanliness and behavior, according to the standards first set.

However, a few people started to complain that the principal terrorized the children about cleanliness and laziness. Because of this, the students began to regress. They treated the director with contempt and never achieved the desired level of performance.

The Italian government, with the permission of the Turkish government, established a school to teach the Italian language, arithmetic, and Hebrew to the Jewish youths.

In the cemetery there are no engraved markers. It is only in recent years that, from time to time, an engraved marker has been placed with the name of the deceased, the date, and so forth. The reason for this is that the Mohammedans are jealous of the Jews, and they break the markers that are built on the Jewish graves. At a later period, the burial grounds were walled in.

In 1906, when I traveled with my friend, the researcher Dr. Nahum Slouschz, we searched the area, hoping to find some stones with inscriptions buried in the earth. We found nothing but a few broken pieces of brick inscribed with some strange letters. We were unable to ascertain whether they were Assyrian,[30] Greek, or Samaritan.[31] However, it was quite evident to us that Jews have been living there, without interruption, from ancient times until the present.[32] For should you claim that Jewish settlement had ceased, who told them that the present graveyard was for the burial of Jews?

Far to the east of Benghazi, on the seacoast, is the town of Derna, formerly known as Darnus. The area is rich in grain, cattle, and all sorts of fruit because it is watered by two flowing rivers. One of the rivers even flows through the town. It is well adapted for commerce. The Jews engage in trade and make a very fine living, even though they number only 340 souls. I did not go there personally to investigate their customs. There is one practice, however, that they inherited from their forefathers from Tripoli and all the surrounding area. This is the peddling of cosmetics and perfumes to gentile women. (In the Tractate *'Avodah Zarah,* page 61a, it states:

> In a city where only heathens reside it should also [be permitted without a supervisor] since there are [Jewish] spice-sellers going about the cities.[33] Samuel said, [the Mishnah refers] to a city which has doors and bolts.

On this, the Tosafòt[34] comments:

> Even though Ezra decreed only that they pass through towns where there are Jewish women, so that they would not become repulsive to their husbands, they continued to pass through there [the non-Jewish towns] as was their wont.)[35]

What can be concluded from all that we have said is that in 1906 the total number of Jews in Libya was about 24,850,[36] distributed as follows: In Tripoli proper, 15,000; Jebel Yefren, 2,000; Ghuryan, 800; Zuara, 40; Zawia, 600; Zanzur, 40; Amrus, 2,000; Tajura, 140; Mesallata, 700; Khoms, 400; Zliten, 640; Misurata, 900; Benghazi, 1,200; Derna, 340; and Sirte, 50. In 1906, the total number of Christians, both Catholics and Protestants, in Tripoli was 2,792. The figure does not include the Greek Orthodox mentioned in Section 1. Those Christians to be found in the other towns can be counted on one hand, for there are but a few here and there in Khoms, Zliten, Misurata, and Derna. Benghazi has more

Christians than all the other towns put together (in 1919, I counted 2,850 Christians there).

It is difficult to ascertain the number of Mohammedans, or even to make an estimate. I have seen several books in which the number of settlers in Tripoli is believed to be about one million. It seems that this assumption is incorrect, for there are many, many more.[37] Even the Turkish government cannot accurately gauge the numbers of her citizens in Africa.

In 1919, there were 230 students in the Talmud Torah school in Benghazi. Of these, 130 went to both the Italian school and the Talmud Torah. The Talmud Torah has a Hebrew teacher named Hakham Meir 'Aqnin, from Jerusalem. He teaches a few of the students Hebrew in Hebrew. His students enjoy their lessons very much.[38] The principal of the school is R. Eliyahu Gewili. His assistants are: R. 'Azura Romani, R. Khamus Fallah, Mr. Mokhai Ben David, R. Shim'on 'Arbib, R. Shalom Lighzayil, Mr. Hai Gabizon, and Nimni Huriya.[39] The monthly budget for teachers is 175–250 francs. The general monthly expenses are 1,354 francs. The Talmud Torah is funded in the following way: 58 francs weekly from the communal fund; a merchant's tax of one part in a thousand on the value of goods imported;[40] the sale of *'aliyot* to the Torah in the synagogue of the Talmud Torah school; and the tuition fee paid for sending the children, each person according to his means.

NOTES

1. Presumably a transposition of the ancient name Berenice.

2. Here Hakohen inserts Note 90, a long excerpt from the introduction to a book by E. Lavi (1864). We have set the note separately as the next portion of text.

3. The last statement probably refers to one source of resentment on the part of the Moslems (and Christians) towards the Jews. It appears to have been added after the original draft of the manuscript was completed. There are many such additions in this section. It seems likely that Hakohen modified his text after taking up residence in Benghazi (see the Editor's Introduction).

4. Here, as in other sections, there is a close association between the topic of wealth and the ways of spending money to fulfill religious ends.

5. See Section 95.

6. My lord. The text has the Hebrew *'adon*.

7. The Hebrew *muqṣeh*. The concept of *muqṣeh* concerns additional Sabbath prohibitions, which are designed to keep people from violating the major prohibitions. For example, it is forbidden to write on the Sabbath, so a pencil becomes *muqṣeh* and should not be touched.

8. This appears to be a mistake. Hakohen is probably referring to Avraham Adadi (see the Editor's Introduction), whose grandfather was named Nathan.

9. A technical term. Each activity, slaughtering and inspection, is a specialty in its own right. Often, however, one person is trained in both crafts.

10. The Hebrew *taqqanah*. These are laws that are enacted, supplementary to the Torah, but which enjoy religious backing. Such ordinances may be promulgated by the leaders of individual communities and are binding on members of that community.

11. The Hebrew *herem*.

12. The reference is probably to judicial reforms made under Abdul Hamid (Lewis 1961:179–180).

13. A garment with connotations of sexual intimacy. A woman is expected to keep her hair covered in front of strange men, and does so with a kerchief. The Tripolitanian term for kerchief, *mharma,* comes from an Arabic root that suggests something "forbidden" and "sacred" (*cf.* Antoun 1968:679).

14. To recite a blessing over the Torah when it is read.

15. See Goldberg (1974b:146) on the term *gabila*.

16. This brief section was added later on. Hakohen intended to supply numbers in the blank spaces, but never did.

17. The topic is partially repeated because Hakohen added this part of the account at a later date.

18. I have been unable to identify this Rabbi—a fact that is puzzling because of the important position he claimed to hold. Yaari (1951:677, n. 68) mentions a *shaliah kollel* from Safed named Moshe Ashkenazi, who was in North Africa at approximately that time. It appears that his authorization as an emissary was revoked while he was in Morocco. This *shaliah* may have given false information about his background; many of these visitors attempted to impress the local populace with their importance.

19. There are various degrees of "excommunication" in Jewish law. Two are mentioned here.

20. The Hebrew word for serpent, *nahash,* also forms an acronym of the three degrees of excommunication—*nidui, herem,* and *shamta*.

21. The great synagogue.

22. The most well-known book of the Kabbalah.

23. The written words are central to the sacred quality of the Torah scroll. Adadi's book, *Hashomer 'Emet* (1849) deals with laws concerning the Torah scrolls and begins with the rules concerning the writing of a scroll. On the religious value of writing, see Goldberg (1972a:43–44n) and Deshen (1975).

24. The *widdui*.

25. Here and in other places in the paragraph, Hakohen intended to fill in the information, but never did. In some cases, the additional sentences he did add can be read only with difficulty.

26. A group of individuals who rose in the early morning to recite prayers of supplication and hymns. This was a mild form of asceticism growing out of the Lurianic Kabbalah (Idelsohn 1960:55).

27. Community.

28. A traditional religious school.

29. In the traditional system, everyone studied in one room. Often, the more capable older children were given the task of instructing the younger ones (see the Author's Introduction, in which Hakohen mentions that he earned money working in this fashion).

30. Standard Hebrew script.

31. Hakohen probably uses this term to refer to the ancient Hebrew (pre-exilic) script. This hypothesis is in line with Slouschz' ideas on the antiquity of Jewish settlement in the area.

32. The continuity of Jewish settlement since ancient times is quite problematical (*cf.* Hirschberg 1974:24–39).

33. The question involved is whether wine that has been in the possession of a heathen may be drunk. The assumption is that the non-Jew will refrain from touching wine that is to be used by Jews, for fear of being seen. Consequently he will not be able to sell the wine to Jews. Even if all the inhabitants of the city are heathens, it may be expected that the non-Jew will be careful lest he be seen by a Jewish peddler in the town. Hakohen thus shows the antiquity (and virtue) of the occupation of peddling.

34. A classic commentary on the Talmud (*Encyclopaedia Judaica*, vol. 15, pp. 1278–1283).

35. The Babylonian Talmud (*Baba Qama* 82a) declares that Ezra the Scribe promulgated ten decrees, one of which was that peddlers should be allowed to go about the countryside. It explains that peddlers sold jewelry to women so that they would not become repulsive to their husbands. The Tosafot wish to harmonize this passage of the Talmud, which refers to Jewish towns, with the section quoted by Hakohen, which assumes that the peddlers go into towns inhabited by heathens.

36. This figure seems high (Goldberg 1971).

37. Here again, Hakohen overestimates.

38. Former pupils of 'Aqnin have particularly fond memories of Hebrew plays that he organized in the school (Maurice Roumani, personal communication).

39. The name of a woman who presumably helped 'Aqnin care for the school. Her surname is given before her personal name.

40. This tax was called *khaba* (Goldberg 1974b:625).

Jewish-Christian Conflict in Benghazi
(NOTE 90)

What is unusual is that the Christians sometimes harbor hatred of the Jews. I will present to you a case of false accusation copied from the introduction to a book, *The Redemption of the Lord*, written by Rabbi Eliyahu Lavi, may his soul rest in Eden, who was a Righteous Teacher[1] in the city of Benghazi:

"I shall remember God's mercy accomplished through the person of the wealthy Mr. Shaul Lavi (may his soul rest in Eden)[2] in the year 1862 at the season of Passover. At that time, I was living in the town of Benghazi (may the Lord protect it) and a group of four people went out to the fields to chant the blessing on the trees,[3] as was the custom.

Among the four people was included my eldest son David (may the Lord watch over him). After they had concluded the blessing on the trees, they ate and drank some whisky and wine, as was the custom. They left the field close to nightfall, slightly drunk from the wine, from the holiday, and from the happiness of having performed the commandment of reciting the blessing.

"On the way back, they took herbs and vegetables, and one of them put these on his head. They took the tablecloth on which they had eaten and drunk and made it into a *bandera*.[4] The tablecloth had a stain on it, due to some wine that had spilled during the eating and drinking. They chanted hymns as they made their way, and the people who saw them pass laughed at them. A Christian[5] man and woman saw them and went to complain to more influential Christians, saying, 'This is what we have seen. So and So have made an effigy of Jesus and had a kerchief full of blood in their hands, and they were commemorating the killing of Jesus. The Jews are mocking us and our religion.' The Christians then gathered together and said, 'It must be a Jewish law to do this every year, to commemorate the killing.[6] The proof that this is so is that we have seen the son of the Rabbi with them.' This kind of talk resulted in false accusations, for it never occurred to any Jew to do such a thing. They gathered together to plan a way to erase our name and to rid the whole town of Jews.

"Among the four Jews who were involved were an English citizen and a French citizen. The others were subject to Arab rule. The Christians immediately went to the English and French consuls, who happened to be in Benghazi (may God protect it) at that time, and recounted the incident to them. Immediately upon hearing the tale, these consuls sent for the Jews under their jurisdiction and put them in irons. The Christians gathered together and collected signatures and written testimonies that they saw the Jews do what has been described above. Then they continued to tell whatever lies they pleased. They also collected signed written testimonies from the Ishmaelites. They gathered more than one hundred signatures from one hundred of the most important people of the city. They went to the ruler of the town, called all the gentiles together, and they all testified before the ruler, each one giving different testimony. This one told it one way and another told it differently, but each one was determined to make trouble for Israel. They called in the four people involved. These people said, 'Heaven forbid that we should do such things. It is true,' they said, 'that we took some herbs but only out of the joy of holiday. We know nothing of what they are speaking.' Then they, because of our sins,[7] were put in iron chains. Thirty Jews who saw what was happening were also put in prison, all because of the hatred and wickedness of the two consuls who were in Benghazi.

"The four people mentioned were taken out to the streets of the marketplace on the Sabbath of Passover, and all the Moslems and Christians insulted them and threw stones at them. This was in addition to the pain of being in iron chains. All the Moslems and Christians kept saying, 'In three days these four will be burned and we will put an end to the Jews.'

"When I saw what was happening, I almost collapsed. I went to the English consul and said to him, 'Don't you know that one of the four people is an English citizen?' Then I said to him, 'Do you have the permission of the consul of Tripoli?' He told me, 'It is a small matter, but I want to receive permission in order to burn them.' At first I spoke to him quietly and then harshly, but nothing helped. Because of our many sins, the hatred of the Moslems and Christians against us had increased; both were of one mind to eradicate our name. A war had been declared against us by the Ishmaelites and the Christians. We were surrounded on all sides.[8] All were conspiring to make more false accusations so the punishment meted out to us would be more severe. We could not go out into the marketplace, as we had become fair game to all, and the gentiles could do what they pleased with us. There were Jews who fled to the desert. There were those who hid in caves.

"On the eighth night of Passover, about ten of us went to say the evening prayer. We had just begun to pray when some Christians entered, each with instruments of destruction in his hand, intending to burn the synagogue and the Torah scrolls and kill the Jews (God forbid). We stopped praying. They were accompanied by a Jewish informer, may God erase his name and memory forever. He directed them, saying, 'This is the Jew who was with the four people who were mocking your religion, and this is another one,' until (because of our many sins) no one in the synagogue could escape. The doors were blocked with other Christians besides those who had first entered. Moreover, they took three Jews away, beat them, and threw them in jail.

"Eventually, four people were seized with the zeal of the Lord of Hosts. These four were subjects of the Arab government. They went to the ruler of the town, taking a devious route so that they would not encounter the Christians. They came before the ruler of the city and said to him, 'Tell us, our Lord, is the city under your control, or is it controlled by the Christians? For the Christians have set upon us, though we have committed no crime, and they wish to kill us. If we are guilty and deserving of punishment, we have come before you. Do with us as you will, kill us or let us live!'

"They began to cry before the king. The king took pity on them and sent messengers with them to see them safely home. All this did not help. The Christians continued to collect the signatures of the Ishmaelites. They collected signatures from almost half the city. They paid them money in order that they should testify. They rented a boat for an enormous fee in order to be able to send long letters to Tripoli to the Pasha. They wanted to be able to spread their false charges far and wide and put an end to the Jews.

"The four wealthy and distinguished men, Sir Ḥaim Ḥasan (may God protect him), Sir Mordechai 'Arbib (may God protect him), Sir Yiṣḥaq Teshuva (may God protect him), and Sir Moshe Halevi (may God protect him), saw that worship had been suspended, that the synagogue (because of our many sins) had no worshippers at the appointed times, since all the Jews were confined to their homes. They went to the ruler. They said to him, 'What sin have we committed, what transgressions? Can anyone really believe that we would do such a thing? We would like to inform you that we are not even able to worship.' Then some of the ruler's attendants accompanied them. This happened close to midday, when a quorum of men had just gathered. We said the morning prayer individually[9] and studied the portion of the Torah relating to the holiday, and afterwards publicly recited the additional prayer for the eighth day of Passover. A telegram was sent to Shaul Lavi (may God protect him), and he was informed of the false accusations being levied against us by the Christians. God awakened his spirit, and he was filled with the zealous passion of the Lord, and he went to the English consul of Tripoli. The English consul of Tripoli was a very learned man and a righteous gentile, and he understood the truth. He immediately sent a telegram to the consul of Benghazi, saying, 'When this message reaches you, you are to free the English subjects.' Then the consul of Tripoli and Sir Shaul Lavi (may God protect him) went to the Pasha on behalf of the other Jews, who were subject to the government of the Arabs, to prevail upon him to send a message to the ruler of Benghazi (may God protect it) to free them. He promised that in a few days he would free them, and, God forbid, nothing would happen to them and they need not fear. Sir Shaul Lavi sent us a telegram informing us of all this.

"We went to the consul of Benghazi, and we said, 'How is it that you did not release those Jews who are English citizens from their iron chains when you received orders from the consul in Tripoli who is your superior?' He said, 'I do not care to hear of this. I will not release them from prison.' All this is the handiwork of God in heaven in order to humiliate him, for the consul did as he saw fit and was in contact with the Christians, who promised to give him a great deal of money if he took vengeance upon the Jews. Again we sent word to Sir Shaul that the Benghazi consul persisted in his rebellious stance. Upon hearing of this, the consul of Tripoli sent him a message saying that if he did not release the English citizens his end would be very bitter. At this, he released them and sent them on their way.

"Following this, an authoritative statement came from high places in

London, and from other notables in the English kingdom, that the consul of Tripoli had acted correctly and justly. Further, the consul of Benghazi was directed to release all those who were imprisoned, and if he again should dare to harm the Jews he would be beaten with whips and knotted scourges until he died. Whoever harmed the Jews would be put to death.

"This miracle and redemption was accomplished by the consul of Tripoli and the upright Sir Shaul Lavi. Dear God, watch over them, and insure that they and their children have a long and blessed life.

"It was not long before all the Christians who had falsely libeled the Jews received their just deserts, all manner of misfortune from God in heaven. Also, the English and French consuls in Benghazi who had perpetrated these evil deeds fled the city in humiliation and disgrace, while all the Christians laughed at them and degraded them. Blessed be He who saves Israel."

NOTES

1. A term indicating the Rabbinic leader of a community.

2. The parenthetical remark was added by Hakohen. Shaul Lavi was alive in the 1860s. He served as vice-consul for Austria-Hungary (Hirschberg 1965a) and was president of the Tripoli Regional Alliance Israélite Universelle Committee.

3. The custom of going out to the fields during the month of Nisan (in the spring) to view the trees and recite a blessing often took on the atmosphere of a picnic. In Section 67 (ms. p. 127a), Hakohen describes how this custom was practiced among the Jews of Tripoli. "They view it," he says, "as one of the commandments of the Torah." In Section 38, Hakohen cites another Jewish-Gentile confrontation, from the first third of the nineteenth century, which was prompted by the Jewish celebration of the blessing of the trees (see Goldberg 1978a).

4. Wearing it like a cloak.

5. Here, and throughout, the term used for Christian is *'arel, i.e.* uncircumcised (see the list of words in Section 94).

6. Landau and Ma'oz (1974) have discussed the incidence of blood-libels elsewhere in the Middle East—where Moslems, Jews, and Christians were in proximity—during the nineteenth century.

7. The Hebrew *ba'awon* is an elliptic formula bemoaning the condition of exile in which the Jews are vulnerable to all manner of suffering.

8. *I.e.* we were unable to play off one side against the other, as usual.

9. *I.e.* there were not enough men (less than ten) to say the morning prayers publicly.

CHAPTER SIX

The Italian Invasion of Libya

Editor's Foreword

The last four sections of the *Highid Mordekhai,* which Hakohen calls Part IV, are actually a continuation of Part I. Together they comprise the historical sections of the narrative. Hakohen's primary concern is the Jewish community, and he provides enough general background to make the experience of the Jews comprehensible. As usual, the historical sequence of events is interspersed with data of other kinds, so that we learn of economic conditions or local attitudes and debates in addition to major political events. In Section 65, at the end of Part I, Hakohen describes Tripoli under the regime of the Young Turks (1908–1911), providing the immediate background for his description of the Italian takeover. The following summary presents some of the main points of that account:

The accession to power of the Young Turks was welcomed by the governor of Tripoli, Rajeb Pasha. Already there had been rumors that the Sultan, Abdul Ḥamid, was prepared to cede Tripoli to Italy, and the Pasha felt that the new democratic regime would be able to stand up to the European powers. Although this was also the hope of the local population, at the same time they were wary of the reformist and sometimes antireligious tone of the new rulers.

Rajeb Pasha died in the fall of 1908, and was followed by two more governors (1909–1910), Ahmed Fawzi Pasha and Ahsan Husni Pasha. Both of these were returned quickly to Istanbul since they were unacceptable to the local populace.

We have already mentioned two of the reforms instituted by the Young Turks—elections to the parliament in Istanbul and military conscription. Despite the numerical prominence of the Jews in the city of

178

Tripoli, none were sent to parliament. However, they were represented proportionally among the new recruits. While insisting that the Jews serve in the army, the Turkish authorities were sensitive to their religious needs. The Jewish soldiers were not forced to eat nonkosher food and were given leave on the Sabbath and Jewish holidays. Perhaps in this way the Young Turks demonstrated to the population at large that they were not against religion.

The Moslems and Jews were united on another front. The Turkish reformers tried to institute a law in which the state became the trustee of a man's estate if his children were still below the age of twenty years at the time of his death. The Moslems saw this as an abolition of the traditional rules of inheritance. It seemed that the government was trying to expropriate the land of any person who died without children, keeping it from passing to his brothers or other heirs. Government officials began the administrative work of registering the estates of local people upon their death, despite popular opposition.

The Tripolitan notables were divided over how they should react. Some advocated rebellion against the Turks. Others suggested that they invite Great Britain to take over the country, on the premise that she would not change the traditional Islamic laws. Still others argued that this would not work because they had heard that members of the Triple Entente had agreed to give the Italians a free hand in Libya. All of this discussion came to naught.

In May 1910, a wealthy Jew by the name of Sa'adan 'Atiya passed away, leaving no children. When the government officials came to his house to register the estate, the Jews prevented the officials from entering the house. Jewish artisans and merchants then closed their shops and demonstrated in the streets. Upon seeing this, the Moslems joined the demonstration and also called a strike. When the crowd approached the governor's palace, Ibrahim Pasha agreed to admit a few of the leaders, including both Moslems and Jews. When asked what the protest was about, the leaders declared that they were united in opposition to the new laws of inheritance. The Pasha attempted to argue with them: "Is there not a clear commandment in the Holy Koran that one must establish a guardian for orphans?"[1] Hakohen, who was a member of the group, was quick but respectful in his retort: "The law of the Koran applies to orphaned minors, not to people of legal majority. The Jew Sa'adan 'Atiya was of legal age. Why should the law apply to him?" The Pasha told the leaders to give him two weeks' time to make a decision. He contacted Istanbul about the matter and was told that the issue should be referred to the local council of notables *(idāra)*. The council voted to do away with the new laws.

The picture that emerges in this episode is repeated through the latter sections of Part I. While the Turkish Pashas differ considerably from one another, they do include capable men—notably Ahmed Razem Pasha (1882–1895) and Rajeb Pasha (1904–1909)—intent on improving the condition of the province (Martin 1978) through technological innovation, economic reorganization, and administrative reforms. The local population appreciates technical advance and the establishment of security in the countryside, but when new laws, new taxes, and military conscription are involved, resistance is quickly expressed—often in the name of religion. Hakohen himself reveals an interesting stance. He applauds the attempts at reform, but opposes the conscription of the Jews and the new inheritance laws. Despite this, his narrative helps to correct the one-sided "general condemnation of Turkish rule" (Evans-Pritchard 1949:90) and provides a more rounded picture of these developments.[2]

This brings us to the time of Italian intervention. Evans-Pritchard (1949:101, 108–109), has already discussed the Italian misreading of the disputes between the Turks and the Libyans. Although he focuses on Cyrenaica, his observations hold true for Tripolitania as well. The Tripolitanian Arabs and the Turks had their differences, but when a takeover by a European Christian power became imminent there was little question in the minds of the Arabs that they should unite with the Turks to oppose the invasion. The Turkish government tried to work against the foothold that the Italians had established: a school was built near Jamʻa Maḥmud to compete with the Italian schools; no tenders were accepted from Italian contractors, despite economic loss to the government; local Arab writers urged the people not to use the Bank of Rome. Popular resentment toward the Italians grew, and was expressed in daily incidents. These events led Italy to issue an ultimatum, but this only constituted an excuse for carrying out a plan which had been in the making for years.

NOTES

1. Sura IV, verse 6.
2. Hardly any mention of serious attempts at reform appears in the accounts of Féraud (1927) and Rossi (1968). Rossi gives the following summary statement (1929:817): "The city however remained for 76 years entirely subject to the Ottomans; the conditions of the native population were practically unchanged; the city enjoyed a certain measure of progress thanks only to the foreign colonies, among which the Italian colony predominated as to numbers, influence and private and financial enterprise." Hakohen, while welcoming the Italian conquest, also appreciated the efforts of the Turkish Pashas for the good of the city and the province.

The Italian Capture of Tripoli[1]
(SECTION 111)

In 1911, word went out that Italy had cast her eyes upon Libya with the intention of conquest. This was in spite of the fact that Arab journalists had for a long time been writing venomous, stinging articles, designed to excite hatred against the Italians and demean them in the eyes of the masses. These articles were written to encourage the people to oppose and act coldly toward all Italian subjects.

In the month of Tishrei 5672, September 1911, the Italians seemed bent on putting their intentions into action. The people were divided in their opinions, saying both this and that. However, the majority decided to look upon the Italian scheme as a ploy or a deception. They claimed that Italy could cause no harm to Tripoli because of her fortifications and strong towers. Even if their cannon balls did reach the town, the worst they could do was to make a breach in the wall. On the other hand, the cannon balls from the tower could sink the Italian ships into the depths of the sea.

On the sixth of Tishrei, the twenty-ninth of September, Italian warships came into view. The Italians acted justly, according to the biblical injunction, "When you approach a town to attack it, you shall offer it terms of peace" (Deuteronomy XX:10). When they saw that there were no more chances for a peaceful solution, they evacuated all Italian subjects to Italy,[2] and on that very day they declared war. However, the actual battle remained in abeyance for four days while negotiations went on in hopes that a solution could be found.

(As the main purpose of this book is to write of those matters pertaining to the Jews, I will write only a brief account. The Italians will certainly write all about the war at length.)

On the eleventh of Tishrei, October third, the Mohammedans were prepared and equipped with everything that was necessary for a holy war on behalf of the beloved homeland. They made all the necessary preparations for an offensive war.

Just past midday, the Italian ships began the deadly shelling, firing from amidships and continuing until nightfall without a stop. The earth trembled and was shaken from her foundations. The towers were destroyed first. Many houses were not spared, even in the city proper. The bullets and bursting shells rained down on the city in an unending stream. The Jews lost six souls, who met their bitter end. Thanks are due to the French consul, who opened his doors to all who sought his protection, for his house was filled to overflowing with many Jews.

The gunners in the towers who escaped death in the bombardment fled after seeing, in amazement, that their cannon balls could not reach the Italian navy, which was anchored at a great distance from shore. Their cannon balls fell into the waters a bow's shot away from the Italian fleet. Seeing this, the soldiers, the clerks, and the governmental officers began to flee, narrowly escaping through the desert. Masses of people fled with them because they realized how much they had erred in assessing the situation. Those Jews who had been conscripted into the army prior to the outbreak of the war,[3] and those who had been assigned to guard the Jewish quarter, remained at their stations with their guns ready. They did not let any stranger pass through the Jewish quarter unless he was relieved of his arms. Anyone who, in a fit of religious zeal, attempted to force his way into the area was set upon, relieved of his weapons, and sent on his way.

Peace negotiations were begun, through the efforts of mediators, because the remaining Mohammedans feared for their lives lest the Bedouin do with them as they wished in a city where there was no legal authority and no army to maintain order.

One night, the peasants who lived in the surrounding countryside got together and decided to plunder the Jewish trade market called *suq al-'aṭṭāra*.[4] They said, "The city is wide open, and there are no real guards there, only a handful of policemen. The marketplace is near the city gates. Perhaps no one will stand in our way." They made an armed attack after midnight and battered down the doors of the stores, undisturbed. No one protested because the Jewish owners stayed home at night. Those few policemen who were about did not raise a murmur of protest. Indeed, they assisted the looters, saying, "Take what you can, for it is better that you should have it than that a Christian infidel should benefit. After all, everything is now fair game."

They robbed and looted all the money and goods that were there. Each man took for himself the spoils of the enemies of God, the Jews, who deny the truth of the Mohammedan religion.

When they saw how successful they had been on the fourth of October, they all agreed that they would stage an armed attack on the Jewish quarter after midnight on Friday, October sixth. They would rape the women and young girls, kill, destroy, and take booty as their hearts desired.

The Jews were divided on how to react. While it was still light that Friday, there were those among them who said, "Let us not give up hope. While it is still daylight there is a chance that the flag of peace will be raised before the sunset. But if it be ordained by heaven, then we should be silent like a lamb led dumb to the fleecing."

The others said, "Even though we cannot save ourselves, at least let us die as heroes and defend ourselves. Let not our blood be spilled without a price."

The Mohammedan city-dwellers were filled with fear. They knew very well that should the peasants first attack the Jewish quarter, they would finish their work on fellow Mohammedans. Realizing this, they beseeched the notables of the city, saying, "Finish the negotiations and raise the white flag so the Italians will enter the city and protect it." The peace negotiations were then intensified, but they were not completed.

In broad daylight, the mob broke into the armories and stole all the weapons. Afterwards, they turned their attention to the supply depot, where the army's foodstuffs were stored. After that, they plundered the government palaces and the courthouses and took away furniture, documents, and everything else.

On the eve of the fifth of October, the white flag of peace and surrender was raised over the city, as if to say, "Come, God's blessed ones,[5] and capture the land." Some Italian troops landed on shore while the powerful fleet stood on guard from afar to protect them. On Friday, the generals and the rest of the troops landed. All the notables of the city came out to greet them with joy and gladness, wishing them good luck and success.

The notables among the peasants also came to submit their surrender and to sign a peace treaty. The Jews who were on guard duty quickly took off their military uniforms and weapons and put on civilian clothes. When no sound of shells was heard on the second of October, the Day of Atonement,[6] their joy knew no bounds. Shelling was heard only on the third of October, after the holiday.[7] What's more, they were able to buy palm fronds from the peasants for the festival of Booths, and they were also able to buy the four species. This was because the peasants had returned to working the land, as before, and all fruits and vegetables were available and trade resumed.

However, the army officers and the people who had fled the city poured oil on the flames of discontent among the inhabitants of the region. They proclaimed a holy war against the Christian religion. Their influence on the local population was so great that all commerce and industry ceased and the desert was sealed off.

The government allotted fifteen kilograms of wheat per person to the residents of the city. Each head of a household received an amount in accordance with the number of people in his family. The government also decreed that all weapons must be turned over to officials.

All Jews and some Mohammedans turned in their weapons. The local population adopted the position of the Jews, neither joining forces with the rebels, nor opposing them. On October twenty-third, the local population secretly conspired to start a rebellion to break the peace treaty signed with the Italians.

Whoever called himself a Mohammedan had to sacrifice himself in the holy war, for he had everything to gain and nothing to lose. Should he be victorious, then he would lead a life full of bliss; should he die in battle, he would instantly be divinely rewarded. All his sins would be forgiven, and he would be sent on high to the Garden of Eden. There he would not only be rewarded spiritually, he would also be given an unlimited number of concubines and maidens.

NOTES

1. Hakohen's own title for this section is "The Reconquest of Libya by Rome, as in Ancient Times." See McClure (1913), Askew (1942), and Segrè (1974).
2. In Section 65, ms. p. 121b, Hakohen indicates that Jewish and Christian Italian nationals, and other foreign nationals, started to leave by ship on September 21.
3. Under the regime established by the Young Turks, Jews were conscripted into the army in Tripolitania.
4. Outside of the Jewish quarter.
5. This expression may be understood as sycophancy, on the basis of its use in Genesis XXIV:31.
6. The last day of the Solemn Holidays.
7. The city was shelled on October third and fourth, and the marines landed on the fifth (Askew 1942:83).

The Fighting in the Hinterland

(SECTION 112)

On that very same October twenty-third, while the two sides were fighting each other on the battlefield, the rest of the Italian army was sitting in safety in the outlying areas far from the battle zone. They felt so secure that they were unarmed. Suddenly a wild tumult broke out. The peasants rose up as one man and trained their rifles from the rooftops onto the Italian soldiers.[1] The bullets rained from all sides on the Italian army in a never-ending downpour. Many died a cruel death in the fury of revenge. The peasants prepared to continue their onslaught and turned their attention towards the city of Tripoli, meaning to vent their anger on anyone who did not believe in the Mohammedan religion. They approached the walls of Tripoli, and no author can truly describe the confusion and horror that took place.

The Italian officers, upon seeing the panic and realizing that their souls had reached death's door, rolled up their sleeves and demonstrated both intelligence and bravery. Some took measures to tighten the security of the city and to calm the panic. Others, with a superhuman effort, performed amazing deeds. They killed without mercy and captured untold numbers of prisoners.

There were Mohammedans who had at first accepted Italian rule and had been hired as policemen. On that day of anger, they tore off their government badges and joined forces with the rebellion, but they received the punishment they deserved. The remaining Moslems, who were able to escape by the skin of their teeth, did so by denying that they were Moslems. Hitherto, it had been a terrible disgrace for a Mohammedan to say, "I am a Jew" or "I am a Christian," but on that day the tables were turned. In order to save his life, the Moslem found it expedient to say, "I am a Jew," to fool the Italians, who could not differentiate between the two.

After it was all over, the Italian military government vehemently resolved that after a fixed time anyone caught hiding weapons would be severely punished. All the Jews handed over the weapons in their possession, those that they owned as well as those that they held as pledges against loans. Those Mohammedans who feared for their lives turned in all their weapons, while others hid them. Those who hid their weapons and were discovered received severe punishment.

Many Mohammedans were given government jobs, both high and low. However, the Jews who knew Italian were not given any official positions, except those who were able to work as translators. Despite this, many Jews amassed large amounts in commerce and skilled crafts. This happened in spite of the fact that the roads through the desert were closed, and food prices increased sevenfold. Even so, they purchased everything eagerly, because the profit was greater than the expense. However, when the Italian population increased, the rental for stores and houses rose to such an extent that the local residents could no longer bear it. At this point, the Mohammedans grew rich, because they owned most of the real estate.

The Mohammedan battalion was constantly being enlarged by the addition of troops from surrounding areas. They [secretly] received money for food and weapons by way of the conquered desert, all the way from Tunis. The two armies fought each other daily, and the cannons could be heard thundering from afar without any let-up. Many fell on the battlefields on both sides, but the heavier losses took place in the Ottoman army. Not only did the Italians have long-range guns, they also brought in flying machines to carry out aerial warfare.[2] These were used also for reconnaissance flights, to spy on the land and reveal military secrets. These airplanes filled the hearts of the Mohammedans with terror, as if to say, "Who is so brave of heart that he dares stand up to this 'morning star' which is powerful both on sea and on land and whose reach extends even to the heavens above?" The Turkish officers were constantly trying to boost the courage of the Arabs by saying, "Don't be frightened. We will fight for the honor of our religion and the love of our homeland until the last drop of blood is spilled. We shall die the death of heroes. If we make these sacrifices, either we will find the gates of the

Garden of Eden open before us, or we shall live to enjoy a life of happiness and success."

The first strategic center captured from the Ottomans was the site of the well called bu-Miliana. The second center captured was the area near the wadi 'Ain Ṣahra. This place was captured with great fury and courage. The Ottomans retreated. They suffered heavy losses in both men and artillery as well as having to retreat. The Italians, even though they suffered casualties, at long last achieved their objective. They slowly extended the area under their control to the east and the west. In the process, their artillery shells destroyed vast numbers of houses and trees. It will take many years to replace their loss. (Alas for those that are gone and cannot be replaced.)

The Ottomans spread their retreating camps in various areas. They chose the top of Mount Ghuryan[3] as the most secure place where they could safely store their stock of weapons, ammunition, food, and provisions—in short, everything necessary for an offensive war. They concentrated most of their battalion strength there. The Italians ignored the preparations and troop concentrations. They just kept on advancing, little by little. At every point they reached, they armed and fortified their positions. Since they had not yet pacified the countryside, they continued to build sturdy wooden barracks to house their army and equipment; they built new docks stretching out into the depths of the sea; they put in railroad tracks, wire and wireless telegraph equipment, telephones, electric lights, and many other things to modernize the country.

Whoever disguised himself, to leave the Ottoman ranks, and came to Tripoli as a spy was utterly amazed at what he saw; what the talented Italians had accomplished so skillfully in such a short time. He was particularly astounded by all the wealth. He had gone with the intention of spreading propaganda concerning the Mohammedan camp, saying, "Whoever passes through the ranks of the Mohammedans and sees their tactical strength and their stores prepared for war will say 'Aha! Even if all the governments were to band together they would not be able to muster the strength to stand up to the rich and powerful Mohammedan army.' " But he who actually reached Tripoli soon lost his nerve, saying, "Aha! Only a fool who wished to commit suicide would fight the mighty Italian army. All ten of the Ottoman armies are not a match even for the Italian trucks or mule corps. If only the Turkish government would withdraw its army we would all surrender to the Italians and remain alive and not perish."

On October 15, 1912, Italy and Turkey signed a peace treaty.[4] The news spread quickly, and many people rejoiced when they heard of it. The Turks relinquished their interest in Libya in the hope that they could thus stand up to other enemies who were attacking on all sides.

But some Turkish army officers assigned to the forces in Libya were not willing to accept their government's decision and rebelled against their ruler. They were joined by thugs, men of violence who, in the days when there was no law, found it quite easy to perpetrate crimes of banditry and robbery. These criminals raised their voices and proclaimed, "Even if the government of Turkey has abandoned us and will not fight along with us, still we will not surrender to the Christians who deny the Mohammedan religion."

The first place in the mountains of the interior desert to surrender was the Ghuryan, which yielded in the month of November, 1912. Later Terhuna, Orfella, Fezzan, Yefren, Fassato, Ghadames, and the rest all surrendered. All of Tripolitania was captured by the Italians because the coast already had been conquered.

It is true that the whole country was captured by the Italians,[5] but it was no easy task. A great deal of wealth was lost, and much blood was spilled, including that of the many Italian troops who lost their lives on the battlefields. The Italians did not labor in vain. They finally received their reward, the capture of the land. Not so the Mohammedans. They lost their lives, their possessions, and also the lands in which they lived. In the end, those who did not die in battle surrendered against their will to the Italians.

Let us look at what happened to our brethren, the House of Israel, who live in the villages, none of whom took sides in the conflict.

During the days of upheaval, many suffered from shortages and lack of work, and many, many of them actually died of starvation. However, no harm came to their persons or property so long as they did not venture out where they did not belong. The Turkish government issued special orders to its officers to guard the Jews carefully, and the Jews did not interfere in the dispute.

However, in the interregnum, some Mohammedans, filled with religious zeal, attacked the Jewish synagogue in the town of Zanzur.[6] In the town of Zawia, they vented their anger by tearing the Torah scrolls to bits and then burning them. In the town of Tajura, they also committed murder and pillaged Jewish homes, as well as the synagogue. In the town of Misurata, they began by seizing Jewish property and spent their anger by murdering the Jews. On the twenty-fourth of July, 1912, while these hooligans were busy pillaging the Jews, the Italians appeared suddenly from their stronghold on the coast. They fell upon the city of Misurata with warlike shouts. At this, the brigands fled, escaping only with their lives. For the Jews, who were terrified and expected to die, it was as if they had been reborn. Almost to a man, they had been hiding in fright in the synagogue.

The majority of the people who surrendered were pleased at the Italians' behavior. They regretted all that had happened and said, "Alas for those who are gone and cannot be replaced,'' for the Italian officials treat the public fairly, without favoritism or hypocrisy.

NOTES

1. Askew (1942:100).
2. Italy claims to have been the first nation to use airplanes in warfare.
3. The Ghuryan was also the site of a nationalist congress held by Tripolitanian leaders in 1921.
4. Askew (1942:243–245).
5. The interior of Tripolitania was not fully brought under Italian control until the early 1920s.
6. The instability in the interior had an impact on the small Jewish communities until the Italians finally established themselves in the region (Elmalh 1945).

The Italian Capture of Cyrenaica
(SECTION 113)

In the month of Tishrei (October 1911), all the coasts of Cyrenaica[1] were captured by the Italians with the roar of cannon fire. Afterwards, Sirte, which lies between Misurata and Cyrenaica, was captured. Thus all the coasts of Libya were taken easily. Before this, no one imagined that such a powerful navy could appear on the seas.

At first the Jews sat in fear and trembling, dreading the angry hand of the Arabs, who were immersed in religious hatred. However, their fear was in vain, for no one touched them, taking neither life nor property. Only a few people in Benghazi perished in the shelling from the Italian ships.

In the district of Cyrenaica, where the coastal areas were taken easily, battles continued from time to time between the two sides. Many fell dead on the battlefield on both sides, although the Mohammedans usually suffered the greater losses. Even so, the Italians did not advance quickly into the desert interior because there the Bedouin tribes and the Senusis willingly came forth to accept their lot. They ran towards the death-dealing bullets, rejoicing to reach the grave with steadfast faith in their hearts.[2] Whoever dies in a holy war has his sins remitted, and the heavenly Garden of Eden is opened without any obstacles before him.

The Turkish government came to an agreement with Italy to leave Libya. Even so, Turkish officers in Cyrenaica did not pay attention to the treaty. They infused spirit into the minds of the Mohammedan troops, saying, ''Be strong and have courage. Choose to die as heroes and do not submit to the rule of Christians, who deny the Mohammedan religion.'' They did not let the invaders set foot in the desert interior. Some battles were fought to test the Mohammedans' strength, but they did not succeed in ousting the Italians. On the contrary, in the region of Derna the Italians progressed into the desert despite the spirit of the Mohammedans.

Even though the Turkish officers resisted and ignored the agreement by which Turkey removed itself from Libya, time accomplished what good sense was unable to do. Enver Bey, head of Turkish operations in Cyrenaica, heard of the uproar in Constantinople and how it had been surrounded by enemies. Not only had it lost several provinces, but the pro-Hamidian party was pushing out the Union and Progress party, the Young Turks. On hearing this, he decided to leave Cyrenaica.[3] Disguising himself and hurrying across the desert to Alexandria, he made his way to Turkey. There he successfully returned the Young Turks to power.[4]

Still the spirit of the Cyrenaicans did not weaken, and they did not surrender. They relied on their bravery and on the monetary aid and other backing that they received across the conquered desert from as far away as Egypt.

In April 1913, a zealous heroic spirit arose among the Italians, and they revealed their might. They suddenly attacked the central headquarters and supply depot of the Mohammedans, which was not far from Benghazi. They did wondrously that day, killing, destroying, and looting. They took captives and equipment and whatever else they found, and set them aflame.

In that day, the strength of the Italians became known. It was proven that they do not lack bravery and initiative, even in a desert campaign. Fear of the Italians fell over the remaining population, whose heart gave way from the loss of life and property. Then the population split into two camps. One said, ''We are sick of the war and confusion. Are we any better than our Tripolitanian brethren, who have surrendered and are now enjoying security?'' But the second group said, ''Even if we are beaten seven times over we will not surrender. We will fight till the last drop of blood.''

Before the Italian victory, the price of meat in Benghazi was about four francs per kilogram. After the victory, however, one kilo cost from one to one and a quarter francs. The merchants sent quantities of sheep and cattle to Tripoli and to the other coastal towns.

NOTES

1. On the war in Cyrenaica, see Evans-Pritchard (1949).

2. Evans-Pritchard (1949:110–111) gives the following account of the Bedouin who joined the Turkish forces: ''Full of spirit, courageous to the point of

recklessness, their one aim was to charge the enemy, who was armed with the most modern equipment and generally entrenched. They charged on horseback, firing wildly, wherever they might come across him, without any regard to danger, terrain, or odds.''

3. Askew (1942:83, n. 4).

4. Hakohen may be collapsing two different episodes in Enver Bey's career (Lewis 1961:212–213, 220–221).

The Jews Under Italian Rule

(SECTION 114)

From the time the Italian soldiers set foot upon the soil of Tripoli, they stimulated economic growth and trade among the general population, particularly among the Jews. This was true not merely because most Jews knew the Italian language,[1] but also because many Mohammedan residents took refuge in the desert with the Turkish army. Only the very wealthy were left, those who could not take their possessions with them.

In those days, there were no Mohammedan porters in the city, not even to bring merchandise from the port. However, the Jews who had escaped from the village of ʿAmrus and had come with their donkeys to Tripoli as refugees,[2] who had been left without employment, found an opportunity to support themselves. They put their shoulder to the wheel and became porters, and realized a good profit from their efforts.

At the same time, all the hotels were filled from the influx of Italian visitors, merchants, and so forth. Their numbers swelled, and they could find no lodging. The Jews then invented a new business. They crowded themselves in and rented rooms in their homes for a good price. The Italians were overjoyed at this, for they trusted the Jews more than the Mohammedans.[3]

As most of the Italians were not strict or zealous with regard to religion, they became very friendly with the Jews. After a while, however, some hatred developed among a few of the merchants, and they spread it among the masses.[4] This was because the simple merchants among the Italians lost money in business, for two reasons. The first is that they were extravagant in their expenditures. Second, they were not expert in running businesses. It was otherwise with the Jews, who were familiar with business. Sometimes they undersold the Italians, and still they achieved a shining success, making a lot of money. They became well known as businessmen, so much so that Italian customers preferred buying from them over others, saying, "The Jews profit by restricting their consumption."

It appears, moreover, that resentment of the Jews grew elsewhere: among the police, in the courts, and in the hearts of the officials in the customs house. It was as if they were ordered to belittle the Jews and treat them with hostility, and to honor the Mohammedan in his claim, even if he were a simple man arguing against a respected Jewish merchant. The Jews were thus made light of in the eyes of the poor Mohammedan masses.

The Jews could not hold their peace; they complained before God, saying, "What has God done to us? Was it not better for us in former days than now? Even though, during the days of Turkish rule, the Mohammedan majority practiced religious hatred, still a Jew could slyly abate this hatred by appealing to the vanity of the Mohammedan and calling him Lord.[5] Also, the government officials did not treat the claim of a Jew lightly, as they knew very well that in Istanbul there were respected Jews working for liberty and freedom. The words of these Jews were as sharp arrows and were heeded by the government. They would demand redress for an insult to the Jews, and equal treatment [?] from the officials who ___[6] between the two religions. How, then, can the Italian government, which is more civilized, allow its officials to act with hostility toward members of other religions, and to humiliate the Jew for having done nothing except be Jewish? Do they not remember that the Jews were involved in nothing against them? That when the government decreed that everyone hand in their weapons the Jews did so willingly, even bringing the weapons that had been given to them as deposits against loans? It was otherwise with the Mohammedans. Only a few of them brought their weapons, while others were found to have hidden them after a search had been conducted."

A few of the Jews gave the officials the benefit of the doubt and said, "Perhaps it is only a temporary measure, to entice the loyalty of the Mohammedan rebels. It is like one who places bait on a fish hook. He does not intend to feed the fish, but only to tempt him and to catch him."

On the thirtieth of November, 1912, the Great and Honorable Rabbi Shmuel Zvi Margoliot, Chief Rabbi of the city of Florence[7] (may God protect it), arrived in Tripoli. He was sent by the government (may its glory be increased) to investigate the ways of the new Italian subjects, the Jews of Libya, both their customs and their situation. On the fifteenth of December, he was joined by the Honorable Isolomo Colombo, secretary of the general committee of the Jewish community of Rome (may God protect it). In that month both returned, fully satisfied, to their homeland.

NOTES

1. See Section 112. Italian had been taught in schools for several decades (Kahalon 1972). Many adults probably picked up the language through commer-

cial ties with the Italian-speaking population. McClure (1913:277–278) describes
the Jews' activities as interpreters at length:

Among the difficulties which hampered the Italians during the
early days of the occupation was the lack of efficient and trustworthy interpreters. There was a disposition, at first, to rely upon the
Tripoli Jew as the medium of communication between Italian and
Arab, and while the Tripoli Jews are a remarkable and worthy community, the class from which the interpreters were largely drawn did
not supply the type of man that was wanted. The whole Jewish
community welcomed the Italian occupation, but it is an unfortunate
fact that a proportion of its lowlier members saw in the occupation,
and in the part which they were able to play, a chance of revenging
themselves for numberless slights and injuries endured at Arab
hands. The game was easy during the weeks which followed the
revolt, when a mutual suspicion informed the minds of Italian and
Arab. At that time cases of deliberate false interpreting, calculated
to prejudice the authorities against individual Arabs or Arabs in
general, were not altogether rare; and many things were wrongly
coloured. Fortunately, in matters of first-class importance the duty
of translation was entrusted to Italian officers or to others whose
integrity was above suspicion. Capital errors were thereby avoided;
but it is not too much to say that at one time the relations between
the Italians and the Arab community were in danger of being most
gravely prejudiced—they were considerably affected—by the perpe-
tration and nourishment of misunderstandings that ought never to
have arisen.

The employment of Tripoli Jews worked double mischief. In the
first place, a number of them, quite naturally, used their position as a
means of 'getting some of their own back,' sowing mischief between
Italians and Arabs. In the second place, the quasi-confidential position occupied by these Jews, and the semblance of authority which it
gave them, was regarded as an outrage by the Arabs. For in Tripoli
the Jew is held in peculiar contempt, so much so that the Moslem
women are careless if a Jew should see them unveiled. 'A Jew is not a
man,' they say. Under such conditions it is clear that the employment
of Jews on a large scale, in positions of trust and as the connecting
links between the Arabs and the Italians, was a very unfortunate
error.

Happily, the error was realised, partly owing to some indiscreet
expressions of triumph on the part of the Jews, partly owing to the
chance detection of some false translations, partly through a better
apprehension of Arab feeling. The fear, at one time widely spread,
that the despised Jew was to be exalted above the Arab who had
scorned him, was successfully combated; a quiet warning was addressed to the Jewish community, and some changes were made on
the staff of interpreters. The question of interpreters was not easy of
solution, for those who were qualified were almost all Jews, Levan-

tines or Maltese; and, but for the special disabilities that arose from the circumstances, the Jews were undoubtedly the best. A process of supervision and selection, accompanied by the overworking of those who could be trusted, soon led to a better condition of things, and the rapprochement between Italian and Arab, where such rapprochement could take place, was gradually confirmed.

2. In Agostini's survey (1917), the Jews constituted about one third of the population of the city. This may reflect, in part, the flight of some of the Moslem population and the influx of Jews who had sought safety during the war.

3. See McClure (1913:142).

4. In 1923, there were disturbances in the town between Jewish and Italian merchants (*Paix et Droit* 1923).

5. *Sīdī*. The Hebrew text is *'adon*.

6. A word is unclear here.

7. He was also the head of the Collegio Rabbinico Italiano in that city (Roth 1946:506–508) and founded the pro-Falasha committee concerned with the native Jews of Ethiopia.

APPENDIX I

Table of Contents of Parts I and II of the Highid Mordekhai

The following table of contents shows the wide range of topics covered in the portions of the *Highid Mordekhai* that have not been translated here. Hakohen does not include a table of contents in the manuscript, but there is a partial listing in the excerpt he sent to Slouschz (see the Editor's Introduction, n. 53). In the following table I have noted the main topic dealt with in each section, but many sections treat more than one topic. Sections 1–65 (Part I) deal with general and Jewish history, while Sections 66–89 (Part II) concern the customs and institutions of the Jews of Tripoli.

Section	Manuscript Pages	Main Topic Discussed
1	1a–3a	Tripoli: geography, population, and architectural features
2	3b–4b	Public institutions: schools, hospitals, houses of worship, and language
3	5a–6a	Antiquities
4	6a–8a	Climate, water supply, flora and fauna, and natural resources
5	8b–12a	Religious practices and relations between religious groups
6	12b–14b	Physical characteristics of the inhabitants; dress; food; local administration
7	15a–15b	Food preparation and local manufacture
8	16a–18b	Commerce and banking
9	19a–21b	Ancient history from biblical times to 400 B.C.
10	22a–23b	History from 400 to 134 B.C.
11	24a–25b	The Roman period: Jewish settlement in Libya

Section	Manuscript Pages	Main Topic Discussed
47	90a–94a	The Jewish community in the 1830s and 1840s; list of heads of the Jewish community throughout Turkish rule
48	94b–95a	Confrontation with France (1852)
49	95a*	An explosion in the armory
50	95b–96b	The building of the New Gate (1865)
51	96b–97b	The Jews invite the intervention of the Alliance Israélite Universelle (1870)
52	98a–98b	Confrontation with the U.S.A.
53	99a–100b	Modernization and reform (1860–1865)
54	101a–101b	Turkish governors and reform (1870–1882)
55	102a–102b	Foreign powers in Tripoli: opposition to the slave trade and establishment of the postal service
56	102b–105a	The 'Isawiya Order and its decline under foreign pressure
57	105b–107a	Italian schools and the Bank of Rome
58	107b–108a	Ahmed Razem Pasha: the attempt to introduce military conscription
59	108b–112a	Hafez Pasha: attempts to introduce new taxes and local opposition
60	112a–112b	Further reforms of Hafez Pasha (1902)
61	112b–113a	The attempt to establish the military exemption tax
62	113a–115a	The Jews oppose the imposition of the military exemption tax
63	115a–116b	The Jews oppose the imposition of the military exemption tax (1904)
64	115a†	Rajeb Pasha
65	116b–121b	The Young Turk regime in Tripoli
66	122a–123b	Jewish beliefs: the Sabbath
67	124a–129a	Jewish beliefs: holidays and fasts
68	129b–130b	Jewish beliefs: Ḥanukkah and Purim
69	130b–134a	Minor celebrations, including local Purims; Rabbi Abraham Khalfon
70	134a–137a	Miscellaneous local customs
71	137b–141b	Excerpts from *Ha-shomer 'emet* (Adadi 1849)
72	142a–151b	Excerpts from *Maqom she-nahagu* (Adadi 1865)
73	152a–155b	A list of personal names among Tripolitanian Jews
74	156a–158a	A list of patronyms culled from marriage contracts
75	158b–160b	The Arabic dialect of the Jews and the use of Hebrew
76	161a–163a	Jewish education
77	163b–164b	The schools of the Alliance Israélite Universelle

*There is a mistake in the page numbering. Page 95 appears twice.

†Page 115 appears twice.

Section	Manuscript Pages	Main Topic Discussed
78	165a–166b	The economic institutions of the Jewish community
79	166b–167a	The welfare institutions of the Jewish community
80	167b–168a	Burial societies
81	168a–168b	Funerary customs
82	169a–170b	Events concerning the Jewish cemetery
83	171a–175a	The Jewish quarters; a list of 23 synagogues
84	175b–176a	The Jewish old age home
85	176b–177a	Religious practices of women
86	177b–186b	The Rabbinic court
87	187a–191a	Jewish antiquities; books published by Tripolitan authors
88	191b–193a	Customs concerning the life cycle: menstruation, childbirth, circumcision, and religious majority
89	193b–196a	Marriage and wedding customs

Newspaper Items by Mordechai Hakohen

This list reflects all the items identified thus far; others are likely to be found after further research.

Published in ha-Sefirah *(Warsaw)*

1904	Vol. 31	no. 57	pp. 2–3

Published in ha-Yehoody *(London)*

1905	Vol. 9	no. 21	p. 8
	Vol. 9	no. 27	p. 8
1906	Vol. 9	nos. 44–45	pp. 19–20
	Vol. 10	no. 11	p. 5
	Vol. 10	no. 29	p. 8
1907	Vol. 10	no. 38	p. 5
	Vol. 10	no. 45	p. 5
	Vol. 11	no. 6	pp. 4–5
	Vol. 11	no. 9	p. 5
	Vol. 11	no. 15	pp. 4–5
	Vol. 11	no. 21	p. 3
	Vol. 11	no. 28	p. 8
	Vol. 11	no. 29	p. 8
	Vol. 11	no. 34	p. 4
	Vol. 11	no. 37	p. 3
1908	Vol. 11	no. 40	p. 5
	Vol. 11	no. 42	pp. 8–9
	Vol. 11	no. 44	p. 4
	Vol. 11	no. 48	p. 8

	Vol. 12	no. 1	pp. 3–4
	Vol. 12	no. 10	p. 5
	Vol. 12	no. 12	p. 16
	Vol. 12	no. 13	p. 5
	Vol. 12	no. 17	p. 5
	Vol. 12	no. 22	p. 6
	Vol. 12	no. 25	p. 3
	Vol. 12	no. 29	p. 4
	Vol. 12	no. 35	p. 4
	Vol. 12	no. 40	p. 16
1909	Vol. 13	no. 5	p. 16
	Vol. 13	nos. 14–15	p. 4
	Vol. 13	no. 25	p. 16
	Vol. 13	no. 27	p. 5
	Vol. 13	no. 30	p. 13
	Vol. 13	no. 40	p. 5
1910	Vol. 13	no. 46	p. 16
	Vol. 13	no. 48	p. 16

Published in ha-Herut *(Palestine)*

1909	November 11	p. 2
1913	June 20	pp. 1–2
	November 6	p. 2
	December 4	p. 2
1914	May 3	pp. 1–2

APPENDIX III

Contents of the Archive of Mordechai Hakohen's Papers

The archive, located at the Jewish National and University Library, Jerusalem (no. 4° 1256), is divided into five files. These contain personal papers and two manuscripts. The letters among the personal papers have been indexed according to the name of the addressee or the sender, as the case may be. Listed below are some of the major contents of the archive:

1. Copies of letters sent to newspapers abroad (see Appendix I).
2. Notes (such as population figures) relating to Hakohen's work.
3. Letters to Nahum Slouschz and M. M. Moreno (see the Editor's Introduction).
4. Letters dealing with Rabbinic law addressed to various individuals and institutions. These include: (a) the court in Tripoli, (b) the Chief Rabbi (Ya'aqov Me'ir) of the Sephardic community in Palestine, (c) Rabbi Aharon Mendel Cohen in Cairo, and (d) Rabbi Ḥizqiyahu Shabbetai in Aleppo (see the Editor's Introduction). The archive also contains replies to these letters.
5. Letters to communal leaders abroad requesting funds for a school or for other charitable purposes, and remittances by Hakohen to religious institutions in Palestine.
6. Accounts, receipts, and other letters concerning financial affairs.
7. Form letters for use in correspondence and documents such as (a) a letter of condolence, (b) the appointment of a Chief Rabbi, and (c) a bill of divorce.

The first manuscript is a book concerning Rabbeinu Gershom Me'or ha-Golah (see the Editor's Introduction, IV). The second, entitled *Neṣah Yisra'el,* is a short history of the Jewish people from antiquity to modern times, written in Hebrew. Neither of these has been published.

The library also contains a portion of *Highid Mordekhai* (Sections 32–45) which Hakohen copied and sent to Slouschz (see the Editor's Introduction). This pamphlet also contains section headings for the whole book. It is numbered 28° 5775 and was given to the library by Professor Dov Sadan, who received it from Slouschz.

Bibliography

Abun-Nasr, J. M.
 1971   *A History of the Maghrib.* Cambridge: Cambridge University Press.
Aby-Serour, M.
 1870   L'établissement des Israélites à Tombouktou (A. Beaumier, trans.).
        Bulletin de la Société de Géographie 19:345–370.
 1880   Les Daggatoun (I. Loeb, trans.). *Bulletin d'Alliance Israélite Univer-
        selle,* January (supplement).
Adadi, A.
 1849   *Ha-shomer 'emet.* Leghorn, Italy: Ben Amozag. (In Hebrew.)
 1865   *Maqom she-nahagu.* In *Vayiqra' 'Avraham.* Leghorn, Italy: Ben
        Amozag. (In Hebrew.)
Adler, M. N. (ed. and trans.)
 1911   *The Travels of Benjamin of Tudela.* London: Frowde.
Africanus, L.
 1847   *The History and Description of Africa and of the Notable Things
        Therein Contained.* Works of the Hakluyt Society, vols. 92–94. Lon-
        don.
Agostini, E.
 1917   *Le popolazioni della Tripolitania: notizie etniche e storiche.* Tripoli:
        n.p.
Ahmar, A. S. al-
 1976   *The Changing Social Organization of a Libyan Village.* Unpublished
        Ph.D. thesis, University of Leeds.
Alport, E. A.
 1954   The Mzab. *Journal of the Royal Anthropological Institute of Great
        Britain and Ireland* 84:34–44.
Antoun, R.
 1968   On the Modesty of Women in Arab Muslim Villages. *American An-
        thropologist* 70:671–692.
Askew, W.
 1942   *Europe and Italy's Acquisition of Libya, 1911–1912.* Durham: Duke
        University Press.
Attal, R.
 1973   *Les Juifs d'Afrique du Nord: bibliographie.* Jerusalem: Ben-Zvi Insti-
        tute.

Azulai, H. Y. D.
  1864   *Shem ha-gdolim*. Vienna: Schlesinger. (In Hebrew.)
Baier, S.
  1977   Trans-Saharan Trade and the Sahel: Damergu, 1870–1930. *Journal of African History* 18:37–60.
Baron, S. W.
  1942   *The Jewish Community: Its History and Structure Through the American Revolution,* vol. I. Philadelphia: Jewish Publication Society of America.
  1957–   *Social and Religious History of the Jews,* vols. III, V, and VIII. New
  1958   York: Columbia University Press.
Barth, F.
  1971   Role Dilemmas and Father-Son Dominance in Middle Eastern Kinship Systems. In *Kinship and Cultures,* F. L. K. Hsu, ed. Chicago: Aldine.
Barth, Heinrich
  1890   *Travels and Discoveries in North and Central Africa*. London: Ward, Lock.
Bazin, R.
  1923   *Charles de Foucauld: Hermit and Explorer* (P. Keelan, trans.). London: Burns, Oates, and Washbourne.
Behij ud-Din, Mehmed
  1867–   *Ta'rikhi Ibn Ghalbun*. Istanbul.
  1868
Benet, F.
  1957   Explosive Markets: The Berber Highlands. In *Trade and Market in the Early Empires,* K. Polanyi, C. M. Arensberg, and H. W. Pearson, eds., pp. 188–217. Glencoe: Free Press.
Benjamin, I. J.
  1859   *Eight Years in Asia and Africa, from 1846–1855*. Hanover.
Ben Yehudah
  1934   *Limdu 'ivrit*. Tripoli: Zionist Organization of Tripolitania.
Ben Zvi, Y.
  1964   The Travels of an Emissary of Safed, by Rabbi Ya'aqov Siqli Hakohen. *Otzar Yehudei Sefard* 7:77–86. (In Hebrew.)
Bequinot, F.
  1942   *Il Berbero nefusi di Fassato: grammatica, testi, raccolti dalla viva voce, vocabolarietti*. Rome: Istituto per l'Oriente.
Bergna, C. P.
  1925   *Tripoli dal 1510 al 1850*. Tripoli: Arti grafiche.
Bezirgan, N. A.
  1974   The Islamic World. In *The Comparative Reception of Darwinism,* T. F. Glick, ed. Austin: University of Texas Press.
Blake, G.
  1968   *Misurata: A Market Town in Tripolitania*. Durham Research Papers, No. 9. Department of Geography, Durham College, University of Durham, England.

Bodin, J.
1945   *Method for the Easy Comprehension of History* (B. Reynolds, trans.).
        New York: Columbia University Press. (Originally published in 1566.)
Bono, S.
1967   Untitled communication appearing under "Notizie varie." *Oriente
        Moderno* 47:825–827.
Bourdieu, P.
1977   *Outline of a Theory of Practice.* Cambridge: Cambridge University
        Press.
Bowie, L.
1976   An Aspect of Muslim-Jewish Relationships in Late Nineteenth-
        Century Morocco: A European Diplomatic View. *International Jour-
        nal of Middle East Studies* 7:3–19.
Brauer, E.
1947   *The Jews of Kurdistan: An Ethnological Study* (R. Patai, ed.). Jerusa-
        lem: Palestine Institute of Folklore and Ethnology. (In Hebrew.)
Brown, K.
1977   Changing Forms of Patronage in a Moroccan City. In *Patrons and
        Clients in Mediterranean Societies,* E. Gellner and J. Waterbury,
        eds., pp. 304–328. London: Duckworth.
Buffon, G. L.
1812   *Natural History, General and Particular . . . the History of Man and
        the Quadrupeds* (W. Smellie, trans.; W. Wood, ed.). XX vols. Lon-
        don: Cadell and Davies. (Originally published in 1749.)
Bulugma, H. M.
1968   *Benghazi Through the Ages.* Tripoli: Dar-Maktabat al Fikr.
Burke, E.
1972   The Image of the Moroccan State in French Ethnological Literature:
        A New Look at the Origin of Lyautey's Berber Policy. In *Arabs and
        Berbers,* E. Gellner and C. Micaud, eds., pp. 175–200. Boston: Heath.
1975   Towards a History of the Maghrib. *Middle Eastern Studies* 11:306–
        323.
Cachia, A. J.
1945   *Libya Under the Second Ottoman Occupation.* Tripoli: Government
        Press.
Cahen, C.
1965   Dhimma. In *Encyclopaedia of Islam* (2nd ed.), vol. 2, pp. 227–231.
        Leiden: Brill.
Calassanti-Motylinski, A. de
1898   *Le djebel Nefousa.* Paris: E. Leroux.
Càzes, D.
1890   Israélites de la Tripolitaine. *Bulletin d'Alliance Israélite Universelle*
        14:106–112.
Cesàro, A. (trans.)
1933   *Santuari islamici nel secolo XVII in Tripolitania.* Studi e monografie
        coloniali. Tripoli: Governo della Tripolitania.
1939   *L'Arabo parlato a Tripoli.* Rome: Mondadori.

CHIÈ
    1940   *Dizionario degli Italiani d'oggi* (4th ed.). Rome: Lenacolo.
Chouraqui, A.
    1952   *Marche vers l'Occident: les Juifs d'Afrique de Nord*. Paris: Presses
            Universitaires de France.
    1965   *Cent ans d'histoire: l'Alliance Israélite Universelle*. Paris: Presses
            Universitaires de France.
Cohen, D.
    1964   *Le parler arabe des Juifs de Tunis: textes et documents linguistiques
            et ethnographiques*. Paris: Mouton.
Cohen, M.
    1912   *Le parler arabe des Juifs d'Alger*. Paris: Champion.
Darnell, R. (ed.)
    1974   *Readings in the History of Anthropology*. New York: Harper and
            Row.
d'Beth Hillel, David
    1832   *Travels from Jerusalem through Arabia, Kurdistan, Parts of Persia
            and India to Madras*. Madras. (Reissued in 1973. New York: Ktav.)
De Ambroggio, K.
    1902   Notes succinctes sur les tribus tripolitaines situées entre la frontière
            tunisienne et le méridien de Tripoli, III: Berbères de l'intérieur. *Revue
            Tunisienne* 9:266–276.
Dearden, S.
    1976   *A Nest of Corsairs: The Fighting Karamanlis of Tripoli*. London:
            John Murray.
De Cenival, P.
    1925   La légende du Juif Ibn Mech'al et la fête du sultan des tolba à Fès.
            Hesperis 5:137–218.
De Felice, R.
    1978   *Ebrei in un paese arabo: gli Ebrei nella Libia contemporanea*. Bo-
            logna: Il Mulino.
De Foucauld, C.
    1939   *Reconnaissance au Maroc*. Paris: Société d'éditions géographiques.
De Marco, R.
    1943   *The Italianization of African Natives: Government Native Education
            in the Italian Colonies, 1890–1937*. New York: Columbia University
            Teachers College.
Deshen, S.
    1970   *Immigrant Voters in Israel*. Manchester: Manchester University
            Press.
    1975   Ritualization of Literacy: The Works of Tunisian Scholars in Israel.
            American Ethnologist 2:251–260.
Despois, J.
    1935   *Le djebel Nefousa: étude géographique*. Paris: Larose.
    1965   Djarba. In *Encyclopaedia of Islam* (2nd ed.), vol. 2, pp. 458–461.
            Leiden: Brill.
Dumont, L.
    1970   *Homo Hierarchicus*. London: Weidenfeld and Nicolson.

El-Bekri, A.
  1913   *Description de l'Afrique septentrionale par Abou-Ubeid el-Bekri* (MacGuckin de Slane, trans.) Paris: Librairie d'Amerique et d'Orient, Adrien-Maisonneuve.
Elmaleh, A.
  1945   'Arei ha-pra'ot be-tripolitania. *Hed ha-Mizrah* (Jerusalem), vol. 4: no. 28:6–7, no. 30:6, no. 31:8–9, no. 32:8, no. 33:9. (In Hebrew.)
Encyclopaedia Judaica
  1972   Jerusalem: Keter.
Evans-Pritchard, E. E.
  1949   *The Sanusi of Cyrenaica*. London: Oxford University Press.
Féraud, L. C.
  1927   *Annales tripolitaines*. Paris and Tunis: Librairie Vuibert.
Finley, M. I.
  1968   Slavery. In *International Encyclopaedia of the Social Sciences,* vol. 14, pp. 307–313. New York: Macmillan.
Frieman, A.
  1945   *Seder qiddushin ve-nisu'in* (Post-talmudic documents on marriage law). Jerusalem: Rav Kook Institute. (In Hebrew.)
Furlong, C. W.
  1909   *The Gateway to the Sahara*. New York: Scribners.
Geertz, C.
  1973   *The Interpretation of Cultures*. New York: Basic Books.
Gellner, E.
  1972   Introduction to *Arabs and Berbers,* E. Gellner and C. Micaud, eds. Boston: Heath.
Gerber, J.
  1975   The Pact of 'Umar in North Africa: A Re-appraisal of Muslim-Jewish Relations. In *Proceedings of the Seminar on Muslim-Jewish Relations in North Africa,* pp. 40–51. New York: World Jewish Congress.
Ghelli, E. Q.
  1932   Matrimoni tripolini. *Rivista della Colonie Italiane* 6(2):71–89.
Goguyer, M.
  1895   Le servage dans le Sahara tunisien. *Revue Tunisienne* 2:308–318.
Goitein, S. D.
  1939   *Mas'ot Habshush* (The Story of Rabbi Hayyim Ben Yahya Habshush Concerning His Travels with Joseph Halevy in Eastern Yemen and the Life of the Jews and Arabs There). Tel Aviv: Shtibel. (In Hebrew; trans. from Arabic.)
  1941   (trans. and ed.) *Travels in Yemen: An Account of Joseph Halevy's Journey to the Najran in the Year 1870, Written in San'ani Arabic by His Guide H. Habshush*. Jerusalem: Hebrew University Press.
  1947   *From the Land of Sheba: Tales of the Jews of Yemen*. New York: Schocken.
  1953   Jewish Education in Yemen as an Archetype of Traditional Jewish Education. In *Between Past and Future,* C. Frankenstein, ed., pp. 109–146. Jerusalem: Szold Institute.

1971   The Concept of Mankind in Islam. In *History and the Idea of Mankind*, W. Wagar, ed. Albuquerque: University of New Mexico Press.

1978   *A Mediterranean Society: The Jewish Communities of the Arab World as Portrayed in the Documents of the Cairo Geniza,* vol. III: *The Family.* Berkeley: University of California Press.

Goldberg, H.

1967   Patronymic Groups in a Tripolitanian Jewish Village: Reconstruction and Interpretation. *Jewish Journal of Sociology* 9:209–226.

1971   Ecologic and Demographic Aspects of Rural Tripolitanian Jewry, 1853–1949. *International Journal of Middle East Studies* 2:245–265.

1972a   *Cave Dwellers and Citrus Growers: A Jewish Community in Libya and Israel.* Cambridge: Cambridge University Press.

1972b   The Social Context of North African Jewish Patronyms. *Folklore Research Center Studies* (Jerusalem) 3:245–258.

1973a   Cultural Change in an Israeli Village: How the Twist Came to Even Yosef. *Middle Eastern Studies* 9:73–80.

1973b   Family Rituals Among Tripolitanian Jews: A Working Paper. Israel Society for Ethnography (Jerusalem). Mimeographed.

1974a   Tripolitanian Jewish Communities: Cultural Boundaries and Hypothesis Testing. *American Ethnologist* 1:619–634.

1974b   On the Language and Culture of Tripolitanian Jewry. *Leshonenu* (Jerusalem) 38:137–147. (In Hebrew.)

1974c   The Science of Custom and the Science of Judaism: Explorations in the Culture History of Tripolitanian Jewry. Paper read at the International Conference on Jewish Communities in Muslim Lands. Jerusalem: Institute of Asian and African Studies and Ben-Zvi Institute.

1975   The Relations of the Jews of Tripolitania with Their Moslem Neighbors. *Proceedings of the Sixth World Congress of Jewish Studies,* vol. II, pp. 123–130. Jerusalem: World Congress of Jewish Studies.

1976   Anthropology in Israel. *Current Anthropology* 17:119–121.

1977a   Culture and Ethnicity in the Study of Israeli Society. *Ethnic Groups* 1:163–186.

1977b   Rites and Riots: The Tripolitanian Pogrom of 1945. *Plural Societies* 8:35–56.

1978a   The Mimuna and the Minority Status of Moroccan Jews. *Ethnology* 17:75–87.

1978b   The Jewish Wedding in Tripolitania: A Study in Cultural Sources. *The Maghreb Review* 3(1):1–6.

1980   Turkish Rule in Libya as Viewed by the Jewish Community. *Proceedings of the Conference on Moslems and Jews in North Africa during the Last Century.* Aix-en-Provence: Institut d'histoire des pays d'outre-mer.

Goldberg, H.; Schoenberg, M.; Walerstein, M.; and Ziv, O.

1980   Social and Demographic Aspects of the Jews of Tripoli in the Colonial Period. *Proceedings of the First International Congress for the Study of North African Jewry.* Jerusalem: Centre de recherches sur les Juifs d'Afrique du Nord.

Greenberg, J.
1966 *Universals of Language.* The Hague: Mouton.
Griffin, E. H.
1924 *Adventures in Tripoli.* London: Phillip Alland.
Gruber, J.
1965 Brixham Cave and the Antiquity of Man. In *Context and Meaning in Cultural Anthropology,* M. E. Spiro, ed., pp. 373–402. New York: Macmillan.
Hachaichi, M. el-
1903 *Voyage au pays des Senoussia a travers la Tripolitaine et les pays touareg.* (V. S. Lasram, trans.) Paris: Librairie maritime et coloniale, Challamel.
Hakohen, M.
n.d. *Highid Mordekhai.* Ms. no. 8°, 1292, Jewish National and University Library, Jerusalem. (In Hebrew.)
1969 Letters to Nahum Slouschz. *Genazim: Collections Concerning the Modern History of Hebrew Literature,* vol. III, pp. 45–90. Tel Aviv: Masada. (In Hebrew.)
1978 *Higgid Mordecaï,* H. Goldberg, ed. Jerusalem: Ben-Zvi Institute. (In Hebrew.)
Harris, M.
1968 *The Rise of Anthropological Theory: A History of Theories of Culture.* New York: Crowell.
Harrison, R.
1967 Migrants in the City of Tripoli, Libya. *The Geographical Review* 57:397–423.
Hazzan, E.
1874 *Zikhron Yerushalayim.* Leghorn, Italy: Ben Amozag.
1884 *N'veh Shalom* (The Customs of Alexandria). Alexandria: Ben 'Attar.
Heffening, W.
1929 Wakf. In *Encyclopaedia of Islam* (1st ed.), vol. 4, pp. 1096–1103. Leiden: Brill.
Hertz, J.
1948 *The Authorized Daily Prayer Book* (revised edition). New York: Block.
Hilal, J.
1969 Meaning and Symbol in Some Marriage Ceremonies in Arab Rural Communities: A Case Study from Tripolitania, Libya. *A Monthly Journal and Record of the Departmental Societies of the Faculty of Arts and Education,* no. 4:14–17. Cyrene: University of Libya, Benghazi.
Hirschberg, H. Z.
1963 The Problem of the Judaized Berbers. *Journal of African History* 4:313–339.
1965a Tripolitania. In *A History of the Jews of North Africa, from Antiquity to Our Time,* vol. II. Jerusalem: Bialik Institute. (In Hebrew.)
1965b An Evil and Bitter Experience of the People of the Maghrib. In Bar-Ilan University decennial volume, pp. 415–479. Ramat-Gan, Israel: Bar-Ilan University. (In Hebrew, with an English summary.)

1969   The Oriental Jewish Communities. In *Religion in the Middle East: Three Religions in Concord and Conflict*, A. J. Arberry, ed., vol. I: *The Family*, pp. 119–225. Cambridge: Cambridge University Press.

1974   *A History of the Jews of North Africa*, Vol. I: *From Antiquity to the Sixteenth Century*. Leiden: Brill.

Hocart, A. M.
1969   *The Life-giving Myth*. London: Tavistock.

Hodgen, M.
1964   *Early Anthropology in the Sixteenth and Seventeenth Centuries*. Philadelphia: University of Pennsylvania Press.

Ibn Ghalbun, A. ('Abdullah Muhammad Ibn Khalil Ghalbun)
1929–   *Ta'arīkh Ṭrablus al-Gharb*. Cairo: n.p. (In Arabic.)
1930

Ibn Khaldun
1925   *Histoires des Berbères et des dynasties musulmans de l'Afrique septentrionale*, 4 vols. (le Baron de Slane, trans.). Paris: Librairie orientaliste Paul Geuthner.

Idelsohn, A.
1960   *Jewish Liturgy and Its Development*. New York: Schocken.

Jason, H.
1975   *Studies in Jewish Ethnopoetry: Narration, Art, Content, Message, Genre*. Taipei: Chinese Association for Folklore.

Jastrow, M.
1950   *A Dictionary of the Targumim, the Talmud Babli and Yerushalmi and the Midrashic Literature*, 2 vols. New York: Pardes.

Johnson, M.
1976   Calico Caravans: The Tripoli-Kano Trade after 1880. *Journal of African History* 17:95–117.

Joseph, R.
1974   Choice or Force: A Study in Social Manipulation. *Human Organization* 33:398–401.

Kahalon, Y.
1972   La lutte pour l'image spirituelle de la communauté de Libye au XIXe siècle. In *Zakhor le-Abraham: mélanges Abraham Elmaleh*, H. Z. Hirschberg, ed., pp. 79–122. Jerusalem: Comité de la communauté marocaine. (In Hebrew, with a French summary.)

Katz, J.
1961   *Exclusiveness and Tolerance*. London: Oxford University Press.

Khadduri, M.
1963   *Modern Libya: A Study in Political Development*. Baltimore: Johns Hopkins University Press.

Khalfon, A.
1861   *Hayei 'Avraham*. Leghorn, Italy: Tobiana. (In Hebrew.)

Khuja, M.
1960   Garian Town. In *Field Studies in Libya*, S. G. Willimot and J. I. Clarke, eds., pp. 120–124. Durham Research Papers No. 4. Department of Geography, Durham College, University of Durham, England.

La Mettrie, J. O. de
1912 *Man a Machine.* G. Bussey, ed. Chicago: Open Court. (Originally published in 1748.)

Landau, J.
1969 *Jews in Nineteenth-Century Egypt.* New York: New York University Press.

Landau, J., and Ma'oz, M.
1974 *Jews and Non-Jews in Nineteenth-Century Egypt and Syria.* Paper read at the International Conference on Jewish Communities in Muslim Lands. Jerusalem: Institute of Asian and African Studies and Ben-Zvi Institute.

Lavi, E.
1864 *Ge'ulat Hashem.* Leghorn, Italy: Tobiana. (In Hebrew.)

Le Tourneau, R.
1949 *Fès avant le protectorat.* Casablanca: Institut des hautes études marocaines.

Lévi-Strauss, C.
1963 *Structural Anthropology.* New York: Basic Books.

Lewicki, T.
1971 al-Ibaḍiyya. In *Encyclopaedia of Islam* (2nd ed.), vol. 3, pp. 648–660. Leiden: Brill.

Lewis, B.
1961 *The Emergence of Modern Turkey.* London: Oxford University Press.

Littman, D.
1975 Jews Under Muslim Rule in the Late Nineteenth Century. *The Weiner Library Bulletin* 28:65–76.

Loeb, L.
1976 Dhimmi Status and Jewish Roles in Iranian Society. *Ethnic Groups* 1:89–105.

Lowick, N. M.
1974 The Arabic Inscriptions on the Mosque of Abu Ma'aruf at Sharwas. *Society for Libyan Studies, Fifth Annual Report,* pp. 14–19. London.

Lowie, R.
1937 *The History of Ethnological Theory.* London: Harrap.

Lyon, G. F.
1821 *A Narrative of Travels in North Africa in the Years 1818, 1819, and 1820.* London: John Murray.

Maher, V.
1974 *Women and Property in Morocco.* Cambridge: Cambridge University Press.

Mahler, R.
1971 *A History of Modern Jewry, 1780–1815.* London: Vallentine, Mitchell.

Martin, B. G.
1976 *Muslim Brotherhoods in Nineteenth-Century Africa.* Cambridge: Cambridge University Press.

1978 Ahmad Rasim Pasha and the Suppression of the Fazzan Slave Trade, 1881–1896. In *Islamic Slavery and Related Institutions,* J. A. Willis, ed. Princeton: Princeton University Press.

Mason, J.
   1975   Sex and Symbol in the Treatment of Women: The Wedding Rite in a
           Libyan Oasis Community. *American Ethnologist* 2:649–661.
McClure, W. K.
   1913   *Italy in North Africa: An Account of the Tripoli Enterprise.* London:
           Constable.
Mercier, M.
   1927   *Etude sur le waqf abadhite et ses applications au Mzab.* Algiers: J.
           Carbonel.
Midrash Rabbah
   1939   Freedman, H., and Simon, M., eds. London: Soncino. (There have
           been many earlier editions.)
Midrash Tanhuma
   1969   Jerusalem: Lewin-Epstein. (In Hebrew; there have been many earlier
           editions.)
Mishneh Torah
   1962   *Maimonides' Mishneh Torah.* Jerusalem: Rav Kook Institute. (In
           Hebrew; there have been many earlier editions.)
Misurati, 'A. M. al-
   1960   *Ghuma: faris al-sahra'.* Tripoli: n.p. (In Arabic.)
Moreno, M. M. (trans. and ed.)
   1924   *Usi, costumi e istituti degli Ebrei libici, fascicolo 1: religione e magia,
           feste e cerimonie, vita e morte,* by M. Cohen [Mordechai Hakohen].
           Officio studi, Governo della Cirenaica; Rapporti e monografie coloni-
           ali. Benghazi: Unione tipografia editrice.
   n.d.   *Gli Ebrei in Libia: usi e costumi,* by M. Cohen [Mordechai Hakohen].
   (1928) Collezione di opere e monografie a cura del Ministero delle colonie.
           Rome: Sindicato italiano arti grafiche.
Norris, H. T.
   1977   *The Pilgrimage of Ahmad: Son of the Little Bird of Paradise.* War-
           minster, England: Aris and Phillips.
Noy, D.
   1967   *Seventy-One Folktales of Libyan Jews.* Jerusalem: Folklore Archives.
           (In Hebrew.)
Ohel, M.
   1962   *Ish Nidham.* Jerusalem: published by the author. (In Hebrew.)
Osther, A.
   1912   *The Arabs in Tripoli.* London: John Murray.
Paix et Droit
   1923.   A yearly publication of the Alliance Israélite Universelle (Paris).
Patai, R.
   1971   *The Tents of Jacob.* Englewood Cliffs, New Jersey: Prentice-Hall.
Peters, E. L.
   1965   Aspects of the Family among the Bedouin of Cyrenaica. In *Compara-
           tive Family Systems,* M. Nimkoff, ed. Boston: Houghton Mifflin.
   1968   The Tied and the Free. In *Contributions to Mediterranean Sociology,*
           J. Peristiany, ed., pp. 167–190. The Hague: Mouton.

1977 Patronage in Cyrenaica. In *Patrons and Clients in Mediterranean Societies*, E. Gellner and J. Waterbury, eds., pp. 275–290. London: Duckworth.

Pitt-Rivers, J.
1968 The Stranger, the Guest and the Hostile Host: Introduction to the Study of the Laws of Hospitality. In *Contributions to Mediterranean Sociology*, J. Peristiany, ed., pp. 13–30. The Hague: Mouton.

Raccah, G.
1945 *Rabbinical Manuscripts from Tripolitania: Excerpts and Biographies of the Authors*. Tripoli: n.p. (In Hebrew.)

Redfield, R.
1948 *The Folk Culture of Yucatan*. Chicago: University of Chicago Press.

Richards, A.
1956 *Chisungu: A Girls' Initiation Ceremony Among the Bemba of Northern Rhodesia*. London: Faber.

Rosen, L.
1968 A Moroccan Jewish Community During the Middle Eastern Crisis. *The American Scholar* 37:435–451.
1972 Muslim-Jewish Relationships in a Moroccan City. *International Journal of Middle East Studies* 3:435–449.

Rossi, E.
1929 Tripoli. In *Encyclopaedia of Islam* (1st ed.), vol. 4, pp. 814–818. Leiden: Brill.
1968 *Storia di Tripoli e della Tripolitania della conquista araba al 1911* (M. Nallino, ed.). Rome: Istituto per l'Oriente.

Rossi, E. (trans. and annotator)
1936 *La cronaca araba tripolina di Ibn Galbun*, sec. XVII. Bologna, Italy: Licinio Cappello.

Roth, C.
1946 *The History of the Jews of Italy*. Philadelphia: Jewish Publication Society of America.

Roumani, J.
1973 Libya and the Military Revolution. In *Man, State and Society in the Maghreb*, I. W. Zartman, ed., pp. 344–360. New York: Praeger.
1974 Review of *Libya* by J. Wright and *Libyan Independence and the United Nations* by A. Pelt. *International Journal of Middle East Studies* 5:222–230.

Sahli, O.
1970 Some Social Aspects of Fassato: A Nafusah Berber Community in Western Libya. Unpublished M. A. thesis. Lawrence, Kansas: University of Kansas.

Sapir, Y.
1866 *'Even Sapir*. Lyck, Poland, and Mainz, Germany: Ziabat-Brill. (In Hebrew.)

Schneider, D.
1968 *American Kinship: A Cultural Account*. Englewood Cliffs, New Jersey: Prentice-Hall.

1976   Notes Towards a Theory of Culture. In *Meaning in Anthropology*, K. Basso and H. Selby, eds. Albuquerque: University of New Mexico Press.

Scholem, G.
1946   *Major Trends in Jewish Mysticism.* New York: Schocken.
1965   *The Kabbalah and Its Symbolism.* New York: Schocken.

Schulmann, K.
1877   *Mosdei 'Eres, 'Afriqa.* Vilna, Poland: Ram. (In Hebrew.)

Segrè, C. G.
1974   *Fourth Shore: The Italian Colonization of Libya.* Chicago: University of Chicago Press.

Semach, Y.
1928   Un rabbin voyageur marocain: Mardochée Aby-Serour. *Hesperis* 8:385–399.

Slouschz, N.
1907   Tripoli and Cyrenaica: Report to the Council of the Jewish Territorial Organization. Paris.
1908a   La Tripolitaine sous la domination des Karamanli. *Revue du Monde Musulman* 6:58–84, 211–232, 433–453.
1908b   *Hebraeo-pheniciens et judéo-berbères: introduction à l'histoire des Juifs et du Judaisme en Afrique.* Archives marocaines, vol. XIV. Paris: Leroux.
1913   Les Juifs de Debdou. *Revue du Monde Musulman* 22:261–269.
1926   In the Mountains of Libya. *Reshumot* (Tel Aviv) 4:1–76. (In Hebrew.)
1927   *Travels in North Africa.* Philadelphia: Jewish Publication Society of America.
1938–   *My Travels in Libya,* 2 vols. Tel Aviv: Vaad Hayovel. (In Hebrew.)
1943

Stahl, A.
1979   Ritualistic Reading among Oriental Jews. *Anthropological Quarterly* 52:115–120.

Stillman, N.
1975   Muslims and Jews in North Africa: Perceptions, Images, Stereotypes. *Proceedings of the Seminar on Muslim-Jewish Relations in North Africa,* pp. 13–27. New York: World Jewish Congress.

Stone, R.
1974   Religious Ethic and the Spirit of Capitalism in Tunisia. *International Journal of Middle East Studies* 5:260–273.

Streicker, A.
1970   Government and Revolt in Tripoli Regency, 1795–1855. Unpublished M. A. thesis. Evanston, Illinois: Northwestern University.

Stumme, H.
1898   *Märchen und Gedichte aus der Stadt Tripoli in Nord Afrika.* Leipzig.

Tefilat Yesharim
1958   *Mahzor shalosh regalim* (prayer book for the festivals). Jerusalem: Bickel. (In Hebrew.)

Toledano, Y. M.
1911   *Ner ha-ma'arav: A History of the Jews in Morocco.* Jerusalem: A. M. Luntz. (In Hebrew; reissued in 1973 by Hama'arav Press.)
Toschi, P.
1934,   *Le fonti inedite della storia della Tripolitania.* Tripoli: Airoldi.
Tully, R.
1957   *Letters Written During a Ten Years' Residence at the Court of Tripoli* (introduction and notes by S. Dearden). London: Arthur Baker. (Originally published in 1816.)
Turner, V.
1962   *Chihamba, the White Spirit: A Ritual Drama of the Ndembu.* Rhodes-Livingston Papers, no. 23. Manchester: Manchester University Press.
1969   *The Ritual Process.* Chicago: Aldine.
Voinot, L.
1948   *Pèlerinages judéo-musulmans du Maroc.* Paris: Larose.
Waterbury, J.
1972   *North for Trade: The Life and Times of a Berber Merchant.* Berkeley: University of California Press.
Westermarck, E.
1916   *The Moorish Conception of Holiness.* Helsinki: Akademiska Bokhandeln.
World Jewish Congress
1975   *Proceedings of the Seminar on Muslim-Jewish Relations in North Africa.* New York: World Jewish Congress.
Wright, J.
1969   *Libya.* New York: Praeger.
Yaari, A.
1951   *Emissaries of the Land of Israel.* Jerusalem: Rav Kook Institute. (In Hebrew.)
Zafrani, H.
1972   L'enseignment traditionel juif au Maroc. In *Zakhor le-Abraham: mélanges Abraham Elmaleh,* H. Z. Hirschberg, ed. Jerusalem: Comité de la communauté marocaine. (In Hebrew, with a French summary.)
Zimmels, H. J.
1958   *Ashkenazim and Sephardim, Their Relations, Differences and Problems as Reflected in the Rabbinical Responsa.* London: Oxford University Press.
Zohar
1933   Sperling, H.; Simon, M.; and Levertoff, P., trans. and eds. London: Soncino. (There have been many earlier editions.)
Zuaretz, F., *et al.,* eds.
1960   *Yahadut Luv* (Libyan Jewry). Tel Aviv: Va'ad Qehillot Luv be-Yisrael. (In Hebrew.)

Subject and Name Index

For spelling conventions see the Note on Orthography, p. xii. The symbol *n* in this index refers to one of the author's Notes at the bottom of a page, not to the editor's notes. The article *a-* or *al-* is ignored for alphabetical purposes. Following this index is a special index of Biblical citations.

Index of Biblical Citations